D1175673

EUROPEAN POLITICS I

The Restless Search

EUROPEAN POLITICS I

The Restless Search

A Comparative Government Biennial

Edited by

WILLIAM G. ANDREWS

Contributions by

CARL J. FRIEDRICH, *Harvard University*
ANTHONY KING, *Oxford University*
WILLIAM G. ANDREWS, *Tufts University*
STANLEY HOFFMANN, *Harvard University*
ELMER PLISCHKE, *University of Maryland*
SAMUEL HENDEL, *The City College of New York*

D. VAN NOSTRAND COMPANY, INC.

PRINCETON, NEW JERSEY

TORONTO　　NEW YORK　　LONDON

D. VAN NOSTRAND COMPANY, INC.
120 Alexander St., Princeton, New Jersey
(*Principal Office*)
24 West 40 Street, New York 18, New York

D. VAN NOSTRAND COMPANY, LTD.
358, Kensington High Street, London, W.14, England

D. VAN NOSTRAND COMPANY (Canada), LTD.
25 Hollinger Road, Toronto 16, Canada

Published simultaneously in Canada by
D. VAN NOSTRAND COMPANY (Canada), LTD.

PRINTED IN THE UNITED STATES OF AMERICA

Preface

THIS BOOK ATTEMPTS TO BRIDGE TWO GAPS IN COMPARATIVE GOVernment teaching materials: the time lag between last year's textbook and this morning's headlines, and the intellectual cleavage between the level of sophistication of text materials and that of scholarly journals. Each of the contributors was asked to help fill those gaps. The four essays dealing with individual countries take one or two major political developments (British leadership changes, the rise of French presidentialism, the Adenauer legacy, the continuing relevance of ideology in the U.S.S.R.), describe and analyze them in depth, and present, through them, scholarly theses. The introductory essay dissects the nub of current constitutional problems with a theoretical and comparative analysis.

I wish to express my appreciation to the contributors and, in advance, to those teachers of comparative government who, if this volume serves their needs as well as I hope, will make a second volume possible two years hence.

WILLIAM G. ANDREWS

Belmont, Massachusetts

Introduction

THROUGHOUT HISTORY POLITICS HAS BEEN A SEARCH. THE ANCIENT Greeks sought an instrument to create the ideal society. Medieval man sought order. The early moderns sought liberation. The Bolsheviks seek Marx's Elysian Fields.

Western man—pragmatic and cynical—seeks simply improvement. The tools are familiar. The basic building blocks of modern political systems were created long ago and are solidly in place in most Western systems. The main problems confronting the West concern adjustments, refinements, and the recruitment of competent managers. No radical improvements are expected imminently. No utopias are just around the corner. No panaceas find mass markets.

Perhaps this stability has drained from Western democratic politics some of the thrills and excitement of fifty years ago. This is the real meaning of the end of ideology, of the "depoliticization" that has been so widely discussed on both sides of the Atlantic. Man has not become more "alienated" from his political system. He has not withdrawn into apathy or anomie. He has merely come to recognize the limitations of politics. He does not believe that politics have no further, expanded services to render society. But he does see that the remaining gains must be won slowly and cautiously lest those already accumulated be endangered.

Professor Friedrich calls attention to both these aspects of modern politics in his introductory essay. He points out the general failure of governmental systems to meet all the demands placed upon them by modern man. He also shows that relatively superficial institutional alterations—especially federalism—may help close the remaining gap. At least, he rightly notes this as one major area that has elicited interest and activity in many countries.

The authors of the essays on Britain, France, and West Germany, have all dealt with closely related leadership problems.

In the three Western nations the problems are similar because all three are laboring high up the same slope near timberline, in the zone where further refinements of institutions or changes of personnel can be expected to yield only marginal gains in extracting greater service from Leviathan.

In 1964, unlike 1945, the British expected no sweeping changes either from the transfer of leadership in the two parties or from the replacement of the Conservatives by the Labour Party at Whitehall. Indeed, in the first matter they were concerned almost entirely with the question of whether the procedures being used were adequate for a modern democracy and in the second very largely with the relative ability of the competing party teams. Dr. King's account of the party leadership changes is the first published, other than newspaper reports or polemical defenses by participants or their advocates. His analysis of the election is the first between book covers West of the Atlantic.

The French travel the road from parliamentarism to presidentialism with special reluctance because they see so little likelihood that political salvation lies at its end. Professor Hoffmann and the editor present here the first account of that journey, including the development of presidential electoral politics, and anticipate its culmination in the December 1965 presidential elections. Professor Hoffmann wrote section II and parts of section I; the editor wrote the rest. Each author reviewed and commented upon the parts written by the other. Especially, the conclusions benefited from Professor Hoffmann's criticism.

The Germans, having learned from tragic experience the dangers of radical solutions, sought to build the Bonn Republic on solid and respectable, though unspectacular, foundations. Professor Plischke uses Konrad Adenauer's resignation (not retirement) as a benchmark for an appraisal of the edifice over whose construction he had presided. The editor has added a short note in which the brief period of Ludwig Erhard's chancellorship is scrutinized for evidence indicating which parts of the structure were merely ephemeral extensions of Adenauer's personality and which are permanent features of German politics. Once again, these are the first scholarly treatments of these topics in English.

Unlike the Western countries, the Soviet Union is saddled with an apocalyptic ideology which obviously promises far more than it can produce and is also an irritating impediment to the solution of practical but important problems, such as agriculture. Those who ignore the continuing force of that ideology, Professor Hendel makes clear, misunderstand the system. Most of his essay is an original contribution to a lively scholarly debate on the relevance of Marxism to current Soviet policies.

All five essays call attention to problems of political leadership, the constant struggle to hitch an effective, yet controllable, governmental team to society and through such means to "remedy," as Professor Friedrich says, "an existing political order." It is highly revealing of the differences among the systems that the British and German attempts involve mainly changes in political personnel, while the Soviets and some Frenchmen compound their problems by seeking to make increasingly brittle ideological harnesses fit without excessive chafing.

One can see in these four systems various stages of refinement in the modern political search. The Soviets and many Frenchmen have not yet given up hope of reconciling ideology with reality. The British and Germans have let the scales fall from their eyes, have turned from "The Book" to "Life," and deal with politics primarily in pragmatic, managerial terms. Perhaps, then, this is the modern political search, for means to discard the servitudes of 19th century ideology in the same ashbin of history where the 19th century liberals and socialists cast so many relics of the Middle Ages. The search is restless because Man knows not always for what he seeks.

Contents

Contributors

WILLIAM G. ANDREWS, Associate Professor of Government, Tufts University, is author of *French Politics and Algeria* and editor of *Soviet Institutions and Policies* (forthcoming).

CARL J. FRIEDRICH, Eaton Professor of the Science of Government, Harvard University, and past president of the American Political Science Association, is author of *Constitutional Government and Democracy* and *Man and His Government.*

SAMUEL HENDEL, Professor of Political Science and Chairman, Russian Area Studies Graduate Program, The City College of New York, is editor of *The Soviet Crucible* and (with Hillman M. Bishop) *Basic Issues of American Democracy.*

STANLEY HOFFMANN, Professor of Government, Harvard University, is author of *Le Mouvement Poujade* and (with others) *In Search of France.*

ANTHONY KING, Fellow at Magdalen College, Oxford, has been appointed Senior Lecturer in Government, University of Essex, and is author (with D. E. Butler) of *The British General Election of 1964.*

ELMER PLISCHKE, Professor and Head, Department of Government and Politics, University of Maryland, is author of *Contemporary Government of Germany* and *Government and Politics of Contemporary Berlin.*

European Politics I

The Search for a Model Political Order

by Carl J. Friedrich

CLASSICAL POLITICAL THEORY REVOLVED AROUND THE QUESTION of the "ideal" political order. Plato and Aristotle made this search for the perfect *polis* the key problem of their discussion of politics. For many generations it remained the universally acknowledged task. Machiavelli challenged this tradition most explicitly and radically. "Many have imagined republics and principalities which no one has even seen or heard; for between life as it is, and life as it should be, there is a vast difference. . . . I leave aside all that has been imagined about rulers and speak only of the reality." Modern political science has followed him in searching for the reality of government and politics. But the argument continues about a good political order, about what *ought* to be the reality of government. More particularly, the breakdown of many established regimes, the emergence of new states, and the worldwide revolutionary challenge of totalitarianism have raised the ancient problem with renewed insistence. Political science and political theory cannot and in fact do not escape from the task which the search for standards implies. Whoever has been asked what kind of "constitution" to advise for Germany, France, Puerto Rico, India, or Nigeria—to mention a few random examples—has had to consider what the findings of political science may be able to contribute to this universal quest. Yet few, if any, political theorists would think that this search should be pursued in terms of the ideal or the perfect state. The marginal chance of its realizability so poignantly put in Plato's *Republic* appears too discouraging to the activist modern mind. What ought to be, is not to be deduced from abstract notions of right and wrong, from metaphysical speculation about ideas and ends, but is to be concluded from concrete observation. It is not final, definite, and eternal, but constellational, tentative, and temporal.[1]

Other papers in this symposium are concerned with the search for particular solutions of specific regimes, a more or less radical improvement in their specific political order. They describe and analyze what political power-wielders, actors and ideologues alike, have thought and done to revamp a system or a theory, to re-establish leadership or its legitimacy. Beyond these situations, a fairly universal search can be observed throughout the world for some kind of model political order, to be adapted to the concrete and detailed givens of tradition and culture, of technical need and economic potential, but nonetheless a model which would suit a modern industrial society functioning on the basis of an advanced technology. Practical politicians and theorists alike recognize that the increasing assimilation of living conditions and standards suggests—nay, demands—a corresponding assimilation of the political framework within which men are to live and work.

In the early 1950s many thought that the opposition between constitutional democracy and totalitarian dictatorship as represented by the United States and the Soviet Union was absolute and permanent, that indeed the future of mankind hinged upon which of the two systems would prevail. It was never a correct view, but the intervening decade has produced much practical experience which tends to show that there are not only many intermediary forms, such as de Gaulle's France and Nehru's India, Franco's Spain and Nasser's Egypt, but that the USSR and the United States increasingly incline to take over certain institutions and practices from each other and thus resemble each other at least in some important respects more than they used to do. To be sure, a recent careful inquiry into this matter has produced a rather skeptical estimate. "Every healthy political system changes, but if the change is gradual it tends to be shaped by the present and the past. Unless it is possible to prove that there has been or will be a major shift in the development of either the American or the Soviet system's relationship with society, or unless it is possible to prove that the past models of development of the two societies are fundamentally alike, then the very fact of evolution makes convergence unlikely." [2]

The search for a model as well as the comparison of contemporary regimes raises the problem of typology. In fact, the ancient question of an adequate typology of forms of government has acquired a new urgency by these developments and inquiries. Neither the traditional triad in terms of the number of rulers, nor the Platonic and post-Platonic variations on it, nor yet the more recent attempts to classify governments according to their class character, as was done by Marx, Michels, and others, nor yet Max Weber's triad in terms of rationalism and its supposed opposites of traditionalism and inspirationalism have proved satisfactory. A strictly empirical review of the forms of government which have appeared [3] discloses a bewildering multiplicity of forms —fourteen in all—which do not readily fall into any rational pattern. Some dichotomies suggest themselves, by our contemporary concerns, more especially that between autocratic and non-autocratic regimes. Yet, generally speaking, it seems rather that forms of government correspond to the state of the community in terms of development, its values, beliefs, and interests. The recent tendency has been to highlight this interdependence by combining the word state with whatever appears to be the outstanding and hence characeristic goal of the particular political order: welfare state, police state, legal state, administrative state, and so forth.[4] The true task of theoretical analysis is often bypassed by such terms. A typology should be related to the core of the phenomenon whose types are being sought. In the case of governments, i.e., institutionalized systems of rule, this is a matter of who rules and how, and to what end or purpose. The egalitarian belief in the common man led to an overemphasis on the first problem; it all seemed to be a matter of "Who rules?" the answer being: the more, the better. Totalitarianism, while not explicitly rejecting the egalitarian presumption, nonetheless stressed the role of an elite, whether in terms of class-consciousness (i.e., an elite with insight into the dialectics of history) or in terms of presumed national or racial excellence and an insight into the role of such nations or races. This challenge being cast in terms of a stress on goals produced forms of governmental operation that were markedly autocratic without fitting into the older historical patterns of autocracy. Industrialization and expansion, though not originally primary focal points, became the keys to totalitarian operations. Their "how" turned out to be a novel form of autocracy with built-in ideological and inspirational leadership.

At the same time, the problem of how to govern presented itself in a large number of communities which confronted unprecedented situations as they emerged both from colonial rule and from traditional forms of government which had become compromised by their subservience to their colonial masters. Attempts to adopt and adapt either constitutional or totalitarian forms of government have not been strikingly successful in achieving the universally desired goal of a rising standard of living, in fact often have failed even to maintain the standard achieved under colonial rule. As a result, anarchy has been spreading, with Vietnam and the Congo the most striking examples at the moment.

As a result of all these developments, there is a universal and growing dissatisfaction with government everywhere. Why is it that men everywhere are more dissatisfied with government, *their* government, than they were only two generations ago? Is it that the world is drifting into misgovernment? Or are excessive demands being made upon the rulers? Or has the situation with which governments have to cope become utterly unmanageable? Or is it perhaps a combination of all three of these constellations? Whatever may be the right answer to these questions—and at present our data certainly do not suffice to answer them—they all imply that governments fail to achieve adequate results in the view of the governed. In short, they imply that men are not governed well. Yet, in response it must be said that contemporary man is not searching for an ideal or perfect state, even if he is willing to concede that such a quest has meaning (which many would, with Hobbes, deny). They *do* want to find out what makes a government function well. Hence, they search for a model that can serve as a measuring rod by which to assess existing regimes. It is evident that such a model is not going to be discovered in one of the existing forms of government, all of which are proving defective. This search leads beyond communism, liberalism, and conservatism, as it has already led beyond fascism.

Yet, since the Second World War the builders of states and the makers of constitutions have manifested a striking disinclination to face up to these problems. The prevailing negativism led to a number of radical reverses which have been called "negative revolutions." [5] The establishment of the constitutions of post-war France, Italy, and Germany were not motivated by any constructive belief in the value of the institutions which these constitutions embodied. Rather they were a result of the widespread disillusionment with the preceding Fascist regimes. Hence, a restorative tendency was generally prevalent. It can be observed from the vantage point of 1965 that the French constitution which was most nearly a revamping of the institutions of the Third Republic has already been swept away, while the German one which had to meet the challenge of the totalitarian East has survived. But even the basic law of the Federal Republic has no broad support among either intellectuals or the common people, and particularly characteristic institutions, such as its federalism, its constitutional judiciary, and its parliamentary bodies, have more critics than friends. Numerous more or less detailed studies have been produced by political scientists and historians in recent years to document these general developments.[6] One subject, federalism, has been particularly explored. The reason for the ever broader interest in federalism is unquestionably related to a world-wide trend to which we should devote some comments, before indicating the analytical views developed in the field of federalism proper.

Throughout the contemporary world there is a trend for political orders to transcend the narrow confines of the national state. Yet, the force of nationalism continues so strong that this trend can only make slow headway. This is particularly dramatic in Europe, where the national state is entrenched behind centuries of historical growth embodied in ever more powerful national bureaucracies. Even so, the trend has become more pronounced in recent years, responding especially to economic needs. But it is not only an economic matter; the pan-movements are clear signs that the uniting of larger cultural entities has a powerful appeal and responds to strong emotional needs and aspirations. Under these circumstances federalism offers a potential solution, provided the necessary constitutional underpinning can be created. Unfortunately, the advocates of such federal unions often forget how strong is the interdependence of federalism and constitutionalism. What goes under the name of federalism in totalitarian systems is largely a species of decentralization.[7] It is curious that, nonetheless, the interest in federalism is widespread. It testifies to the universal inclination to envisage more comprehensive orders. In spite of great obstacles in the way of realization, the emotional and ideological appeal of pan-movements has been sufficiently strong in various parts of the world to have persuaded politicians to advocate unification even when generally convinced that they have little chance of success at present, as is the case in Africa. Even here, a certain amount of progress is being achieved.

This universal trend suggests an emergent world structure composed of a limited number of rather large units, running from 100-700 million people each. They would be held together by a common culture and tradition reinforced by religious ties at times. For in spite of a good deal of conflict, the great world religions with all their varied subdivisions constitute important integrators. Christianity in Europe and the Commonwealth as well as in Latin America and the United States, Islam in Arab countries, Buddhism in Southeast Asia, and a Confucian tradition in China, even if at present perverted by Communism, are examples of this integrating effect. Nor is this to be wondered at; religion has since the ancients been recognized as a significant community builder. If one is willing to interpret Communism as a secular religion, the proposition is thereby reinforced.

It will be many decades before these large cultural entities are really effectively organized in a political and economic sense, yet there is much ground for believing that they will eventually become so organized. Modern technology and the disintegration of the older orders everywhere thrust men forward into attempting these broader communal structures. They may of course fail, and anarchy may eventually spread ever farther afield. As already noted, the anarchical potential is fairly universally present and may indeed overtake the men who are trying to build political orders in their race with the mounting tasks of industrialization and democratization.[8]

The unification of Europe thus fits into a world-wide development and need not be dependent upon the external threat of the Soviet Union (or of the United States, in President de Gaulle's view). For this threat merely provides the occasion, and there is a deeper impulse involved. Europe is seen by many of its ablest exponents, whether political or literary, as a citadel to be defended against the mounting dangers of materialism, emanating from both the superpowers which at present dominate the scene. Such an argument, while oblivious to the powerful spiritual convictions at work elsewhere in the contemporary world, has nonetheless real meaning as an expression of Europe's creating for itself a new self-understanding which is inclusive rather than exclusive, cultural rather than national. It also provides something of an example in the task of federalizing an emergent cultural whole.

The discussions on federalism, precipitated by new federal experience and the efforts to use federal forms to solve problems of complex community organization, constitute one of the areas in which the search for a model political order has taken concrete form. The unification movements by which large cultural entities seek to achieve unity while preserving diversity, and such special situations as Berlin, Puerto Rico, and other former colonial dependencies, have directed attention to the fact that the federal relationship is not only one of pattern, i.e., of designing a suitable division of powers and competencies. It is also a continuing process of adaptation to a changing community and social structure. Then, too, there has been a significant broadening of the understanding of the parallels between international and constitutional processes, and the underlying dynamics of social change.[9] In this connection, it should be noted that the process of federalizing political entities is not restricted to states, but plays a highly significant role wherever autonomous groupings organize cooperation on a permanent basis for the pursuit of common goals and interests, e.g., trade unions, churches, educational institutions (Oxford, Paris!) and others. In all these cases, federalism may be interpreted both dynamically, as the effective organizing of diversity, and statically, as a description of the resulting pattern or structure.[10]

Federalism is thus seen to be a process as well as a design. Any particular design or pattern of powers is merely a phase, a momentary pattern in a kaleidoscopically evolving relationship. That does not mean that it is unimportant: describing a federal order means ascertaining its existing distribution of power[11] and the (always partial) institutionalization of this pattern of competencies. It is very important that this pattern correspond to the actual community structure, and that procedures exist for adapting it as that structure evolves. This has led to an increasing interest in the way federal systems are founded, how they grow and decline. Involved in such inquiries are the problems of contemporary political science: how decisions are reached in federal unions, and more especially how federal decision-making may be combined with parliamentary systems, with the requirements of the welfare state (particularly economic planning), and with the interaction between federal governmental structures and political parties and interest groups. This range of inquiries leads into the problems of totalitarian federalism, because of the predominant position of one political party in totalitarian systems. None of these specific topics are capable of scientific treatment without a general theory of federalism. Like all political theory, such a theory will have not only a morphological content, but a genetic and an operational or functional content (federalism in terms of design in morphological theory).

The core of such a general theory of federalism is that a federal union is a grouping of groups, united by one or more common objectives, but retaining their distinctive group character for other purposes. A federal union appears to be on the group level what association is on the interpersonal level. It unites the members without destroying them and is meant to strengthen them. Functionally speaking, federalism is the process of federalizing divergent groups, and more especially states. If thus understood, it becomes apparent that it may operate toward either integration or differentiation. Both the transformation of the British Empire into the Commonwealth of Nations and the uniting of Europe's national states into a United States of Europe are federalizing processes. Indeed, both integration and differentiation may be going on at the same time, as can be seen in India.

Operationally, then, federalism describes the process of federalizing a political community which is composed of several subcommunities which are sufficiently differentiated to live a life of their own. Federalizing is *either* the process by which a number of separate political organizations enter into arrangements for working out solutions together, that is to say, adopting joint policies and making joint decisions on common problems, *or* the process through which a hitherto unitarily organized political community, as it becomes differentiated into a number of separate and distinct political subcommittees, achieves a new order in which the differentiated communities, now organized for autonomous life and action, become capable of working out separately those problems they no longer have in common. This generalized description of what has at times been called the federal bargain—a term which is too limited and one-dimensional—seeks to explicate the dynamic on-going characteristic of federalism, both in its founding and in its operating complexity.[12] It has been noted that a federalizer may often be at work in bringing about the kind of bargain upon which a federal design comes to rest.

Yet federalism may not be, and need not be, the result of a bargain or of the work of a federalizer. Instead, it may be the consequence of a constitutional decision on the part of men who wish to divide power territorially (areally, as some would prefer to call it), just as they may divide it functionally. Indeed, since any territorial (spatial) division of power necessarily calls for a distribution of competencies, such a territorial or spatial division involves a functional division as well. It may be desirable to distinguish such instances by speaking of a federally organized unitary state.[13] It is, in a way, the characteristic form of federalism in totalitarian regimes where, however, it is decided upon in response to other considerations than the desirability of dividing power—for the concentration of power is the key principle of totalitarian systems.

It would be appropriate at this point to devote some attention to the evolution of totalitarian regimes. For there can be little doubt that they have been developing, even though it is very controversial just how the nature of this evolution should be interpreted. The hope that it may tend in the direction of constitutionalism and democracy has caused a good deal of wishful thinking. It seems more nearly in line with the reality that can be ascertained to see this evolution in terms immanent to these sytsems.[14] A growing consensus is providing the leadership (power-wielders) with increasing authority and legitimacy which in turn enables them to relinquish the use of instruments of bald and brutal coercion which their totalitarian operations formerly called for. This emergence of a totalitarian legitimacy and authority is coupled with the search for a more adequate structuring of the dictatorship (popular democracy) itself. The program of the CPSU projects a model of the future political order which is not without appeal to many who view the present political order in the Soviet Union with doubt, if not with hostility. This is not the place to discuss either the feasibility or the adequacy of this model, but it seemed necessary to recall its existence, before turning to a brief delineation of an alternative which the empirical review of political orders, past and present, seems to suggest.[15]

A political order is an operational whole which enables a group of human beings to arrive at decisions and to evolve policies by way of institutions which provide them with the means of effective cooperation. If such institutions and processes operate to the satisfaction of a substantial number of those subject to them, the order will rest on consensus. The power which the rulers or governors wield will be considered beneficial, even when it constrains or compels. Under such conditions, legitimacy and authority are assured. This is crucial, for in our complex industrial societies no political order can hope to succeed on the basis of brute power; it needs authority and legitimacy. For if power is largely coercive, the vast amount of conforming activities fails to occur; only consensual power can elicit them. Rulers must, therefore, organize voluntary support on a large scale. Hence, integrating political parties may be obliged to predominate over long periods of time. Several parties are necessary, but it is not necessary that they alternate in ruling the country. As long as they can exercise effective restraint, they operate as guardians of the order and of the rights of its members. They also channel the participation of all members in the actual operation of public functions. Thus, not only freedom of independence, but freedom of participation is safeguarded. Such participation requires decentralization to the greatest possible extent. The two most dependable ways of insuring such decentralization are local self-government and federalism, and therefore both ought to be organized effectively. Much present dissatisfaction with both is the result of antiquated patterns and rigid operations.

Three tasks present themselves as central for the operation of a satisfactory government. No existing system is actually governing so as to fulfill them adequately. They are: (1) to organize the political community in such a way that its continuous renovation can take place; (2) to plan the needed actions and policies; (3) to effectuate the plans and policies. Part of the difficulty of existing systems results from their claim of being optimal solutions to these problems, when in fact they fail to achieve the needed minimum.

This minimum calls for the following. First, there must be a government that can act effectively, i.e., take all measures necessary to cope with the technological requirements of survival, both economically and militarily, and more especially comprehensive planning. Second, some enforceable restraints upon the government's operations must function to protect the citizen's right to become and remain a political person. Third, some operative participation of all adult and sane members of the community must be provided for in the making of general rules, especially the basic rules of the game, as implied in the first, second, and third propositions. This means, of course, that there must be such general rules embodying the permanent shared values, beliefs, and interests of the community. Fifth, then, such an order requires a judiciary which will interpret the rules and particularly define the terms of settlement for disputes. Sixth and finally, there ought to exist at least two voluntary political associations (parties) which provide the organizational channels for developing alternative policies, and thus educating the people, for developing political leaders, and for securing the orderly succession of the rulers. Existing political orders fall short of this model in one or more respect, whether we consider local, national or world-wide structures. There is nothing very startling in this empirically derived model, but its concretization has succeeded nowhere so far, since formidable obstacles are encountered in any efforts to remodel existing establishments in light of these "minimum requirements."

Their general validity suggests at least one explanation for the gradual assimilation of the various kinds of democracy, as well as for the continued confusion of democratic and totalitarian "solutions." It may well be that totalitarian systems will eventually turn into regimes resembling the model. But such a development, even if gradual, would mean an abandonment of the totalitarian core of these systems: namely the single party, ideologically motivated and effectively claiming a monopoly of power, authority, and legitimacy. Such a party is excluded by the model, as are the operational manifestations to which it gives rise.

The chapters which follow describe in turn efforts in a number of important national systems to remedy an existing political order by searching for an element which now is believed to be lacking. The story of these searches is not overly encouraging. But even if they succeeded, they would not bring these regimes close enough to the model that has been delineated to make it likely that they would become really good governments. Nor is it at all likely that the search for a workable political order for the world at large will produce anything like the model. This most crucial search has hardly begun, because the parochial systems now dispensing what governing there is in the world muddle along benumbed by their several traditions. Will it take another holocaust to generate the will and the insight without which good government cannot be achieved?

NOTES

1. For a more extended discussion of this and what follows see Chapter 35 of *Man and His Government,* New York, 1963.

2. Zbigniew Brzezinski and Samuel P. Huntington, *Political Power: USA/USSR,* 1964, p. 436.

3. Such a review was attempted by me, *op. cit.,* Chapter 10.

4. This trend is probably traceable to the German language, in which such word combinations are common and provide both rich suggestiveness and abundant confusion: *Rechtsstaat, Wohlfahrtsstaat, Polizeistaat, Staendestaat, Verwaltungsstaat* are expressions which suggest the link while leaving it unclear what the nature of the link is, whether it is teleological, procedural, or what. Be it recalled here that stress on the *telos* seemed to the ancients the crucial point, beyond the question of who participates in ruling.

5. Cf. my *Constitutional Government and Democracy,* pp. 151-154.

6. The bibliographical references in the papers which follow give a good overview of these writings.

7. For a penetrating analysis, see K. von Beyme, "Federal Theory and Part Reality in the Soviet Union" *Public Policy,* vol. 13, pp. 395ff. This paper was read at the IPSA conference mentioned below.

8. For a more detailed discussion of these problems within a broader framework see my paper "Panhumanismus: die Kommende Weltordnung und die Einigung Europas" in *Europaarchiv,* 52, 1964. It will soon be published as part of the proceedings of the Basle Congress of the Council of Europe, held September 1964.

9. One of the major sections of the triennial Congress of the International Political Science Association, held at Geneva, 1964, was devoted to this range of issues. The author served as general rapporteur, as he had the previous year at an IPSA round table held at Oxford, and entitled "Federalism—National and International." Cf. also the symposium edited by Elmer Plischke, *Systems of Integrating the International Community,* 1964, with contributions by the author, Francis O. Wilcox, Arnold J. Zurcher, W. W. Kulski, and the editor. The

papers of the Geneva Congress will, it is hoped, be published before long.

10. See the author's "New Tendencies in Federal Theory and Practice" which constituted the general report of the session referred to in the previous note; it will be published presently in *Jahrbuch des Oeffentlichen Rechts,* 1965 (in English).

11. Cf. Arthur Maass, ed., *Area and Power,* 1959, which develops the separation of powers aspect of federalism suggested in Friedrich, *Constitutional Government and Politics,* 1937, Chapter XI. Recently, William H. Riker has published *Federalism—Origin, Operation, Significance,* 1964, which contains some interesting, if one-sided observations; unfortunately the author seems not to be familiar with recent work in the field and imagines himself to be the first to abandon "normative and legalistic" treatment into which he himself falls back under different headings. Thus to speak in dichotomic terms of centralized and peripheralized federalism is little better than to talk about the federal state versus the federation of states.

12. I have undertaken to place this theory within the broader context of general political theory and more particularly to contrast it as a process with imperialism in *Man and His Government,* 1963, Chapters 31 and 32.

13. Cf. Konrad Hesse, *Der Unitarische Bundesstaat,* 1963, who would claim this type of federalism to be the basis of the Federal Republic of Germany.

14. Cf. Zbigniew Brzezinski and Samuel Huntington, *Political Power: USA/USSR,* 1964, and the new edition of Friedrich and Brzezinski, *Totalitarian Dictatorship and Autocracy,* 1965, where these trends are assessed in detail.

15. For what follows compare *Man and His Government,* 1963, especially Chapter 35, where the matter is elaborated and placed within the context of general theory.

Great Britain: The Search for Leadership

by Anthony King

THE TWO YEARS BEGINNING IN JANUARY 1963 WERE YEARS OF almost convulsive change for the British people and their government. On New Year's Day, despite premonitory warnings from across the Channel, most Englishmen could still assume that Britain would shortly enter the European Common Market. Then on January 14, President de Gaulle abruptly vetoed Britain's application, declaring that Britain was an "insular, maritime" power, and that the nature of the European community would be "completely changed" if she were allowed to join. Only four days later, Hugh Gaitskell, Leader of the Labour Party and an increasingly outspoken opponent of the Common Market proposal, died suddenly after a short illness. He was succeeded in February by Harold Wilson, hitherto the party spokesman on foreign affairs and a one-time critic of Gaitskell.

The spring and summer of 1963 brought the Profumo affair and mounting criticism of Harold Macmillan, the Prime Minister. On June 5, John Profumo, army minister in the Conservative Government, resigned from office. He admitted that two months earlier he had lied to the House of Commons in denying rumors which linked his name with those of Christine Keeler and a former Soviet naval attaché, Captain Ivanov. In the ensuing debates, grave doubts were cast on the efficiency of Britain's security services, and on the very standards of the country's public life. On June 27, twenty-seven Conservatives refused to support the Macmillan Government on a vote in the House of Commons. Nevertheless, the Prime Minister was apparently determined to carry on when, on the eve of his party's annual conference in October, he was stricken with a painful prostatic obstruction and forced suddenly to resign. His successor, Sir Alec Douglas-Home, emerged only after the most prolonged, public, and bitter struggle for power in the recent history of the Conservative Party.

For nearly a year after October 1963, British politics were conducted under the shadow of an impending general election. Within days of the new Prime Minister's taking office, it was announced that the election would not be held until sometime in 1964. The Government proceeded with its legislative program (including the highly controversial abolition of resale price maintenance), and during the early weeks of the new year both Sir Alec and Harold Wilson toured the country in what was dubbed a "pre-election campaign." Anticipating defeat, however, the Prime Minister announced in April that Parliament would not be dissolved until the autumn—the last moment at which an election could, by law, be held. A relatively calm summer was followed by a strangely muted election campaign and, finally, on October 15, by the first change of Government in Britain for thirteen years. The Labour Party, after having lost ground at four successive elections during the 1950s, gained fifty-five seats but was returned to power with a parliamentary majority over Conservatives and Liberals of only four. In mid-1965 it was still not yet clear how long Harold Wilson's new Government could remain in power (or would want to) with such a small majority.

The events of 1963 and 1964, and their significance for British politics, cannot be dealt with fully in the course of a short essay. In what follows, therefore, I have chosen to concentrate primarily on three developments: the succession of Harold Wilson to Hugh Gaitskell as Leader of the Labour Party; Harold Macmillan's replacement as Conservative Leader by Sir Alec Douglas-Home; and the general election itself, Each of these events will be discussed in turn, following a brief sketching in of the background.[1]

I. THE LABOUR PARTY RALLIES

The result of the 1959 general election, constituting a massive vote of confidence in the *status quo,* was accepted calmly enough by the British public. The Conservatives had proved themselves capable administrators and, on the whole, humane and enlightened legislators; the country had never been more prosperous. There seemed no particular reason to change. In the press and among political scientists, however, the result was taken more seriously. Labour had been defeated for the third successive time, despite a vigorous and momentarily successful election campaign and in defiance of the "swing of the pendulum." The London *Daily Mail* commented: "Some general elections come and go like a shower of rain, freshening things up a bit, but not changing anything radically, not penetrating to the roots of our political soil. This is not likely to be said of the general election of October 1959. It will be remembered as a major upheaval, a turning point, a political watershed." D. E. Butler and Richard Rose, in their study of the election, suggested that the result "at least opened up the possibility that the old demarcations of the two-party struggle were obsolescent."[2] It began to be asked whether the Labour Party could ever again win power in Britain.

Defeat reopened old wounds in the Labour ranks and led to a renewal of the bitter factional fighting which had marked the "Bevanite" controversies of the early and mid 1950s. The struggle lasted two years and fell into two phases, the first concerned with domestic policy, the second with foreign. At a special party conference in November 1959, Gaitskell forced the domestic issue by advocating the amendment of clause IV—the public-ownership clause—of the party's constitution. He wished to emphasize publicly that Labour did not stand committed to wholesale nationalization. His proposal attracted widespread support, particularly in the parliamentary party, but the Left remained adamant. "Is the Labour Party," Michael Foot, a leading Bevanite, asked in *Tribune,* "seeking power for the purpose . . . of extending public ownership to such a degree that the nature of capitalist society is seriously transformed?" He demanded an affirmative answer. More important, many in the Center and on the trade-union wing of the party, while sharing Gaitskell's general views on policy, objected to his seemingly irreverent attitude towards Labour's traditional ideals. "I am quite unrepentant," a leading trade unionist wrote, "in my adherence to the ideals of socialism which are written into the constitution of the Labour Party." Confronted with an alliance between the extreme Left and these more moderate elements, Gaitskell was forced to back down. On March 16, 1960, the National Executive Committee agreed to an "amplification" of the party's aims; but clause IV itself was retained intact.

The second phase of the struggle opened almost immediately. It concerned the independent nuclear deterrent and Britain's role in the Western alliance. Since before the 1959 election, a large and growing Campaign for Nuclear Disarmament had advocated the abandonment of Britain's independent nuclear weapons and the withdrawal of foreign nuclear bases from Britain. A large section of the Campaign advocated outright neutralism. Suddenly, in the summer of 1960, several of the largest trade unions adopted "unilateralist" resolutions in opposition to the official party policy. At the annual conference in October, despite an eloquent plea from Gaitskell, the official policy was narrowly defeated and two unilateralist resolutions carried. But Gaitskell was determined to "fight and fight and fight again" to reverse this decision, and by mid-1961 he had succeeded. Three of the major unions which had deserted him a year earlier now renewed their support. At the 1961 annual conference, unilateralism was overwhelmingly rejected and support for the NATO alliance reaffirmed. "Last year," Gaitskell said, "our task was to save the Party. This year it is to save the nation." Gaitskell's victory, achieved by dint of assiduous campaigning and effective grass-roots organization (especially in the unions), ensured that for the foreseeable future Labour would be united under his leadership.

Throughout this period, Labour's divisions were reflected faithfully in by-election results and the public opinion polls. Asked by Gallup in October 1960 whether their opinion of Labour had gone up or down since the election, exactly 50 per cent of a sample said it had gone down; the main reason given (by 35 per cent) was "lack of unity" in the party. But the Government's popularity was also beginning to suffer. A continuing balance of payments deficit forced Selwyn Lloyd, the Chancellor of the Exchequer, in July 1961, to introduce deflationary measures, including what he called a "pay pause." Enforced mainly at the expense of public employees (including nurses and teachers), the pay pause aroused passionate opposition and led during late 1961 and 1962 to a sharp decline in the Conservatives' standing in the opinion polls. The Government suffered a number of spectacular by-election losses, including one to the Liberals in the prosperous London dormitory suburb of Orpington. In July 1962 the Prime Minister responded by dismissing at short notice a third of his cabinet; Selwyn Lloyd, author of the pay pause, was the chief victim. The Government's popularity declined further during the winter of 1962-63 when deflationary economic policies combined with wind, sleet, and snow to produce the highest level of unemployment in Britain for more than ten years.

The country's economic difficulties, together with Harold Macmillan's personal desire for a dramatic new departure in foreign policy, prompted the Government to announce in July 1961 that after earnest consideration it had decided to apply formally for British membership in the European Common Market. The Government's initiative was taken without consultation with Labour, and divided both public opinion and the two major political parties. The Conservative Party as a whole ratified the Prime Minister's initiative, but many Tories were less than enthusiastic and a few openly disaffected. Labour at first contented itself with defending Commonwealth interests, and insisting upon an election on the issue; but, despite the presence of a pro-Common Market element in the party, Gaitskell himself gradually moved into a position of opposition. At the 1962 annual conference, he carried the great bulk of the party with him in declaring his open hostility. What, he asked, does a federal Europe mean? "It means the end of a thousand years of history." Among the public, the number approving of the Government's initiative exceeded the number who disapproved at almost every stage; but the proportion with no opinion remained high, and there were many who agreed with Gaitskell that an election should be fought on the issue. In December 1962 a Gallup survey found that 37 per cent would support the Government if it decided that Common Market membership was in Britain's best interest; 29 per cent disagreed, and 24 per cent had no opinion.

In the early period of the Government's unpopularity, the Liberals (with only six seats in the House of Commons) rather than Labour were the chief beneficiaries. Although derided by the Labour *New Statesman* as "a convenient refuge for temporary deserters from the other two parties" and by the Tory *Spectator* as an "aimless all-purpose wish-fulfillment machine," the Liberals' median standing in the Gallup poll rose from 10 per cent in the year after the 1959 election to 19.5 per cent in 1962; in six months, the party's support topped 20 per cent. But towards the end of 1962 the Liberals began gradually to decline and Labour to advance. In November 1962 the proportion declaring Labour sympathies exceeded 45 per cent for the first time in three years. The party's revival coincided with Macmillan's "purge" of ministers and with the first signs of mounting unemployment; it seemed to reflect the public's growing preoccupation with domestic affairs, and appeared (if anything) to be accelerated by Gaitskell's hostility to the Common Market. By the end of 1962, Labour's lead over the Conservatives in the opinion polls was beginning to lengthen; during the year three seats were gained at by-elections. The public increasingly expected a Labour victory at the next election. The years of Conservative dominance in British politics were, it seemed, drawing to a close.

II. WILSON SUCCEEDS GAITSKELL

Battle Lines

Hugh Gaitskell died at the Middlesex Hospital, London, of a virus infection on January 18, 1963. He was 56. He had had in front of him, the *Economist* wrote, "all that a high, fair and unenvious mind, a precise, even punctilious intelligence, a real warmth and gaiety of companionship, stubborn application to the task, equally stubborn loyalty to his comrades, an unselfish vanity and an honesty of always patriotric purpose had earned for him." The *Times* attributed to him "a great belief in the British character and the abilities of his countrymen. He would never consciously have done anything that would have been untrue to either." Harold Macmillan referred to his death as "a grievous loss to the whole of the nation." On January 22 the Prime Minister testified to the country's grief by moving the adjournment of the House of Commons—a tribute hitherto reserved for those who had held the office of Prime Minister.

But, until the very end of his life, Gaitskell had always been the subject of controversy.[3] Following Labour's defeat at the polls in 1951, he had quickly emerged as the most trenchant spokesman for the Right of the party among the younger generation. While Aneurin Bevan established himself as the darling of the militant workers in the constituencies, Gaitskell won the loyalty of Labour's members of Parliament and, increasingly, of the most powerful trade union leaders. In 1954, when the party treasurership fell vacant, the trade unions swung behind Gaitskell and inflicted a crushing defeat on Bevan. On Clement Attlee's retirement from the leadership in December 1955, Gaitskell easily defeated Bevan on the first ballot. From then till the 1959 election, the party's internal life was comparatively placid. Bevan accepted the verdict of 1955 and remained loyal to his former rival until his death in the summer of 1960. But the years 1960-61 were marked, as we have seen, by acrimony, turmoil, and factional strife.

Labour's internal conflicts assumed different forms, but underlying them all was an essential clash of principle: whether the party should play the Gaitskellite role of a moderate, reformist alternative government, or whether it should adhere to the more radical, revolutionary faith of the left-wing militants. To Gaitskell and his supporters, socialism meant concern for the less fortunate, equality of opportunity, the abolition of restrictive social barriers, racial equality, an element of personal idealism, and the insistence "that pursuit of private gain should not take precedence over the public good." [4] These were the ends; specific proposals for nationalization or the redistribution of income were but means. But to Michael Foot, Ian Mikardo, and Bevan's successors, socialism meant the explicit rejection of the mixed economy and the complete overturn of capitalist society. Contemporary British society the Left characterized as "evil and disgraceful and rotten." [5] Although each side claimed that its conception of Labour's goals coincided with the desires of the British public, the conflict had elements in it of what Max Weber described as the tension between the "ethic of ultimate ends" and the "ethic of responsibility"—between those who sought "to rekindle the flame of pure intention" and those who accepted the limitations of practical political action.[6]

A Leader other than Gaitskell might have sought to bridge these gulfs. But by conviction, political instinct, and temperament, Gaitskell was not a compromiser. Morally, he repudiated the totalitarianism implicit in much left-wing thinking. Politically, he believed that for electoral reasons Labour must move towards the Center, and that it would be inexpedient as well as timorous to surrender to the Left. Intellectually, he had nothing but contempt for what he regarded as the Left's empty slogans and bombast. Although beloved by his intimates for his breadth of interests, his capacity for personal affection, and his invincible integrity and courage, Gaitskell suffered from an inability to conciliate his enemies and to make even symbolic compromises. For all his intellectual (even academic) gifts and his personal gentleness of manner, he was a tough fighter; there were many in the Labour Party whom he had bruised. His donnish disdain for old-fashioned socialist rhetoric offended deeply the sensibilities not only of the Left, but of many on the Right and Center who lacked his intellectual rigor. Nevertheless, by the time of his death, Gaitskell had won the profound respect if not the love of his party, and had re-established himself firmly as its Leader. The choice of a successor did not promise to be easy.

On January 23, the Wednesday following Gaitskell's death, the Parliamentary Labour Party agreed, on the recommendation of the Parliamentary Committee, to hold an immediate election. The new Leader was to be elected by an absolute majority of the Labour members of the House of Commons (abstainers excepted). Five former Labour M.P.s, who had been expelled for repeated breaches of party discipline, could not vote; nor could members of the House of Lords, or other party officials not in the House of Commons. Altogether the electorate numbered 249; if all 249 voted, 125 votes were needed to win. Nominations were to close on January 31. Balloting was to take place during the following week, with the result to be announced on February 7. If no one emerged with an absolute majority on the 7th, the candidate finishing last would drop out and another ballot be held during the following week. Successive ballots would be held until an absolute majority had been secured. In outlining the voting procedure, Herbert Bowden, the Chief Whip, appealed for dignity and restraint. He particularly asked that M.P.s should resist the temptation to take part in broadcasts on the subject. His words were heeded, and during the three weeks the election disappeared to a remarkable extent from public view.[7]

Wilson

Two candidates declared themselves almost at once: Harold Wilson, the 46-year-old party spokesman on foreign affairs, and George Brown, 48, the Deputy Leader.[8] The son of an industrial chemist, James Harold Wilson attended State schools in the north of England before winning a scholarship to Oxford in 1934. He established a brilliant academic record as an economist, and taught the subject at Oxford from 1937 until the outbreak of war. From 1940 to 1944 he served in the higher civil service, first as an economic assistant to the War Cabinet Secretariat, then as director of economics and statistics at the Ministry of Fuel and Power. Elected to Parliament in 1945, Wilson was immediately given junior ministerial office. Two years later he was promoted to the Presidency of the Board of Trade, becoming at the age of 31 the youngest cabinet minister since the early nineteenth century. During most of Labour's years of opposition, he spoke from the front bench on economic and financial affairs, transferring to the foreign field only in 1961. Wilson was elected to the constituency section of the National Executive Committee in 1952 and from 1954 served on the Parliamentary Committee of the P.L.P.

A bald summary of Wilson's career, however, fails to capture the controversy which surrounded much of it. As a minister in the Attlee Government, Wilson did not shine; he was generally considered competent but quite unspectacular. Then in April 1951 he joined Aneurin Bevan in resigning over the scale of the Government's rearmament program. For the next few years he remained close to Bevan and won his place on the National Executive as a spokesman of the Left. But when in 1954 Bevan resigned from the twelve-man Parliamentary Committee in protest against Labour's official foreign policy, Wilson, who had stood thirteenth in the poll, hesitated only briefly before taking his place. Many on the Left were incensed. During the clause IV controversy following the 1959 election, Wilson remained ostentatiously aloof, refusing to back Gaitskell although his views on matters of policy were known to resemble Gaitskell's. "Let us unite," Wilson said, "on policy, not divide on theology." He also refused to support Gaitskell during the unilateralist struggle and, although denying that he was a unilateralist, openly challenged Gaitskell for the leadership in November 1960. He was defeated by 166 votes to 81. Two years later he challenged George Brown for the deputy leadership, losing this time by 133 to 103. Like many others in the Labour Party, he refused to commit himself on the Common Market at the outset, though his qualified approval gradually hardened into less qualified antagonism.

By January 1963, Harold Wilson had earned a reputation—at least on the Right of the party—for disloyalty and deviousness. Although his views on policy were not in themselves extreme, Wilson appeared to court the Left assiduously, and positively to go out of his way to avoid committing himself to the leadership's positions. He was widely believed to be unscrupulously ambitious; he was distrusted. Even the Left had its doubts. Not only were Wilson's policy views moderate, but he refused to align himself openly with the anti-Gaitskellite faction. During the 1960 annual conference, the *New Left Review* commented acidly: "If the Labour Party ends this week facing in two directions, it is certain that the figure of Mr. Wilson will be there, at the end of both of them."[9] It was widely accepted that Wilson had stood against Gaitskell in November 1960 only because the appearance of another candidate, Anthony Greenwood, had forced his hand. As a person, Wilson was known to be capable of acts of great kindness; but he was a shy man, often likened to "the cat who walks by himself." Friendly to all, he was particularly friendly to none.

Nevertheless, in the coming struggle for power, Harold Wilson had certain enormous assets. An undistinguished parliamentary performer as a minister, Wilson had used the years of opposition to perfect a debating style that was brilliantly caustic. He delighted the Labour benches with his sardonic phrasemaking and his manifest contempt for the Eden and Macmillan Governments. Of his assault on the "pay pause" in 1961, a Conservative M.P. wrote: "It was a speech laced with class-hatred, venom and brilliant invective. It made many a Government backbencher wince."[10] Nor were his gifts merely polemical. Wilson's speeches evinced a firm grasp of many subjects, particularly in the economic field, and he had had a distinguished career as a wartime civil servant. He knew his way around Whitehall and the academic and industrial worlds. Perhaps equally important, despite his somewhat rasping voice and north country accent, Harold Wilson had about him an air of educated middle-class respectability. With an election believed imminent, this fact alone was to weigh with many Labour M.P.s.

Brown

Wilson's chief rival, George Alfred Brown, presented an almost complete contrast. Born into poverty in Lambeth, south of the Thames River in London, he left school at the age of 15 and worked successively as an invoice clerk and a fur salesman before becoming a full-time trade union officer. In the evenings he attended Workers' Educational Association classes. Elected to Parliament, like Wilson, in 1945, Brown rose to junior ministerial office in 1947, and when the Attlee Government fell in 1951 he was Minister of Works. His early career in opposition was comparatively undistinguished, except for his readiness to engage in verbal slugging matches with Aneurin Bevan. When Nikita Khrushchev visited Britain in 1956, Brown achieved momentary notoriety by provoking the Soviet leader into a violent outburst at a private dinner party. During this period Brown spoke from the front bench mainly on agricultural, economic, and defense topics. Later, after the 1959 election, he achieved considerable stature as official party spokesman on defense, consistently criticizing the ill-fated Skybolt agreement with the United States. Brown stood well to the Right of the party, and in 1960, at the height of the unilateralist controversy, was elected Deputy Leader in succession to Bevan. He fended off Wilson's challenge without too much difficulty two years later.

Although sometimes privately critical of Gaitskell's tactics as Leader, George Brown had publicly supported him throughout the unilateralist controversy. Unlike both Gaitskell and Wilson, he favored Britain's entry into Europe. An Oxford professor once said of him: "Brown has the greatest untrained mind I've ever experienced."[11] A man of generous impulses and undoubted courage, he was well liked by the parliamentary party, especially among his own trade union group. But, although an infinitely more accomplished platform orator than Wilson, Brown lacked his rival's finesse on the floor of the House of Commons. He often rambled, or misjudged the mood of the House and lost its ear. The emotionalism which endeared him to some alienated others; his pugnacity frightened even his friends. Moreover, Brown lacked formal education and, although in fact a literate and cultivated man, gave the impression of being aggressively proletarian. Particularly on television, Brown's boisterousness often contrasted sharply with the more modulated performances of Harold Wilson.

Right-wing Strategy

With 125 votes needed to elect, the backers of the two candidates felt they could count on about 80 votes spiece. Wilson's solid support would come mainly from the Left. Prior to 1959, the Left in Parliament had consisted disproportionately of white-collar workers (journalists, social workers, insurance agents, and party publicists and organizers); the Right generally had the support of both manual workers and the learned professions (doctors, teachers, and lawyers). Trade union sponsored M.P.s were generally right-wing, with Cooperative members leaning far to the Left; the group backed by the constituency parties was mixed.[12] But by 1963 the hard core of the Left appeared to have grown slightly (from perhaps 55 to 70) and to have broadened its base somewhat. On December 13, 1960, 72 out of 258 Labour members abstained from voting on an official party defense motion in the House of Commons; their number included approximately a fifth of the 92-member trade union group. Afterwards several abstainers claimed they were objecting to Gaitskell's decision to defy the party conference's unilateralist decision, and it may be that over a period of years Gaitskell's stubborn style of leadership alienated a small number of M.P.s who would otherwise have supported him.[13] Eighty-one members, most of them left-wing, voted for Wilson against Gaitskell in 1960, and Wilson's backers were certain he could rely on their support again. Despite the defection of a few trade unionists to the Left, Brown could bank on some 65 or 70 trade union votes, plus a dozen or so from confirmed right-wingers.

To win, therefore, each candidate needed some 45 additional votes. Superficially, the stronger position seemed to be Brown's. As the candidate of the Right, he could hope to match the 166 votes amassed by Gaitskell in defeating Wilson in 1960; he himself had beaten Wilson for the deputy leadership only three months before. But, between the earlier elections, Wilson's poll went up from 81 to 103. Some of the increase might be accounted for by Center M.P.s seeking to balance Gaitskell with the more radical Wilson; but more was probably the result of a widespread sense of Brown's personal limitations. In either case, it seemed reasonable to suppose that some members would support Brown for the deputy leadership but not for the leadership itself. Even some former Gaitskellites doubted Brown's ability either to lead the party effectively in Parliament or to impress the floating voters on whose support Labour depended to win the coming election. During the week before nominations closed, increasing skepticism was expressed about Brown's ability to defeat Wilson in a straight fight. The possibility loomed that Harold Wilson might be elected in default of a stronger right-wing candidate.

Confronted with this possibility, many of the most prominent parliamentary figures nevertheless determined to support Brown. They liked him personally and valued his abilities; they believed he could win. Their number included James Griffiths and Sir Frank Soskice, both former members of the Attlee administration, Tom Fraser, a prominent Scottish M.P., and Alice Bacon, a former party chairman. In time they were joined by Patrick Gordon Walker, an ex-minister and front bench spokesman on defense. But other former Gaitskellites were caught in an agony of indecision. They desperately wanted to defeat Wilson, whom they deeply despised for his equivocations and disloyalty to Gaitskell; but they were not sure whether Brown could do it. The Gaitskellite pressure group within the party, known as the Campaign for Democratic Socialism, split wide open, some of its leading members finally deciding to back Brown, others preferring to seek an alternative candidate. C. A. R. Crosland, a CDS supporter and the Gaitskellites' most brilliant and profound thinker, took the latter course. In this he was joined by Douglas Jay, an intimate friend of the late leader and party spokesman on Board of Trade affairs, and from outside CDS by Denis Healey, another Labour defense expert, and Michael Stewart, increasingly prominent as an initiator of housing policy.

For six days the third-candidate faction searched anxiously for an acceptable alternative to Wilson and Brown. As one mourning Gaitskellite put it, "It's like a child being asked which step-mother he would prefer." James Callaghan, the "shadow" Chancellor of the Exchequer, seemed the obvious choice, but Gordon Walker, Soskice, and Stewart were each at some stage approached. Each in turn refused, and by February 1, when nominations closed, Leonard James Callaghan had emerged as the candidate whom Jay, Crosland, and their allies hoped could rally the moderates. He seemed well cast for the role. At 50 he was only slightly older than his rivals. A former assistant secretary of the Inland Revenue Staff Federation, he had served in the navy before entering Parliament in 1945. He served under Attlee first at the Ministry of Transport and later at the Admiralty. In the House of Commons, Callaghan could be as pugnacious as George Brown and had first become prominent as the bitterly aggressive critic of Conservative Colonial Secretary Alan Lennox-Boyd. But in private, and on television, he had more of Harold Wilson's smoothness. During the years of party dissension, he had backed Gaitskell consistently without incurring the deep antagonism of the Left. Although probably less able than either Wilson or Brown, Callaghan possessed personal charm and a certain brisk competence.

His intervention hugely delighted Wilson's supporters, and threw the Brown camp into a near paroxysm of fury. Coming from the Gaitskellites, it constituted the most pointed possible personal rebuff to Brown. Callaghan agreed on all substantial issues with Brown and could only be standing because his backers lacked confidence in Brown. Not only would Callaghan almost certainly take more votes from Brown than from Wilson; his candidature in itself would raise questions in the minds of Brown supporters. Equally serious, Callaghan's intervention would probably necessitate a second ballot. If Wilson led on the first ballot, as now seemed likely, Callaghan supporters might then switch to Wilson rather than to Brown in order to ensure that the eventual winner was returned by a substantial, unquestionable majority. In other words, a Wilson bandwagon might begin to roll. Between February 1 and 7, Brown's leading backers tried in every way possible to get Callaghan to withdraw. George Brown himself threatened to retire from the front bench if Callaghan was elected. But they failed, and all three names remained on the ballot paper.

Campaign and Election

The week-long campaign was quiet but intense. The declared backers of Wilson and Brown were left more or less alone, but the other eighty to a hundred Labour M.P.s found themselves subjected to continuous pressure. Telephones rang, letters were written, and members found themselves joined for lunch by colleagues they scarcely knew. Harold Wilson's campaign was managed by R. H. S. Crossman, the brilliant but unpredictable sometime *enfant terrible* of the party's left-wing intelligentsia, and by George Wigg, a mildly eccentric retired service officer who combined left-wing views with love of horseracing and the army. George Brown ran his campaign with the aid of a London M.P. and former party official named Gerry Reynolds. The original supporters of Callaghan attempted to look after his interests. During the week, Parliament continued in session, and the three candidates each made a major speech; all three did well, and probably few votes were affected. Wilson's campaign received a fillip on January 27 when a Gallup poll showed Wilson enjoying a small lead over Brown among all voters; Brown was favored by Labour supporters, but Wilson (despite his left-wing views) had the edge among Conservatives. At the outset the two leading contenders had agreed to discourage their supporters from abusing each other, but the agreement had little impact, and by February 7, when the first ballot closed, feelings were running high. Predictably, greatest heat was generated by the Brown-Callaghan clash.

At a meeting of the Parliamentary Labour Party on February 7, the result of the first ballot was declared. It confirmed Brown's worst fears. Wilson had 115 votes, twelve more than when he challenged Brown for the deputy leadership, and only ten short of the required 125. Brown's vote had dropped from 133 in November to 88, scarcely more than his minimum support. Callaghan, with 41 votes, had apparently done Brown serious damage. There were five abstentions (including that of a 90-year-old member who explained that he had been moving house and would certainly vote for Wilson on the second ballot). Callaghan, having finished third, automatically dropped out, and the rest was anticlimax. Despite pleas for his withdrawal, Brown insisted on remaining in the race; in a public statement, he alluded vaguely to important questions of principle which were at stake. But the anticipated Wilson bandwagon developed, and when the second result was announced on February 14 it was clear that a majority of Callaghan's votes had gone to Wilson. With only two abstentions, Wilson had defeated Brown decisively, by 144 votes to 103. Thus at the age of 46 James Harold Wilson became at once the heir to MacDonald, Attlee, and Gaitskell, and the prospective Prime Minister of the United Kingdom.[14]

Criteria

In choosing their new Leader, the Labour members of Parliament had been guided by at least seven criteria. Most M.P.s had all seven in mind, though of course different members ranked them differently. First, the new Leader had to be capable of leading the party in the House of Commons; he must be a fluent speaker and an able tactician. Second, he must know how to appeal beyond staunch Labour supporters in the country to uncommitted voters; he must be an asset to the party at the coming election. Third, the new Leader had to be someone who, if Labour won the election, would make a good Prime Minister. Fourth, he must not be a divisive influence; he must be capable of holding the Labour Party together (if possible, more successfully than Gaitskell had done). On the first three of these criteria, and probably on the fourth, Harold Wilson scored. His superiority over Brown as a parliamentarian was universally acknowledged. The Gallup poll of January 27 underlined his greater appeal to non-Labour voters; perhaps surprisingly, many working-class Labour M.P.s doubted whether a man so conspicuously working-class as Brown could command widespread public respect. Wilson seemed altogether more plausible than Brown as Prime Minister. And it was widely believed that Wilson, unlike Brown, could hold the party together; as a man of the Left, he would be temporarily immune from left-wing criticism, while at the same time he would inevitably be forced to carry with him the large Gaitskellite majority.

The remaining criteria were more personal. By contrast with American convention delegates, British members of Parliament must live on a day-to-day basis with their chosen Leader; he must therefore not be personally obnoxious to them. On this narrow fifth criterion, of personality, Wilson probably also gained with all but Brown's closest friends. Where serious doubts arose were on the sixth and seventh criteria: those concerning the two candidates' integrity and trustworthiness, and their substantial political views. The Left doubted whether they could count implicitly on Wilson, but, since his views certainly resembled theirs more closely than did Brown's, they had no choice. The Right trusted Brown and shared his views; they distrusted Wilson and did not share his views (or at least had not shared them in the past). Many in the

Center also distrusted Wilson, but felt, nevertheless, he would make the more impressive Leader. In the end, the Right's qualms were submerged by the Left's enthusiasm for Wilson, by the Center's lack of enthusiasm for Brown, and by their own divided counsels.[15]

Considerations of ambition probably played little part in the election. This was not because Labour M.P.s were not ambitious; a large proportion of them were (and are). Undoubtedly calculations of personal advantage entered the mind of almost every elector before the contest was over. But most of the prominent figures—those most likely to hold ministerial office in a future Labour Government—were already committed to one or the other wing of the party and therefore, in practice, to either Wilson on the one hand, or Brown or Callaghan on the other. For these electors to have changed sides in mid-battle would have laid them open to charges of blatant opportunism. In any case, it grew increasingly apparent that whoever won would have to take extraordinary precautions to placate all sections. (A few M.P.s may conceivably have campaigned especially vigorously for a particular candidate in hopes of being rewarded if he won, but bought off if he lost.) Thus, insofar as a bandwagon mentality developed, it was of a fairly disinterested sort. The main purpose of plumping for Wilson on the second ballot was to give the new Leader a decisive majority, one whose significance could not subsequently be disputed.

Wilson Takes Hold

On January 19, 1963, the day after Gaitskell's death, the *Times* Political Correspondent had written of his successor: "Anybody who knows the history of the Parliamentary Labour Party will be sure that he . . . will not establish his authority as Leader without an exhaustive and perhaps damaging struggle." In the event, this prediction was wholly falsified. Beginning with a victory address at Transport House, the Labour headquarters, Harold Wilson firmly grasped and held the reins of power. Within months even the most stalwart Gaitskellites freely conceded that Wilson was proving himself a skillful, even brilliant Leader. "I'm trying to forget," said one of them, "that I ever voted for Brown." Wilson worked comfortably and well with all sections of the party, and at no stage was there the remotest likelihood of his authority being formally challenged. Although some ill-feeling lingered on between

Brown and Callaghan, neither disputed Wilson's primacy. There was no exhaustion, no "damaging struggle."

What accounted for Wilson's success? Undoubtedly Harold Wilson benefited enormously from the imminence of a general election and from the simple fact of not being Hugh Gaitskell. For all his qualities of intellect and courage (and despite his temporary popularity with the Left for opposing Britain's entry into Europe), Gaitskell would almost certainly have constituted something of an irritant, an ever-present potential source of discord, if he had continued to lead the party. Wilson at least could not be attacked from the Left. More important, the new Leader benefited immeasurably from being able to build on the solid foundations laid by Gaitskell. Under Gaitskell's leadership, Labour had accepted a major statement of domestic policy, *Signposts for the Sixties;* this remained official party policy for the election. Wilson also inherited the consequences of Gaitskell's decisive and irreversible triumph over the unilateral nuclear disarmers; for the foreseeable future, there seemed no prospect of defense again emerging as a major source of intraparty tension. Wilson recognized these facts. In his victory address, he paid open tribute to Gaitskell's success in reforging party unity, and pledged himself to carry forward Gaitskell's policies.

But Wilson's success contained an equally large, more positive element. In the year following his election, he established himself as one of the most brilliant and adroit party leaders in British political history. He won the support of former Gaitskellites by consulting them freely, and by appointing them to (if anything) more than their share of frontbench posts. By contrast with Gaitskell, who relied heavily on the advice of a few intimate friends, Wilson talked to everyone—and then made up his own mind. On occasion, he made symbolic gestures to the Left, but his major decisions were firmly in the Gaitskellite tradition. Moreover, Wilson excelled in the House of Commons, on television (where he projected an image of intelligence and candor) and in his relations with the press. His standing with the public soared above Gaitskell's. From 1959 onward the Gallup poll had asked each month: "Do you think Mr. Gaitskell [Mr. Wilson] is or is not proving a good Leader of the Labour Party?" While Gaitskell lived, the proportion replying in his favor exceeded 55 per cent only twice, and reached 50 per cent only ten times; often his standing dropped to 43 or 45 per cent. By contrast, during his period as Leader of the Opposition, Wilson only once fell below 50 per cent (in the first month of his leadership) and often exceeded 60 per cent. By late 1964, one of the most experienced observers of British politics could refer to Wilson as "the most professionally equipped Leader since Lloyd George." [16]

Nevertheless, the circumstances of Harold Wilson's election illustrated dramatically one of the permanent problems posed by the British political system: the problem of recruitment to high political office. In choosing their new Leader in January 1963, the Labour members of Parliament were forced by their own Standing Orders, and by the whole weight of British tradition, to select from among their own number. Unlike delegates to a presidential nominating convention, they could not recruit from other branches of government, local authorities, the judiciary, or business.[17] Their range of choice was therefore narrow. It included only men and women who had climbed the same political ladder: nomination by a constituency Labour party, election to the House of Commons, long parliamentary service on the front bench. In practice, the choice was narrowed further by the fact that Labour had languished in opposition for twelve years. Some able M.P.s had been defeated; others had retired, having lost all hope of attaining ministerial office; others had not even sought election to Parliament, believing the prospects to be too poor. Harold Wilson recognized the consequences of this process of attrition. On becoming Prime Minister in October 1964 he appointed to office several distinguished outsiders, who then either moved directly to the House of Lords, or else remained outside Parliament until they could find seats in the House of Commons. But the scope for such action was strictly limited. The narrowness of the recruitment base remains one of the weaknesses inherent in the British form of parliamentary government.

III. HOME SUCCEEDS MACMILLAN

Harold Wilson succeeded Gaitskell as Labour Leader on February 14, 1963. In eight months' time, the Conservative party, too, was to change its Leader, but in vastly different circumstances.

Labour's election was occasioned by the sudden and unexpected death of Hugh Gaitskell. It took place over a period of three weeks and was conducted according to a clearly defined set of rules. Partly because of the sobering influence of Gaitskell's death, it attracted minimal publicity. The number of candidates was small, and when the election was over, Labour quickly closed its ranks. By contrast, the change of Conservative leadership climaxed a prolonged period of tension and uncertainty. Few rules existed beforehand; they had to be invented *ad hoc* by the participants. Partly because of the timing of Macmillan's resignation, the struggle to succeed him attracted maximum publicity. The number of candidates was large. Long after Sir Alec Douglas-Home had kissed hands as Prime Minister, leading Conservatives privately cast doubt both on his title to lead the party and on the method of his selection.[18]

The Macmillan Era

At the time of Wilson's election, Harold Macmillan had been Prime Minister for almost exactly six years.[19] It seemed inevitable that the post-Suez period would be known to history as the "Macmillan era," so completely did he dominate the Government of which he was head. Yet he remained something of a mystery to the British public and even to his colleagues. A man of courage and ruthless determination, he cultivated an air of almost gentle world-weariness. In the 1930s, he had fought hard within the Tory party for Roosevelt-style social reforms. During 1961 and 1962, he championed the cause of Britain's entry into the Common Market. Yet, although his policies were progressive, Macmillan seemed as a person to hark back to an earlier, more self-contained era. With his drooping eyelids and slightly old-fashioned clothes, he seemed in some ways a figure from another age. The idealism which impelled him to strive for improved Soviet-Western relations and which reached fruition in the nuclear test-ban treaty was hidden behind a debonnaire Edwardian mask. Only occasional outbursts of passion—as when he angrily dismissed Gaitskell as being "incapable of rising to the level of great events"—suggested a latent emotionalism. Harold Macmillan was a brilliant, far-sighted, and essentially solitary man. He may have understood the Conservative party; it almost certainly did not understand him. The ties uniting them had always consisted more of respect than affection. From 1961 onward they grew increasingly frayed.

The first four years of Macmillan's premiership had been brilliantly successful. Having succeeded Sir Anthony Eden at the nadir of the Tories' fortunes following Suez, he had reunited the party, restored its morale, and led it to a resounding victory at the 1959 general election. By 1960 he was being hailed by the popular press as "MacWonder" and "SuperMac," and in April his personal standing in the Gallup poll soared to 79 per cent. But then, very gradually, his troubles began. The Government's African and Common Market policies caused unrest on the Conservative back benches, and the "pay pause" contributed to a slow but steady decline in the party's standing in the opinion polls. In August 1961, Labour edged ahead in the Gallup poll for the first time since the election. Although Macmillan's own standing also began to slump, the Prime Minister himself remained relatively free from personal attack until early 1962. On February 2 a distinguished Conservative backbencher, Sir Harry Legge-Bourke, called attention in his constituency to Macmillan's advancing age and suggested that the time had come for him to give way to a younger, more dynamic Leader. Many observers had detected an increasing fuzziness in the Prime Minister's public pronouncements, and Legge-Bourke alluded to an impression of "indecision, uncertainty and lack of direction." But, although Legge-Bourke's remarks undoubtedly echoed in the minds of many Conservatives, many more were scandalized. Letters reprimanding him appeared in the press, and within a few days he was forced to resign his chairmanship of the Tory backbench defense committee.

Macmillan's troubles did not disappear, however; they multiplied. The spring and summer of 1962 brought a further decline in the Conservatives' standing in the polls and a series of stunning by-election reverses. Then suddenly on July 13, Macmillan reacted with a brutality that staggered the political world. At one blow, he sacked a third of his cabinet, including Selwyn Lloyd, the Chancellor of the Exchequer, whose fortitude in withstanding public uproar over the pay pause had won him much admiration. Many Tories were aghast. When Macmillan next took his seat in the House of Commons, he was met with stony silence. No revolt occurred at the time, but many Conservative M.P.s later looked back to July 1962 as their moment of final disillusion. And worse was yet to come. Although Macmillan won a great personal triumph at the annual party conference in October, when the Government secured an overwhelming vote of confidence for their Common Market policy, the harsh winter of 1962-63 brought further by-election setbacks, de Gaulle's veto, and the highest level of unemployment since 1947. Labour's lead in the polls lengthened; the Prime Minister's personal standing plummeted to 35 per cent. Conservatives began to voice their doubts privately in increasing numbers. But Macmillan was not ready to go, and on April 10, 1963, announced his determination to carry on: "I shall be leading you into the General Election and I shall be with you in the new Parliament." For a brief moment, his announcement cleared the air.

Profumo

But then, on June 5, the news of John Profumo's resignation burst like a thunderclap. Macmillan had appointed Profumo to high office, had sat beside him in the House of Commons while he lied about his relations with Christine Keeler, and as head of Britain's security services could be held responsible for their failure to detect the Profumo-Keeler-Ivanov triangle. Rumors spread, following a cabinet meeting on June 10, that a number of the younger, more able ministers were contemplating resignation. But, whatever their doubts about the Prime Minister's handling of the situation, ministers had no desire to embarrass him; it was far from certain that he had been at fault. Nor was it clear what purposes resignation would serve. If the Government did not fall, those who left it would still be accused by their fellow Conservatives of self-seeking and treachery; if it did, the consequences would be incalculable. The cabinet held together. But backbench M.P.s could voice opinions somewhat more freely; the Government would fall only if they abstained or voted against it on a massive scale. When the Commons debated Profumo on June 17, Macmillan was a shadow of his former self—nervous, hesitant, at times almost maudlin. Nigel Birch, an ex-minister speaking for the Conservative dissidents, hoped that the Prime Minister's resignation would not be too long delayed. In the ensuing division, 27 Conservatives deliberately abstained, signifying their lack of confidence in Macmillan and sharply reducing the Government's majority.

Predictably, in the weeks that followed the Profumo debate, Macmillan's ordeal produced a wave of sympathy. Although his standing in the Gallup poll fell back to 35 per cent, Conservative Central Office reported a wave of pro-Macmillan sentiment among party workers in the country. The Prime Minister declared that he had no intention of being driven from public life by a sordid intrigue; on television, he repeated his April formula: "All being well, if I keep my health and strength, I hope to lead the party into the election. . . ." Nevertheless, Randolph Churchill records that during August and September 1963, Macmillan devoted much anxious thought to the succession. "Though he had not yet taken a decision as to his own future he realized that if he were going to resign he ought to do so before Christmas so as to give the new party leader and Prime Minister a chance to establish himself firmly." [20] He was apparently still wavering in early October, on the eve of the party's annual conference. By October 7, however, Churchill reports that Macmillan had all but decided to announce at the conference his intention of leading the party into the election. Then suddenly, the next day, the Prime Minister was stricken with a painful prostatic obstruction; the doctors feared it might be malignant and insisted upon operating immediately. Two days later, on October 10, Lord Home read Macmillan's announcement of his intention to resign to the 4,000 Conservative delegates assembled at Blackpool. An era had ended. A struggle for power unprecedented in the history of the Conservative party had already begun.

Removing Prime Ministers

Before continuing, however, I think it is worth considering the implications for the British political system of Harold Macmillan's last eighteen months in office. In the revised second edition of *British Political Parties,* Robert McKenzie asks what he admits is an unanswerable question: "Had it not been for the Prime Minister's illness, could he if he had wished have carried on as Party Leader into the next election?" He goes on to suggest that Macmillan could have survived only in the event of a dramatic upturn in the party's fortunes. "In the absence of such a development very powerful pressures for a change of Leadership before the impending general election were building up within the Party." Far from Macmillan's illness having caused his resignation, McKenzie suggests that it was no more than a pretext; he points out that within nine weeks Macmillan was taking part in a House of Commons debate as a backbencher. "It is difficult to escape the suspicion that he would have done so as Prime Minister, having taken his illness in his stride, had it not become clear that Party opinion had hardened in favor of fighting the forthcoming election under a new Leader." McKenzie concludes: "Harold Macmillan's is perhaps a marginal case, but he is nonetheless a serious candidate for the list of Conservative Leaders in this country who have, in effect, been forced from office." [21]

This view seems to me considerably to underestimate the difficulty of dislodging a British Prime Minister determined to defend his position. In principle, a Prime Minister whose Government enjoyed a majority in the House of Commons could be forced from office (royal intervention apart) in one or the other of two ways: either by a revolt of his supporters in Parliament, or by a *coup* in the cabinet. In practice, both methods are, except in the rarest of circumstances, virtually precluded. A revolt by the Government's backbenchers would have to be staged either on the floor of the House of Commons, or at a party meeting upstairs (of either the Conservative 1922 Committee or the Parliamentary Labour Party). If it occurred on the floor of the House, it would run the risk of toppling not only the Prime Minister but the entire Government; a small-scale demonstration, designed to avoid this consequence, might embarrass the Prime Minister but would probably not be enough to destroy him. For this reason, M.P.s determined to oust a Prime Minister would be more likely to attempt a vote of no confidence at a party meeting; such an attempt might be more difficult to organize than a House of Commons revolt, but it would obviate the danger of defeating the Government.

Either technique could be used by dissident backbenchers, but in normal times neither is likely to be. The Carlton Club revolt of Conservatives in 1922 forced the resignation of a Prime Minister, Lloyd George, who was in fact the Leader of another party; the Conservatives believed that in rebelling against him they were fighting for the very existence of their party, which might otherwise be "smashed in atoms and lost in ruins." [22] Similarly, the

House of Commons revolt which drove Neville Chamberlain from office in 1940 was motivated by the belief that the World War could be prosecuted successfully only under a national government. In normal times, backbenchers are powerfully inhibited by their feelings of loyalty to the party Leader, and by the fear that any display of internal party divisions will be exploited by the other side; the very prospect of electoral defeat, which might lead a party to want to depose its leader, would in itself act as a powerful incentive not to do so.[23] For a revolt to succeed, too, the dissidents would probably have to agree on an alternative Leader (or at least on a range of more or less equally acceptable alternatives); otherwise, potential rebels would almost certainly be restrained either by divisions among themselves or by the fear that their actions might have unforeseen (and undesired) consequences. Finally, before rebelling, most M.P.s would need to be virtually certain of success; an abortive revolt would not only split the party, but might bring down on the rebels' heads the wrath of their colleagues and constituents.

In Macmillan's case, a determined backbench revolt never got under way. His persistent individual critics—men like Lord Lambton and Anthony Fell, both of the extreme Right—were generally dismissed as irritating but harmless cranks. The June 17 abstentions were far more serious, but even they were intended not to force the Prime Minister's immediate resignation, but to indicate the strength of backbench feeling; Nigel Birch and others said afterwards that the number of abstainers, 27, was "just about right"—not large enough to defeat the Government, but quite large enough to show that discontent was spreading. The discontent was further expressed at a meeting of the 1922 Committee held three days after the Profumo debate. According to Churchill, the Committee met "in a divided and mostly hostile mood to the Prime Minister" and was held in check only by being warned that, if Macmillan were driven from office, the Queen might be compelled to send for Harold Wilson. But when the Committee met a few days later, the Prime Minister announced the signing of the nuclear test-ban treaty, whereupon, according to Randolph Churchill, "the bitterest critics swallowed their bitter cups of criticism": "The 1922 Committee, from all accounts, had recalled Macmillan to its heart."[24] The ease with which this reconciliation was consummated is almost certainly the measure of the backbench M.P.s' extreme reluctance to rebel against their Leader.

The other possible way of deposing a British Prime Minister is by means of a cabinet *coup*. This method entails a willingness on the part of ministers to tell the Prime Minister that they will resign unless he himself retires. To succeed, the dissident ministers must be so powerful that the Government could not carry on without them; their number would probably have to include three or four of the most senior men in the cabinet. But all the factors inhibiting backbenchers—loyalty, desire not to divide the party, fear of unforeseen consequences, and fear of failure—impinge even more powerfully on cabinet ministers. In the event of failure, they have more to lose; moreover, only in highly unusual circumstances would senior and probably ambitious ministers combine against a Prime Minister in order to put one of their own number in his place. In fact, only one Prime Minister in this century has been driven from office by the action of his colleagues: Asquith, who fell in 1916 at the height of the First World War, having lost the confidence of both his Liberal lieutenant Lloyd George and the Conservative members of his coalition. Efforts to oust Attlee in 1947 foundered on the inabilty of the leading ministers to agree on his successor.[25] The same inability undoubtedly restrained Macmillan's ministers during the Profumo crisis and would have gone on restraining them beyond October. In resigning, Macmillan was almost certainly responding in part to his followers' sense that it was time for a change; he may have been privately relieved when his illness intervened. But Macmillan resigned only when his will to continue had left him; he was not forced from office. Indeed, his experience suggests that a British Prime Minister determined to remain in office occupies a position which is, in normal times, virtually impregnable.

Some time afterwards, Iain Macleod observed: "I was, I think, at the end perhaps the only member of Macmillan's Cabinet to hold steadily to the view that the Tory party would do better under Macmillan's leadership at the polls than they would under any of the possible alternatives."[26] McKenzie cites this remark as an indication of Macmillan's weakness. But it could be taken, on the contrary, as evidence of his strength. Despite their loss of confidence in him, the cabinet made no move whatever to depose

Macmillan. At the end of the last cabinet meeting held before the Blackpool conference, Macmillan informed his colleagues that he intended to announce at the conference his decision on whether or not to remain in office. According to Randolph Churchill, he asked for their advice but was given no clear indication of their views. "The Prime Minister then withdrew, deliberately leaving his colleagues there so that, if they wished, they could dispute his decision and make other recommendations." [26a] He adds: "Though some of them doubted that he would be well enough to speak in Blackpool, and none of them can genuinely have believed that he would be able to fight the election, they dispersed without further discussion." In other words, the cabinet refused to repudiate Macmillan's leadership even though he all but invited them to do so. Having failed to act then, they would have found it extremely difficult to act later. Nor, despite Churchill, is it likely that "none of his colleagues" genuinely believed that he could carry on; only two days earlier, on Churchill's own admission, Macmillan's son and his son-in-law were both urging him to stay on till the election. It is improbable, therefore, that the Prime Minister's colleagues were exercising restraint merely because they knew he could not go on much longer.

Macmillan Resigns

The news of Macmillan's illness was received by the assembling delegates at Blackpool with consternation. Many Conservatives welcomed his imminent retirement, but even they were saddened by the cause of it. The party's chronic anxiety about the future of the leadership at once became acute; for no obvious successor to Macmillan had emerged, and no agreed procedure existed for selecting among the unusually large number of possible claimants. At times during the preceding two years, it had seemed that one of the younger ministers—Reginald Maudling, Edward Heath, or Iain Macleod—might succeed in establishing his claim. But, for a variety of reasons, none had done so, and during August and September 1963, Macmillan's own thoughts turned to two peers, Lord Hailsham and Lord Home. The passage of the Peerage Act that summer had incidentally made both men eligible to return to the House of Commons. According to Churchill, Macmillan sent for Hailsham on September 30 and told him that, in the event of his resignation, Hailsham would probably be most acceptable to the party. A week later, the Prime Minister and Home agreed that Hailsham was the best man, but Macmillan (not for the first time) sounded out Home himself. Nevertheless, as the party conference opened, the most senior member of the cabinet, R. A. Butler, still loomed as probably the most formidable contender.[27]

Butler

An M.P. since 1929, Richard Austen ("Rab") Butler, 61, had been a minister almost continuously since 1932. During the five years of Labour government after 1945, he acted as chairman of the Conservative Research Department and played a decisive part in modernizing Tory policy. More recently, he had served as Chancellor of the Exchequer, Home Secretary, and First Secretary of State. In 1957 he had been edged out for the premiership by Macmillan. A man of acknowledged intellectual force and administrative ability, Butler was especially admired by those who had worked most closely with him. As a symbol of the new, more liberal Toryism, he was believed to appeal to the crucial "center" element in the British electorate. But Butler had many enemies in the party, including Macmillan himself who, although an admirer of Butler's talents, hardly bothered to conceal his conviction that Butler was quite unfitted for the highest office. This conviction sprang from a number of sources. Butler, unlike Macmillan, had been a man of Munich in the late 1930s; later he had incurred widespread Tory mistrust, first by appearing cool towards the abortive Suez expedition, and then as Home Secretary by sponsoring what many Tories regarded as "soft" penal legislation. As a person, Butler seemed to lack warmth; many suspected him also of lacking courage. He was a mediocre platform speaker and on television lacked any element of personal magnetism.[28]

Hogg

Quintin McGarel Hogg, Viscount Hailsham, 55, had entered Parliament at a celebrated by-election in 1938 and remained in the House of Commons until succeeding to his father's peerage in 1950. He reached the cabinet in 1957, serving subsequently as Minister of Education, Leader of the House of Lords, and Minister for Science. In the summer of 1963, he had helped negotiate the nuclear test-ban treaty. Unlike Butler, Hailsham had captured the hearts of rank-and-file Tories both in Parliament and in the country. Where Butler appeared cool and dispassionate, Hailsham exuded gaiety, passion, and anger. A man of tremendous vivacity and exuberance, he combined perfervid partisanship with puckish good humor. Intellectually, he was Butler's equal; rhetorically—both from the platform and on television—he was far superior to Butler. But even many of Hailsham's admirers doubted his ultimate suitability for the premiership. His showmanship lacked an element of dignity and restraint, and it was widely believed that his verbal extremism might alienate the very "center" voters whom Butler would attract. Hailsham was thought by many to lack a Prime Minister's essential self-command and soundness of judgment.

Home

Like Hailsham, Sir Alexander Frederick Douglas-Home, Knight of the Thistle, Lord Douglas of Douglas, Lord Hume of Berwick, fourteenth Earl of Home, 61, had been educated at Eton and Christ Church, Oxford. With the courtesy title of Lord Dunglass, he sat from 1931 to 1945 in the House of Commons. He succeeded his father, the thirteenth Earl, in 1951, and served as Minister of State at the Scottish Office and as Commonwealth Secretary before becoming Foreign Secretary in 1960. His period at the Foreign Office had been marked by competence, if not distinction. Less well known in the country than either Butler or Hailsham, Home was also less controversial. He lacked the other two men's intellectual gifts, but was nevertheless highly regarded for his decisiveness and shrewdness of judgment. He seemed a more amiable, more straightforward man than Butler, but was not handicapped (or helped) by the ebullience of Hailsham. Above all, Home was a gentleman, with a pleasant, shy smile and wholly unaffected manner. He had made no enemies and, at a time of confusion and uncertainty, appealed to the desire of thousands of rank-and-file Conservatives for reassurance and guidance.

Younger Men

Among the younger ministers, Reginald Maudling, 46, the Chancellor of the Exchequer, appeared the favorite. Having served his political apprenticeship under Butler in the Research Department, Maudling was identified with the modern, progressive wing of the party. Earlier in the year, following the introduction of his first budget, he had enjoyed a brief boom among Conservative M.P.s; for a moment it looked as though he might "emerge." But Maudling suffered from what many Tories regarded as an excess of affability; his partisanship was tempered by a certain professional detachment, and by an amiable sensitivity to the other fellow's difficulties. He suffered, too, from being still in his 40s. Despite President Kennedy, many Conservatives still instinctively preferred age to youth; at the very least, an older man who proved a failure might be expected to retire sooner.[29] The same handicap also affected the chances of Edward Heath, 47, Lord Privy Seal and Foreign Office spokesman in the House of Commons, and of Iain Macleod, 50, party Chairman and Leader of the House of Commons. Like Maudling, both men represented the modernizing wing of the party. Heath's brilliant success as Chief Whip during the Suez period and his ruggedness and skill in conducting the Common Market negotiations had excited widespread admiration; but he had never held high office, and was inevitably closely associated with the Common Market failure. Macleod, a dedicated exponent of African decolonization, had profoundly impressed many younger Tories during his period at the Colonial Office; but his actions in Kenya and Central Africa, especially his apparent indifference to the white minorities there, had angered and embittered the imperialists.

Traditional Methods

Not only were the possible contenders numerous; it was by no means clear how it would be decided which of them had won. In the past, Conservative Leaders had been formally elected only after they had somehow "emerged." The classic description of this process is provided by McKenzie:

> A potential Conservative Leader in the process of his "emergence" first establishes his prowess in oratorical battle in the Commons; he is called into the councils of the party by the current Leader. . . . Increasingly he is groomed by the old Leader and recognized by the party as the heir apparent. If the emerging Leader has rivals they must either outshine him or supersede him in the affections of the old Leader and of the party. And they must do so long before the party meeting assembles to elect a new Leader. There can be no question of forcing

a contest at that late date. Convention requires that on that occasion all potential rivals should affirm their unswerving allegiance to the tribal chief. The tribe then speaks with one voice and the new Leader has "emerged." [30]

Critics of the "evolutionary" method had called before for an open system of democratic election; they did so again now. But their proposals evoked little response, and it was clear from the outset that some variant of the traditional method would be employed. In the light of what was about to occur, it may seem strange that Conservatives acquiesced so readily in a procedure whose details were as obscure as its outcome was unpredictable. The method of "evolution" had, however, much to be said for it. It avoided the sort of open, formal clash between rival contenders and factions which had so often disfigured the internal politics of the Labour party. It tended to produce a Leader acceptable to all sections of the party. By minimizing the role of mere "head-counting," it enabled due weight to be given to the more senior, influential men in the party. It could be extended beyond the Conservative party in Parliament to include prospective candidates and leading party workers in the country. And it preserved, at least in form, the prerogative of the Queen to choose her Prime Minister; she could appear to act on advice rather than being forced merely to ratify the party's democratically determined choice.

Moreover, the method had worked well in the past. Altogether, six Conservative Prime Ministers had retired since the turn of the century. Of their successors, three—Arthur Balfour, Neville Chamberlain, and Sir Anthony Eden—had been the heirs apparent; they had had no serious rivals and, even if democratic elections had taken place, there probably would have been only a single candidate. Winston Churchill, similarly, was the obvious choice to succeed Chamberlain in 1940, though he was not formally elected Leader of the Conservative party until he had been Prime Minister for some months. Thus, only two successions while the Tory party was in power prior to 1963 had been in any sense "contested." In 1923, Lord Curzon's seniority and gifts gave him a stronger claim than Stanley Baldwin to succeed Bonar Law; but an interview with the Conservative elder statesman Lord Balfour confirmed the King in his judgment that at that time a peer could not be Prime Minister, and he therefore chose Baldwin. In 1957, on Eden's resignation, the Queen summoned Macmillan in preference to Butler after talks with Lord Salisbury and Sir Winston Churchill; on this occasion, "soundings" were taken in the party before Eden resigned, and the members of the cabinet were individually polled by Lord Kilmuir.[31]

Now, in October 1963, Macmillan's letter to the party conference announcing his impending resignation expressed the hope that it would "soon be possible for the customary processes of consultation to be carried on within the party." But this phrase, although it reassured the rank and file, concealed the fact that the party had never before been called upon to select a Leader in anything like comparable circumstances. Whereas in the past there had never been more than one or two serious contenders, this time there were at least four, possibly six. Whereas in the past the decision had ultimately been made by a handful of Tory elder statesmen, now there were no elder statesmen; Churchill was too old, Salisbury too unpopular, and Macmillan (for the moment) too ill. Nor was it clear who should be "sounded." Until 1957, soundings had been largely confined to members of the cabinet, and possibly also a few leading backbench M.P.s and peers. In that year, the circle had been enlarged to include all of the cabinet and a large proportion, if not quite all, of the M.P.s. But since 1937 the formal electing body had always included representatives of the extraparliamentary National Union, and with the crisis occurring on the eve of the mass party's annual conference, it seemed inevitable that some effort would be made to include this group too. The past thus provided some signposts into the future, but they were neither numerous nor unambiguous.

The coming struggle had another feature which distinguished it sharply from Labour's election eight months before: only with great difficulty could it be characterized as a struggle over policies or ideas. Unlike Labour, the Conservative party lacked fairly clear-cut factions which could be labelled "Right" or "Left." A few Tories consistently took up extreme liberal or conservative positions over a wide range of issues; but they were in a minority. The majority consisted of men of the Center, who might adopt extreme liberal or conservative attitudes on particular matters—like the Common Market, or the abolition of capital punishment—but whose politics were essentially *ad hoc* and nonideological.[32] In

October 1963, Butler, Maudling, Macleod, and Heath were all recognizably candidates of the Left. But Hailsham and Home, although their support tended to come from the Right, could hardly be described as right-wing candidates; on most matters of policy they had been aligned with the moderate majority. Nevertheless, differences of outlook and style did divide them. Butler and the younger contenders represented the party's modernizing, classless, technocratic future, Home and to a lesser extent Hailsham its patrician past. These differences and the inevitable clashes of personality and temperament that went with them gave a hard, emotional cutting edge to what might otherwise have been nothing more than a pure power struggle.

Battle Lines

The Blackpool conference, which opened on October 9 in the vast, ornate Winter Gardens Hall, rapidly became the most dramatic and chaotic in the party's history. Unlike an American nominating convention, the conference itself had no *locus standi;* it was not asked its opinion on the leadership and did not expect to be. But the Blackpool atmosphere, with almost every Conservative politician in the country concentrated along a narrow two-mile strip of sea front, ensured that every maneuver in the struggle for power achieved maximum publicity. Inevitably, the contenders' speeches came to seem enormously important, and many M.P.s feared that they might be stampeded into plumping for a particular candidate; Hailsham's unabashed playing to the gallery was particularly resented. Macleod roused the conference with an urgent, aggressive summons to battle: "Let the faint hearts go their way." Maudling delivered himself of a dry, academic discourse on the state of the economy. Hailsham announced his intention of disclaiming his peerage in a speech which his enemies characterized as vulgar and melodramatic. Home spoke on foreign affairs with authority, modesty, and good humor; he was enthusiastically and affectionately applauded. Home's reluctance to disclaim his ancient earldom was well known, but when questioned on television, he pointedly refrained from asserting that under no circumstances would he accept a draft. Only Heath, who was not scheduled to speak, had no opportunity of making an impression.

Inside the conference hall, the formal sessions proceeded placidly enough, but in the refreshment rooms and corridors near-anarchy reigned. Rumor succeded rumor, the wildest speculations suddenly seemed plausible, and the atmosphere hung heavy with helplessness and uncertainty. For a brief moment, one of the most orderly, tightly disciplined political parties in the democratic world disintegrated into a shambles. By the end of the week, however, a few preliminary steps had been taken. No detailed procedure was laid down; no one had the authority to do so. But it was known in a general way which sections of the party ought to be sounded, and who should do the sounding. The constituency and area chairmen looked naturally to Lord Poole, who, with Macleod, had been Joint Chairman of the party since April. Individual M.P.s voiced their opinions either to Martin Redmayne, the Chief Whip, or to John Morrison, chairman of the 1922 Committee. Conservative peers approached Lord St. Aldwyn, the party's whip in the upper House, and prospective candidates were encouraged to get in touch with their chairman, Harold Montefiore. Lord Dilhorne, following the example set by Lord Kilmuir, spoke to members of the cabinet. But it was accepted that formal meetings of none of these bodies should be held. As the *Times* reported, the 1922 Committee was steering away from meeting to discuss the leadership, "because this might harden positions and because it might end in a vote on names." Flexibility was still the by-word.

Informal soundings had not proceeded far, however, when on Monday, October 14, Macmillan himself felt sufficiently recovered to take a hand. According to Churchill, he wished to be in a position to give the Queen advice of "a realistic and acceptable character." [33] He wished to prevent the Queen from becoming embroiled in the Conservative Party's internal politics, and also to restore order in a still chaotic situation. In addition, Macmillan almost certainly wished to prevent the emergence of Butler. He knew this could best be achieved by expanding the circle to be consulted to include the peers and constituency associations (groups already known to be hostile to Butler), and by placing responsibility for the consultations in the hands of Butler's opponents. Accordingly, since Redmayne and the others who had begun the soundings at Blackpool were all apparently Home or Hailsham supporters, Macmillan could propose with a clear conscience that the informal process initiated there should be continued on a more formal basis. He dictated a memorandum to this effect for his deputy, Butler, and on Tuesday, October 15, it was accepted unanimously by the cabinet. Their later actions suggest that some cabinet ministers, at least, did not fully appreciate to what they were committing themselves.[34]

During the next few days, members of Parliament believed to be wavering were deluged with letters and telephone calls; several complained to the press about the amount of "arm-twisting" going on. Cabinet colleagues buttonholed one another, and the more zealous workers tried to gather support in the constituencies. Butler's active supporters comprised a small liberal clique on the back benches and a larger proportion of the party's officials in Central Office and the Research Department (who, of course, had to act with considerable discretion). Hailsham's backers—dubbed the "blue-blood and thunder group"—included Maurice Macmillan, the Prime Minister's son; Julian Amery, Minister of Aviation and the Prime Minister's son-in-law; and Randolph Churchill, who as Sir Winston's son and a freelance journalist had free access to the top echelons of the Conservative party. The lobbying on behalf of Home, organized by Nigel Birch, was particularly discreet; it took the form mainly of pointing out to M.P.s that, since a deadlock had apparently developed, Home was the obvious person to break it. Little work appears to have been done on behalf of Maudling, Macleod, or Heath, only the first of whom was believed to have a serious chance of emerging.

Soundings

How Lord Dilhorne set about sounding the cabinet remains obscure. He rejected requests that the cabinet (or at least the cabinet minus the chief contenders) should meet to discuss the succession. Instead, he spoke to ministers individually, either in person or on the telephone. What is not clear is how carefully he canvassed ministers' opinions, and how (if at all) he weighted differing views. According to Churchill, Dilhorne's report to the Prime Minister stated that, whereas there had originally been six adherents of Butler in the cabinet and six of Hailsham (out of 19 excluding Macmillan and Dilhorne himself), "the overwhelming consensus now pointed to Home." Macleod, in his version of the affair published the following January, hotly disputes this. He claims not to know what Churchill's word "originally" means, and continues: "From my personal knowledge [on October 18] eleven were for candidates other than Lord Home and two in support. There were some half a dozen others. But even if there wasn't a single one of these for Butler or Maudling or Hailsham, the figures in [Churchill's] book . . . are simply impossible." Macleod argues that there must be some explanation for Churchill's account, and concludes that Dilhorne must somehow have managed to translate the frequent "expressions of genuine regard" for Home into second or even first preferences.

Redmayne's method of assessing backbench opinion he revealed a few weeks later in the course of a radio discussion. He explained that each of the area whips had communicated with the 30 or 40 M.P.s for whom he was responsible. "They gave me just a simple note of the preference of each man, of any second or third preference, and of any particular objection he might have to any of the known candidates. . . ." Redmayne admitted that, in addition to drawing up "a numerical guide about what the situation was," he had weighted some M.P.s' views more heavily than others. He maintained that Home was marginally ahead in the first choices and "outstandingly the leader" when other preferences were taken into account. Macleod does not dispute this point, but professes himself "neither impressed nor surprised." It was, he argues, Redmayne's duty as Chief Whip to consider which man was best for the party and then to do all he could to secure his election. Redmayne believed that Home was the right man and, according to Macleod, worked hard for a week "to secure the maximum support" for him. "That in such circumstances," Macleod adds, "Lord Home achieved a majority of one or perhaps two will amaze few people." [35]

Poole, assisted by Mrs. Margaret Shepherd and Lord Chelmer, two officers of the extraparliamentary party, contacted as many area chairmen, constituency chairmen, and local party dignitaries as he could. According to Churchill, he and the others told Macmillan that at Blackpool roughly 60 per cent of the constituencies had favored Hailsham and 40 per cent Butler. They added that feeling between the two adversaries' supporters was running high, and that Home was increasingly regarded as the man who could hold the party together. Macleod does not dispute this assessment in detail, but he does point out that "the spread was . . . much wider," and quotes a *Daily Express* poll of October 16 showing Butler well ahead of Hailsham among Tory voters, with Home nowhere. "I believe in fact," he says, "that this coincided closely with the actual figures." Macleod accepts completely Churchill's claim that "St. Aldwyn was able to report that the peers were overwhelmingly for Home." The peers could hardly have been expected to repudiate a fourteenth Earl, the first of his rank to be considered seriously for the premiership since 1923. As Macleod tartly comments: "It reminds me of the verse composed in epitaph for Tom Harrisson who with Madge founded Mass Observation—Dr. Gallup's forefather:

> They buried poor Tom Harrisson with his Mass Observer's badge
> And his notebooks: there were twenty thousand odd.
> And he'd not been gone a week when a report arrived for Madge
> Heaven's 83.4 per cent pro God."

Home Emerges

On Thursday, October 17, Macmillan received the four reports. He saw Dilhorne and the others separately at the hospital in the morning, and in the afternoon asked each to repeat his findings in front of the others, so that afterward there could be no misunderstandings or recriminations. "From their advice," Churchill maintains, "it once again became clear that those who wanted Hailsham were violent against Butler and those who wanted Butler were equally violent against Hailsham. Everything pointed to Home." In the evening, Macmillan composed for the Queen a long memorandum on this basis, which he read aloud to her the following morning. That same morning, October 18, the Queen accepted Macmillan's resignation as Prime Minister and summoned Home. At 12:56 p.m. a statement was issued from Buckingham Palace: "The Queen has received the Earl of Home in audience and invited him to form an administration." But Home had not yet become Prime Minister. He had apparently indicated to Macmillan the day before that he did not wish formally to kiss hands until he was assured of sufficient support from among the outgoing ministers. This stipulation either Macmillan or Home repeated to the Queen.

The Earl of Home's caution was well warranted. Macleod has recorded the shocked incredulity with which he and several of his colleagues received the first intimations that Home was to succeed. Macleod, Maudling, Enoch Powell, the Minister of Health, Sir Edward Boyle, the Minister of Education, and a number of other ministers believed passionately in the Tory party as a progressive, modernizing, classless force in British society. They believed that the character of the party had finally been transformed by the reformist "Butlerian revolution" of the immediate postwar years. Yet here was the party apparently on the verge of selecting as Leader an undistinguished aristocrat, a man who in cabinet had dragged his feet on African policy, who admittedly knew little of economic and domestic affairs at a time when these were in the forefront of British politics, and who would inevitably project exactly the image of a tired, old-fashioned Toryism which Macleod, Maudling, and the others were passionately anxious to avoid. Home, moreover, was being evolved by a process almost entirely dominated by the party's upper-class old guard—"the magic circle," in Macleod's acid phrase. "The only interesting part of Churchill's book," Macleod commented in reviewing it, "is the account of the advice Macmillan tendered: of how having first supported Hailsham . . . he switched to Home; of how he organized the collection of opinions by Lord Dilhorne, Lord St. Aldwyn, Lord Poole, Mr. John Morrison, and Mr. Martin Redmayne." He adds bitterly: "Eight of the nine men mentioned in the last sentence went to Eton." [36]

In mid-afternoon on October 17, Macleod learned from a newspaper source of Home's emergence. He was astounded—Maudling and he had lunched together only a few hours before without mentioning Home's name—and decided at once to act. During the afternoon, Macleod and Powell telephoned Home to state their objections to his becoming Leader. Late that night they were joined at Powell's house by Maudling and Frederick Erroll, the President of the Board of Trade; Hailsham kept in touch by phone. Maudling and Hailsham quickly agreed that Home should be stopped, and determined to abandon their own claims in favor of

Butler. "The rest of us," Macleod records, "felt this understanding between those hitherto the three principal contenders was of decisive importance: the succession was revolving itself in the right way." Butler was told of their decision, and Redmayne summoned to convey it to Macmillan. News of the "midnight meeting" also leaked to the press. Thus, when Macmillan awoke the next morning, he found himself confronted with a direct choice. Either he could accept the Maudling-Hailsham verdict and advise the Queen to send for Butler; or he could stand by the memorandum he had composed the night before and advise her to summon Home. If he backed Butler, he would be repudiating the complicated consultations which he himself had set in train only four days before; he would also be ushering into 10 Downing Street a man he believed unfit for the premiership. If he backed Home, he would be openly flouting the wishes of a powerful section of the cabinet; he would also be running the risk that Home could not form a Government. Macmillan did not hesitate. He opted for Home.

The efforts to stop Home, however, continued. At a series of meetings on October 18, Maudling, Hailsham, and Macleod reiterated their objections to a Home Government and worked to stiffen Butler's somewhat half-hearted resistance. Hailsham took the lead in asserting the view that the four chief contenders constituted the party's effective leadership; since three out of four now favored Butler, Home should give way. Everything depended on Butler. It was clear by now that Home could not form a Government without him; it was highly probable that, if Butler refused to serve under Home, he himself would become Prime Minister. Yet Butler continued to waver. He saw Home at least twice on the evening of Friday, October 18, and again on Saturday morning—and then, finally, agreed to join a Home Government as Foreign Secretary.[37] Home was now able to kiss hands as Prime Minister, and during the next two days he completed his cabinet. Only Macleod and Powell stood out; the two men felt that, in view of their strenuous opposition to Home, they could not honorably stay on.

On October 23, the Prime Minister disclaimed his six peerages and expressed the wish to be known henceforth as Sir Alec Douglas-Home. Three days earlier he had been adopted as parliamentary candidate for the safe Scottish constituency of Kinross and West

Perthshire (where the sitting member had died). At the by-election on November 7, the Conservative share of the poll dropped by 10.8 per cent but Sir Alec won easily. On November 11, at the Church House, Westminster, Sir Alec Douglas-Home was unanimously elected party Leader in succession to Harold Macmillan. The formal electorate consisted as usual of the Conservative members of both Houses of Parliament, prospective candidates, and the executive of the National Union. There was no debate. Sir Alec himself spoke for only three or four minutes. His election was proposed by Lord Carrington, the Leader in the House of Lords, and seconded by Butler. It was the second time in eight years that Butler had found himself supporting the election of a man who had snatched from his grasp the highest prize in British politics. The struggle for the Tory leadership was over.

Home Takes Hold

With a general election no more than twelve months away, Sir Alec Douglas-Home had little difficulty in asserting his authority. Like Wilson before him, Sir Alec took care to promote his erstwhile rivals and to pursue policies acceptable to them; he made one of his election themes "the modernization of Britain." But, unlike Wilson, the new Prime Minister never managed to impress the British public. The press treated him coolly at the outset ("Not Smart Alec—just Alec," remarked the *Daily Mirror*), and his popularity in the opinion polls at no time approached Macmillan's at its height. In the Gallup poll, Sir Alec's rating never exceeded 50 per cent; in the National Opinion Poll, more people thought Wilson would make the better premier even at times when the Conservative Party led Labour. In April 1964, only 53 per cent of an NOP sample thought Sir Alec "brilliant" compared with 71 per cent for Wilson; 54 per cent thought him "tough" compared with 82 per cent for Wilson. And, until the brief boom of mid-1964, Conservative morale remained low. Macleod followed up his refusal to join the Government by publishing in the *Spectator* a vivid, acidulated attack on the way the leadership decision had been reached; he reiterated his belief that Home was the wrong man. Early in the New Year, the Government's inept handling of a bill to outlaw resale price maintenance sparked off a major backbench rebellion. Only with the opening of the autumn election campaign did private mutterings against Sir Alec among his senior colleagues die away.[38]

Yet the Prime Minister's buoyancy, good humor, and transparent honesty of purpose continued to endear him to the Tory rank and file in the country. In the section on Labour's leadership struggle, I argued that, in choosing between Wilson and Brown, the Labour members of Parliament were guided by a number of criteria, some political, others more personal.[39] Although interview data is lacking (as it is for Labour), many Conservatives appear to have employed somewhat different criteria—and to have ranked differently the ones they shared with Labour. In Labour's case, electoral considerations undoubtedly played a prominent part, and they might have been expected to do so with the Conservatives as well. Indeed, they were uppermost in the minds of many Tories, especially in Parliament and the cabinet; men like Macleod clearly believed that Home would destroy whatever hope the party had of beating Labour. Yet the two candidates who seemed to most detached observers to have the least chance of appealing to the uncommitted, Home and Hailsham, apparently enjoyed the greatest support among party workers in the country. It is hard to escape the conclusion that the attitudes of many Conservatives were governed less by rational calculations of electoral expediency than by more instinctive considerations of personality, social class, style and age.

Butler, Maudling, Macleod, and Heath were "new men" in outlook and approach; Home and Hailsham represented a more traditional, assured, mellower brand of Toryism. Butler and the others were obviously ambitious; Home, the patrician, seemed to rise above the hurly-burly of ordinary politics. Friends and enemies alike recalled Butler's stand on corporal punishment, Heath's on the Common Market, and Macleod's on Africa. Hailsham's ebullience both attracted and repelled; so did Home's bland self-assurance. Butler's support for Munich long ago and his inscrutable personality undoubtedly did him harm. Home benefited because, unlike Macmillan, he seemed to many Conservatives predictable, straightforward, and safe; with him there would be no adventures in foreign policy, no purges. He repelled many others for exactly the same reason. Insofar as there was a Right-Left clash, it took this diffuse form. The questions of integrity and parliamentary ability hardly arose; the contenders all passed these tests. Only Hailsham (like Brown in the Labour Party) prompted serious doubts about his temperamental suitability for the job of Prime Minister. Oddly enough, the one criterion on which Home undoubtedly scored—that of party unity—appears to have been misapplied. It is extremely unlikely that any cabinet minister would have refused to serve under Butler.

Unfortunately, one of the most intriguing questions raised by the Conservative leadership struggle cannot be answered on the basis of the information so far available. It concerns the extent to which, and why, different strata in the party ranked the various contenders differently. It is certain that the cabinet, M.P.s, peers, and party workers in the country reached their conclusions (even if they happen to have been the same conclusions) on the basis of different types of evidence; few party workers in the country, for example, can have appreciated the qualities in Butler which were detected by his intimate colleagues in the cabinet. And it also seems certain that the different strata employed different criteria; few not in the cabinet, for example, could possibly have rated the contenders in terms of their cabinet performance.[40]

Unresolved Problems

With the emergence of Home, the classical method by which power had been handed on in the Conservative Party finally broke down. It had always depended for its smooth functioning on the means chosen to sound party opinion being universally accepted; in 1963 they were not, and for the first time in Conservative history a change of leadership sparked off a major revolt. In the past, too, the number consulted had always been small; in 1963 it may have exceeded 1,000. Following Home's election, the possibility of adopting a more orderly, democratic procedure was again raised. In January 1964, the Prime Minister indicated privately to a group of interested backbenchers that he would not be averse to holding an enquiry sometime after the general election. It was agreed that some decision should be reached well in advance of the next leadership crisis. Accordingly, a few weeks after polling day in November, Sir Alec Douglas-Home announced that Lord Blakenham, the Conservative Chairman, would begin to sound party opinion. He resisted suggestions that the enquiry should be formal and open.

Indeed, the leading reform spokesman, Humphrey Berkeley M.P., was rebuked at a meeting of the 1922 Committee for daring to vent his side of the question in public.[41]

It is apparent that any new system will have to embody decisions on three extremely difficult points: the exact composition of the electoral college; the question of "weighting"; and the type of ballot to be used. Whether a differently composed electorate would have evolved Home in October 1963 it is impossible to say. But, if constituency activists and peers continued to play a significant role in the selection of party Leaders, occasions might arise when different components of the electorate differed; the M.P.s could conceivably have foisted on them a Leader they rejected. For this reason, any reform is unlikely to allot a major role to either constituency activists or peers. At the same time, "weighting" (at least within any section of the electorate) will almost certainly disappear. In the past, the Conservatives have rejected secret ballots on the ground that "flexibility" is to be preferred to "mere head-counting." Any system of weighting, however, depends on the electors' willingness to accept both the *bona fides* of whoever is charged with allocating the weights, and the principle that some votes should be worth more than others. After October 1963, both of these conditions can probably never again be fulfilled.

More difficult is the type of ballot to be used. Apart from insisting that their Leader be elected by an absolute majority rather than a simple plurality, the Labour Party formally concedes nothing to the view that a consensus and not merely an outcome should be aimed at. By contrast, the Conservatives in 1963 afforded each elector every opportunity to state his second and third preferences, and also to make known the candidates to whom he took the gravest objection. Under any system, of course, electors are apt to vote against, as well as for, particular candidates. But, in situations like both parties' in 1963, where feelings are running high, multi-preference systems—especially ones allowing explicit negative votes—seem certain to encourage blackballing and to facilitate the emergence of compromises. The advantage of multipreference systems is that they may assist deeply divided electorates in finding mutually acceptable compromises; their disadvantage is that they tend to promote candidates whose only virtue lies in their never having caused offense.

Any more formal method of election will inevitably, when the Conservatives are in power, narrow the Queen's prerogative. In constitutional theory, the Queen may ask to form a Government anyone she believes capable of commanding a majority in the House of Commons. It is established by now that, following a general election, the Queen has no alternative but to summon the victorious party's Leader in the House of Commons. On October 16, 1964, for example, Her Majesty had no hesitation in calling for Wilson. But, when a change of Government occurs without an election, the position is less clear. The Labour party has never confronted this situation in practice, no Labour Prime Minister ever having directly succeeded another Labour Prime Minister. The party has indicated, however, that if a Labour premier were ever to retire or be deposed his successor would be elected in the usual manner by the PLP. The Conservatives, by contrast, have in the past recoiled from confronting the Queen with a *fait accompli;* they have insisted that senior party leaders should be no more than prepared to advise Her Majesty. (The Queen could in theory act without advice, but she is most unlikely in practice to do so.) The Conservatives feel more deeply than Labour about the Monarchy's place in the constitution; they have also sought to retain for the Crown some room for maneuver in the event of a national crisis.

The 1963 episode, however, drew attention to the possibility that the Conservatives' failure formally to elect a Leader might embroil the Queen in the party's internal affairs. In 1963 the Queen chose to consult only Macmillan and to act solely on Macmillan's advice. She summoned Home to the Palace with quite unprecedented haste. It has been alleged that, through her private secretary Sir Michael Adeane, she resisted efforts by the dissident Conservatives to approach her directly. But she was in no sense obliged to act in this way; she could have consulted other members of the cabinet and insisted upon a delay until some compromise was reached. No public objection was taken to the Queen's conduct at the time, and Macleod explicitly absolves her from blame. But, following the publication of Macleod's article, a minor furore over the Queen's role blew up in the British press. A writer in the *New Statesman* aroused the ire of Conservatives by asserting that if "there was indeed a conspiracy to foist Lord Home on the nation, it is hard to escape the conclusion that the Palace was a party to it." McKenzie inclines to the same view. Even if, however, Her Majesty acted with perfect propriety in 1963, the danger undoubtedly remains that on some future occasion the Crown's conduct (whether proper or not) might become the subject of a major public controversy. Any formal electoral system which the Conservatives adopt will have the effect of removing this danger. Such a system would probably not, in fact, reduce the Crown's ability to act in time of crisis.[42]

IV. THE LABOUR PARTY TRIUMPHS

With Sir Alec Douglas-Home's election to the Conservative leadership, Britain moved perceptibly into a pre-election period. The new Prime Minister called attention to the fact. In his acceptance speech on November 11, Sir Alec warned that there could be no good government unless there were a Conservative Government: "So from this moment on, the fact that there is a general election ahead of us must never be out of our minds. Every act that we take, every attitude that we strike, every speech that we make in Parliament or elsewhere, must have that in mind. . . ." Labour's leaders replied in kind, and for the next eleven months British politics were conducted in an atmosphere of almost continuous electioneering. Little attempt was made to conceal the fact that critical decisions concerning Britain's defenses and the national economy were being sidestepped or postponed. By the end, both politicians and the public showed signs of having grown thoroughly weary of it all.[43]

The Conservatives' long-term election planning had been largely disrupted, first by de Gaulle's veto of Britain's entry into the Common Market, and then by the prolonged leadership crisis. The party knew it had little time in which to recover. Despite his three years as Foreign Secretary, Sir Alec Douglas-Home was still a comparatively unknown figure, and in the first months of his premiership he set out on a series of "whistle-stop" tours designed to make an impact on the public.[44] Some of the younger ministers felt strongly that, in order to offset the somewhat old-fashioned appearance presented by Sir Alec, the Government should act aggressively and show itself prepared to adopt new policies. As one of them put it: "We cannot tiptoe into these elections; the country will only respect us if we govern." Accordingly, the cabinet in late 1963 and early 1964 approved in principle the digging of a Channel tunnel, accepted the Robbins Report recommendations on the expansion of higher education, and promised within the near future to raise the minimum school leaving age from 15 to 16.

The cabinet also gave its backing to a bill to abolish resale price maintenance—that is, to prevent manufacturers from fixing prices to be charged for their goods in the shops. Conceived by Edward Heath, the new Secretary of State for Industry, Trade and Regional Development, the bill was intended to induce more vigorous competition in the retail trades. Heath meant it to symbolize the Government's determination to revivify the British economy. The public gave the bill a generally favorable reception, but thousands of small shopkeepers, egged on by the *Daily Express,* with its circulation of 4,275,000, protested vigorously. A large section on the Conservative backbenches also objected, and from January through April 1964 Heath had to contend with the most prolonged backbench revolt since the Suez crisis of 1956. It reached its climax on March 11 when 21 Conservatives voted against the Government and at least 17 others abstained; subsequently the Government's majority fell to one. The underlying reasons for the rebellion remain obscure, but it undoubtedly shook public confidence in the Conservatives and further undermined Tory morale. Throughout the first six months of Sir Alec Douglas-Home's premiership, the Conservatives continued to fare badly in by-elections and to trail far behind Labour in the opinion polls.

The Date

It was during the last stages of the "r.p.m." revolt that the most important strategic decision of the entire election was taken—Sir Alec's decision to defer polling day until the autumn. Under a law of 1911, the life of a Parliament could not be prolonged beyond five years. The law had been suspended during both World Wars, but now it was binding, and an election had to be held before the first week in November. The choice of an exact date lay with the Prime Minister. Sir Alec himself favored an election in May or early June, believing that, once the electors had to face the real alternatives, they would desert the Labour Party. Several other senior ministers shared his view. They feared that continuing political uncertainty might damage the economy; they also feared that the voters might grow more, not less, hostile to the Government as time wore on. But other ministers, and the whole weight of party headquarters, came down on the other side. The "Octobrists" insisted on the need for time—time for people to forget the Profumo affair and the resale price maintenance fiasco; time for Sir Alec to make an impact on the country; time for the Tory party to recover its fighting spirit; time for prosperity to recover its hold. Above all, they insisted that the Conservatives had at least a chance of being re-elected in the autumn, but none at all in the spring. On April 9, Sir Alec's decision was announced from Downing Street: the Octobrists had won.[45]

Harold Wilson mocked the Conservatives' obvious relief at the deferment: "It must be the only recorded occasion in military history of a tattered and demoralized army being united in its unfeigned relief at being blessed with a general whose one quality was his ability to run away." Nevertheless, Sir Alec's decision appears to have caught Labour quite badly off balance. To a remarkable extent, Labour's leaders had convinced themselves that polling day could not come later than June. Wilson toured the country from January to April in anticipation of a spring election, and the party used up the bulk of its advertising and publicity funds. Labour's leaders exaggerated the strength of the anti-October pressures building up within the Government and believed that Sir Alec and his colleagues would wish to forestall an economic crisis; they tended to think the public would get increasingly fed up with a Government so obviously hanging on for solely partisan reasons. Equally important, Labour desperately wanted an early election; victory seemed certain, and the strain on M.P.s and front-bench spokesmen was beginning to tell. These considerations almost certainly warped Labour's judgment, and from April onward the Labour campaign lacked something of its former flair.

In mid-1964, however, a Labour victory still seemed inevitable. In April and May the party made sweeping gains in local government elections across the country, and captured by a decisive majority the newly formed Greater London Council. But, as the summer wore on, Labour's lead in the opinion polls gradually but inexorably declined. In the National Opinion Poll, for example, it fell from 8 per cent on June 22 to 4 per cent on July 19, and by August 23 had been converted into a Conservative lead of 1 per cent. Unfortunately, it seems impossible to produce a wholly satis-tory explanation for this phenomenon on the basis of existing evidence. The preponderance of foreign affairs in the summer's political news may have contributed, since the electorate according to the polls placed greater confidence in the Conservatives' handling of foreign policy and defense. Labour's decision not to try to keep up the political pressure during August may also have been a factor. Possibly a series of industrial disputes hurt Labour more than was at first realized. The economy continued to recover well from the difficulties of 1962 and early 1963, but if prosperity was a factor in the Tory recovery, it was remarkably slow to have an impact. It may have been true, as Conservatives contended, that by June the Government had left its worst troubles behind and could afterward be seen to be governing effectively.[46]

The Campaign

Whatever the causes of Labour's decline, the two major parties entered the campaign period in early September running almost neck-and-neck. The Conservatives hoped that the campaign could be kept comparatively quiet. "If the voters are excited," a senior party official remarked, "they'll vote Labour, so we don't want to provide excitement." Sir Alec Douglas-Home, who did not appear to best advantage on television, was scheduled to spend most of the campaign whistle-stopping; he made only six major speeches throughout. Lord Blakenham, the party Chairman, took charge in London. The daily press conferences, which had become a feature of British electioneering in 1959, were taken on the Conservative side by Maudling. Responsibility for the party's television broadcasts was assigned to Heath, who had proved himself a highly competent television performer during the Common Market negotiations. The Labour campaign, in contrast, was largely a one-man affair. Like Vice-President Nixon in 1960, Harold Wilson was determined to keep the day-to-day conduct of the campaign almost entirely in his own hands. He took the daily press conferences himself and made almost all of the party's major speeches. The Liberals, who had attracted less and less attention as their electoral fortunes appeared to decline, built their campaign largely around their Leader, Jo Grimond.

Despite the uncertainty of the outcome, the five weeks of intensive electioneering proved something of an anticlimax—"the lull before the lull," an American journalist remarked in the early days. Most of the parties' speeches and television broadcasts simply repeated arguments that had been used over and over during the preceding twelve months. Few incidents during the campaign aroused much interest, and most of the speeches delivered in the fifth week would have sounded equally appropriate in the first. The two leading opinion polls, Gallup and NOP, somehow contrived to show the electorate moving in opposite directions during more than half the campaign; their oscillations, instead of heightening interest in the outcome, seemed to contribute to the general air of boredom and confusion. Quintin Hogg added one touch of color (and thereby reinforced his critics doubts about his capacity for leadership). At Plymouth on October 6, he accused Wilson of saying that Macmillan had "debauched" the country's public life. When a heckler shouted "What about Profumo?," Hogg retorted: "If you can tell me there are no adulterers on the front bench of the Labour party you can talk to me about Profumo." The ensuing storm rumbled on for several days and delighted Labour's leaders by reviving the Profumo scandal, which they had feared to touch.[47]

Britain's independent nuclear deterrent, which Labour and the Liberals proposed to abandon, dominated the speeches of Sir Alec Douglas-Home. Although few voters seemed interested in the subject, Sir Alec believed it to be of supreme importance and insisted on keeping it to the fore. As one of his colleagues put it: "Every P.M. has one issue he cares about more than anything else. Alec's is the bomb. He'd even be prepared to lose an election on it." Apart from the Prime Minister, however, most leading speakers on both sides concentrated on bread-and-butter domestic issues—pensions, the social services, housing, land prices, health, and education. Labour laid greatest stress on the impending balance of payments crisis and on the weakness of Britain's economy; Wilson warned that Tory economic policy might lead to a new pay pause. Many of the Labour Leader's speeches echoed President Kennedy. "The choice we offer," Wilson said, "is between standing still, clinging to the tired philosophy of a day that is gone, or moving forward . . . to a dynamic, expanding, confident, and, above all, purposive new Britain." The Conservatives sought to undermine public confidence in Labour's capacity to govern and to persuade voters that a Labour Government would risk the nation's hard-won prosperity. Sir Alec dubbed Labour's program "a menu without prices": "There is not a word on where the money is coming from or what the price of the article will be. Without these details the prospectus is void."

What issues interested the electorate? The BBC put on a series of television programs during which the three party Leaders answered questions submitted by viewers. Among the 18,000 questions sent in, five types predominated:

Pensions	23%	Housing and rates	10%
Social services, health, education	15%	Economic issues	9%
		Party political matters	8%

In the penultimate week of the campaign, the National Opinion Poll asked voters which issues were particularly important to them. The answers were:

Cost of living	72%	Economic policy	15%
Education	29%	Nationalization	14%
Housing	27%	Independent deterrent	13%
Pensions	25%	Defense	12%
Unemployment	18%	Foreign Affairs	10%
Modernization	16%		

Domestic issues were rated much more highly than foreign policy in this as in all other polls. Nationalization also appeared to be of interest only to a small minority.

But of course the policy "issues" in which people express an interest do not exhaust the wider variety of "factors" and "influences" which determine their voting behavior. In 1964, British voters were reacting to an immense range of factors—the state of the economy, Sir Alec Douglas-Home's physical appearance, the troubles in Southeast Asia. Their reactions depended on their own political attitudes, moral values, economic well-being, hopes, fears, and expectations. Until the survey data on the 1964 election has been analyzed, efforts to describe what was going on in the voters' minds must necessarily be based on guesswork. Nevertheless, various aspects of the outcome—the narrow Labour victory, the unexpectedly low turnout, and the Liberal resurgence—suggest that many voters were profoundly torn between their desire, on the one hand, to bring to an end a period of Conservative Government which had brought with it economic recessions, scandals, and a decline in Britain's standing in the world, and, on the other hand, doubts about the Labour Party, which had once devalued the pound, which had so often been disunited in the past, and which had been out of office for thirteen years. "The issue at this election," one Conservative remarked, "is time for a change versus fear of change. Who wins will depend on which feeling is stronger."

The Results

Polling day came on October 15, and by noon of the next day all but a few results were known. The outcome was a crushing defeat for the Conservatives, but only a qualified victory for Labour. The Conservatives' strength in the House of Commons fell from 365 in 1959 to 304. Labour had 317 seats compared with 258 five years before. The Liberals increased the number of their M.P.s by 50 per cent—from six to nine. On a lower turnout than in 1959 (77.1 per cent compared with 78.7 per cent), Labour's total vote actually fell somewhat. But the Conservatives fared much worse; their total dropped by nearly 1,750,000—much the largest fall suffered by any party in a single election since the war. Only the Liberals had cause for self-congratulation: their vote rose from under 2 million in 1959 to over 3 million. The proportion of the total poll gained by each party is set out in Table 1.

TABLE 1

	Conservatives	Labour	Liberals	Others
1959	49.4%	43.8%	5.9%	0.9%
1964	43.4%	44.1%	11.2%	1.3%

On October 16, once it had become clear that Labour would have an absolute, if tiny, majority in the House of Commons, Sir Alec Douglas-Home tendered his resignation to the Queen; he had been premier for less than a year. Minutes later, Harold Wilson drove to the Palace to kiss hands as Prime Minister. He declared that Labour did not mean to be destroyed by the smallness of its majority. "Having been charged with the duties of Government," he said in his first broadcast to the nation, "we intend to carry out these duties." Unlike an incoming American President, the new Prime Minister had no breathing space between election and inauguration; instead, Wilson formed his administration within a week of polling day. Three new departments were created—the Ministry of Economic Affairs, the Ministry of Technology, and the Ministry of Overseas Development—and a Minister for Disarmament was added at the Foreign Office. (Legislation providing for the new departments was subsequently enacted by Parliament.) Both of the men Wilson had defeated for the Labour leadership attained high office. George Brown became Minister for Economic Affairs and First Secretary of State (in effect deputy Prime Minister); James Callaghan became Chancellor of the Exchequer.

In general, however, Wilson did not feel himself bound by the "shadow" appointments he had made in opposition. Several "shadow" ministers were not included in the new Government, and a few found themselves cast in entirely new roles; R. H. S. Crossman, who had been groomed for the Department of Education and Science, for example, traded places unexpectedly with Michael Stewart, who had been responsible in opposition for housing and local government. The new Prime Minister took great care to accommodate both the Right and Left wings of his party; Anthony Greenwood, for example, a left-winger who had threatened to challenge Gaitskell for the leadership in 1960, became Colonial Secretary with a seat in the cabinet.[48] Partly because so many holdover M.P.s had legitimate claims to office, the Government included no newly-elected members; at 56, the average age of the 23 cabinet ministers was somewhat higher than expected. It was also the largest Government in British peacetime history, consisting altogether of 103 ministers and junior ministers, eighteen of them in the House of Lords.

In one significant respect, Wilson departed from normal peacetime precedent: he recruited a number of ministers who were not members of the House of Commons and who had not previously been active in parliamentary politics. The Prime Minister wished to strengthen his Government politically by including men who had gained eminence in other capacities,—and in the case of Frank Cousins, a powerful trade union leader, by harnessing the energies of a tough, somewhat unpredictable individual who would probably make a contribution inside the Government but might cause trouble if left out. Cousins became Minister of Technology without, at first, a seat in either house of Parliament; early in 1965 he was elected at a by-election for Nuneaton. C. P. Snow, the novelist and scientist, became Parliamentary Secretary to the same ministry, and entered the House of Lords as Lord Snow. Sir Hugh Foot, a British delegate to the United Nations under Conservative Government, took the title of Lord Caradon and became Minister of State at the Foreign Office and permanent British representative at the UN. Alun Gwynne-Jones, the *Times* defense correspondent (who was reputed to have assisted the Liberals during the election campaign), became Minister for Disarmament as Lord Chalfont. These appointments, most of which were welcomed by the press, opened up the possibility that incoming Prime Ministers in future might accept as routine the inclusion in their Governments of men outside the normal world of politics.

Long-Term Significance

Apart from the change of Government itself, three other aspects of the 1964 election results seemed likely to be of long-term significance. First, the results showed greater variation among the major regions of the country than had been usual in the 1950s; for reasons that are still not entirely clear, London, the North of England, and Scotland showed above-average swings to Labour, while the West Midlands and East Anglia, in particular, moved less to Labour. If marked regional variations in voting were to persist, a completely new dimension might be added to British electoral politics.[49] Second, the Liberals succeeded in amassing more than 3 million votes, although they could not reasonably hope to form a Government (they had only 365 candidates in the field) and despite the closeness of the race between the two major parties. Their success indicates that they may be re-emerging as a major factor in British politics, and that the country may possibly be entering a period of genuine three-party competition. Third, racial antagonisms played a more important part in the 1964 election than ever before. By 1964 the number of West Indians, Pakistanis, and Indians in Great Britain totaled about 800,000 (roughly 1.5 per cent of the population); a large proportion of them had entered the country since 1959, and their concentration in particular geographical areas gave rise to considerable tension. Labour was criticized for having opposed the Commonwealth Immigrants Act of 1961, designed to check the inflow, and of the five seats gained by the Conservatives against the national trend, at least two probably changed hands as the result of white antipathy to the colored newcomers.[50] At this writing, it is still too early to say whether race and color have become permanent features of British political life, but the portents are ominous.

During the closing days of 1964, the new Labour Government still appeared to stand high in the public estimation. On October 15, Labour had squeezed in with a plurality only 0.7 per cent of the popular vote, but by the end of November the party's lead over the Conservatives in the National Opinion Poll had risen sharply to more than 13 per cent. The Government, however, found itself confronted with a staggering balance of trade deficit and a serious drain on the pound sterling. It had to deal with the short-term currency crisis and also to try to overhaul and modernize the British economy, while supported in Parliament by only the slenderest of majorities. Tough measures were required and, although the bulk of the British public accepted the need for them, their implementation would almost inevitably lead to some decline in the Government's popularity. Moreover, Labour was committed to the nationalization of the steel industry, an item in its program which had never been popular except with its own supporters. At the turn of the New Year, the future of Harold Wilson's Labour Government could still not be predicted with any degree of certainty. The years 1963 and 1964 had confronted Great Britain as a nation with a massive challenge to its traditional habits and institutions in the fields of education, technology, government, industry and commerce. In the years to come it would be seen whether the country could provide an adequate response.

POSTSCRIPT

Since the above essay was written, two significant developments have taken place within the Conservative party: the adoption of a new method for selecting the party Leader; and the replacement of Sir Alec Douglas-Home by Edward Heath.

Lord Blakenham was appointed in November 1964 to enquire into the party's method of choosing its Leader. Early in 1965 he presented his report, and on February 25th Sir Alec, after consulting leading figures in all sections of the party, outlined an entirely new electoral system to a meeting of the 1922 Committee. The old method of informal consultation was done away with; so was the practice of weighting. Instead, the Leader was henceforth to be elected by a secret ballot of Conservative members of the House of Commons.

Sir Alec and his advisers still felt unable, however, to adopt Labour's simple-majority system. Under the new Conservative system, a candidate would be elected on the first ballot only if he both received an absolute majority and secured 15% more votes than his nearest rival. If the first ballot failed to produce a winner, a second ballot would be held for which new nominations could be made. To be elected on the second ballot, a candidate needed only an absolute majority. If no one obtained an absolute majority on the second ballot, then a third and final ballot would be held. The names on the ballot paper would be those of the three leading candidates on the second ballot. Voters would be required to indicate their second as well as their first preference. The candidate with the smallest number of first preferences would be eliminated and his second preferences distributed amongst the other two. On the third ballot, one candidate would, in the nature of the system, have to achieve an overall majority. The new system was complicated, but its main purpose was clear. As the *Times* put it on February 26th: "The object of the new procedure, as in the old consultative system, [is] to evolve a Leader with overwhelming majority support."

It had been suggested that Sir Alec Douglas-Home would seek to confirm his authority by standing for election under the new system, but Sir Alec quashed such rumors and throughout the spring and early summer of 1965 repeatedly asserted his determination to lead the Conservatives into the next election. For a time criticism of his leadership, which had revived after the election, died down. But in mid-July the appearance of several newspaper articles attacking the Conservative Leader coincided with renewed unrest on the Tory back benches. An opinion poll indicated that the public still held Sir Alec in low esteem, despite a general Conservative recovery. Then, completely unexpectedly, on Thursday, July 22nd, Sir Alec Douglas-Home announced his resignation. The new electoral system was put into operation immediately. After an intense but discreet weekend of campaigning, the first ballot was held on the following Tuesday. Edward Heath obtained 150 votes, Reginald Maudling 133, and Enoch Powell 15. Heath lacked the required 15% plurality over Maudling, but Maudling, recognizing that he would probably be overwhelmed on the second ballot, at once conceded defeat. Although a few formalities remained, Edward Heath became Leader of the Conservative party, in effect, on July 27th, 1965. As the British press observed, his election had been every bit as orderly as that of Sir Alec Douglas-Home had been chaotic. The new system had passed its first test.

NOTES

1. For a fuller narrative account see Chapter II in D. E. Butler and Anthony King, *British General Election of 1964* (New York, St.

Martin's Press, 1965). Developments in the political parties are described in the Epilogue to Robert McKenzie, *British Political Parties* (New York, Praeger, 2nd ed. revised, 1964). On Britain's relations with Europe see Miriam Camps, *Britain and the European Community 1955-63* (Princeton University Press, 1964), and Nora Beloff, *The General Says No* (Baltimore, Penguin Books, 1963). On the Profumo affair see Clive Irving, Ron Hall, and Jeremy Wallington, *Anatomy of a Scandal* (New York, M. S. Mill Co. and William Morrow and Co., 1963); cf. Wayland Young, *The Profumo Affair* (Baltimore Penguin Books, 1963), and *Lord Denning's Report* (London, Her Majesty's Stationery Office, 1963).

2. *British General Election of 1959* (New York, St. Martin's Press, 1960), p. 201.

3. On the first anniversary of his death, a group of friends and associates published a volume of appreciative essays edited by W. T. Rodgers, *Hugh Gaitskell 1906-1963* (London, Thames and Hudson, 1964). See especially Roy Jenkins, "Leader of the Opposition," pp. 115-131.

4. See Gaitskell's speech to the 1959 annual conference. *Report of the Fifty-eighth Annual Conference of the Labour Party,* pp. 105-114.

5. Michael Foot. *Ibid.,* pp. 122-123.

6. For a discussion of this point, see C. A. R. Crosland, *The Conservative Enemy* (London, Jonathan Cape, 1962), pp. 143-144. Crosland was a leading figure on the Gaitskellite wing of the party, and his earlier volume *The Future of Socialism* (London, Jonathan Cape, 1956) had great influence. For other statements of the moderate position see Douglas Jay, *Socialism in the New Society* (London, Longmans, 1962), and Bryan Magee, *The New Radicalism* (New York, St. Martin's Press, 1963). The Left, though more passionate, was on the whole less articulate. But see R. H. S. Crossman's articles "The Spectre of Revisionism" in *Encounter,* March and April, 1960, and any issue during this period of the weekly paper *Tribune.*

7. For a narrative account see the *Observer,* Feb. 17, 1963.

8. Prior to the 1964 election, there appeared a spate of Wilson biographies. The best on the political side is Dudley Smith, *Harold Wilson, a Critical Biography* (London, Robert Hale, 1964). A more personal account, based on interviews with Wilson himself and his friends, is to be found in Leslie Smith, *Harold Wilson, the Authentic Portrait* (London, Hodder & Stoughton, 1964). On Brown see Cassandra (William Connor), *George Brown, a Profile* (New York, Pergamon Press, 1964).

9. Quoted in Dudley Smith, *op. cit.,* p. 192.

10. *Ibid.,* p. 199.

11. Cassandra, *op. cit.,* p. 31.

12. On the general question of Labour Party organization, and the relationship between the party and the trade unions, see Robert McKenzie, *op. cit.,* and Martin Harrison, *Trade Unions and the Labour*

Party since 1945 (London, George Allen & Unwin, 1960). On the Left-Right split in the parliamentary party, see Chapter II and pp. 134-138 in the pioneering study by S. E. Finer, H. S. Berrington, and D. J. Bartholomew, *Backbench Opinion in the House of Commons 1955-59* (New York, Pergamon Press, 1961). The authors advance tentative explanations for the tendency of different occupational, educational, and sponsorship groups to produce different types of M.P. See also Leon D. Epstein, "New M.P.s and the Politics of the PLP" in *Political Studies,* vol. x, no. 2, June 1962, pp. 121-129.

13. Epstein suggests that the growing number of left-wingers may have reflected the types of candidates being selected by local constituency parties. *Loc. cit.*

14. There followed the curious episode of George Brown's "disappearance." As soon as the result was known, the defeated candidate left for Scotland, leaving no word of his future plans or whereabouts. For several days Labour leaders feared some new eruption. Eventually it emerged that Brown was prepared to remain Deputy Leader but preferred to move from home to foreign affairs. Wilson insisted, however, on naming Gordon Walker "shadow" Foreign Secretary, and only with some difficulty persuaded Brown to accept a general oversight of domestic policy matters. Despite the manifest differences of temperament separating the two men, they worked on the whole amicably and constructively during the long election period and in the early days of the new Government.

15. The terms Right, Center, and Left are used here in a deliberately vague fashion. They should be understood as referring to ideological (even temperamental) tendencies within the party rather than to solid, tightly disciplined blocs. Although Finer, Berrington, and Bartholomew (*op. cit.,* pp. 55ff) identify "syndromes" of right and left-wing attitudes, they lay stress on the fact that all three sections of the party were, for the most part, shifting and inchoate; allegiances changed over time and according to the issue. In connection with the leadership, it would have been perfectly consistent for an M.P. with strongly right-wing Gaitskellite views to feel nevertheless that Wilson for both political and personal reasons would be the best choice. A few did, in fact, take this line.

16. James Margach in the *Sunday Times,* November 8, 1964. Gaitskell's popularity began to increase sharply in the months before his death.

17. Robert McKenzie pointed this out at the time, though he almost certainly underestimated the abilities of Wilson and Brown. See the *Observer,* February 3, 1963.

18. The main sources for the Conservative leadership struggle are Randolph S. Churchill, *The Fight for the Tory Leadership* (London, Heinemann, 1964), and Ian Macleod's extended reply to it in the *Spectator* of January 17, 1964. Churchill's book is highly tendentious (Mr. Macmillan is said to have read and approved the proofs), and

should be read only in conjunction with Macleod's reply. The Macleod article is remarkable for its vehemence and candor.

19. No satisfactory biography of Macmillan exists. For a tendentious and unsympathetic portrait, see Emrys Hughes, *Harold Macmillan* (London, George Allen & Unwin, 1962). Fortunately, Mr. Macmillan is currently engaged in writing his memoirs.

20. *Op. cit.*, p. 94.

21. *Op. cit.*, p. 594h.

22. McKenzie, *op. cit.*, pp. 83-109. The quotation is from a speech at the Carlton Club meeting by Stanley Baldwin. The present 1922 Committee derives its name from this occasion.

23. The importance of loyalty by itself should not be underestimated. What Hugh Dalton wrote of the Labour party is equally true (though they would describe it differently) of the Conservatives: "Though politics is, of necessity, a highly competitive profession . . . we have a strong sense of social security near the top. To do a man out of his job, at that eminence, is against good fellowship." *Call Back Yesterday* (London, Frederick Muller, 1953), p. 191.

24. *Op. cit.*, pp. 78-79, 83. If Macmillan had been driven from office, the Queen would almost certainly not have called on Harold Wilson to form a Government, except in the highly unlikely event of the Conservatives' failing to agree on a new Leader. That the back-bench M.P.s were impressed by such an argument (if indeed they were) suggests the degree of their disinclination to rebel, and reinforces the point made above concerning their fear that "their actions might have unforeseen (and undesired) consequences."

25. See Hugh Dalton, *High Tide and After* (London, Frederick Muller, 1962), especially Chapter XXIX.

26. *Spectator, loc. cit.* 26a. *Op. cit.*, pp. 78-79.

27. Churchill, *op. cit.*, p. 95. On Macmillan's talk with Home, see John Dickie, *The Uncommon Commoner, a Study of Sir Alec Douglas-Home* (London, Pall Mall, 1964), p. 166. It will long be argued what Macmillan's real desires with respect to the Leadership were. He certainly did not wish to be succeeded by Butler, though prior to October 1963 he did not place any particular obstacles in his way. (Cf. Churchill, *op. cit.*, p. 94, and Macleod, *op. cit.*) He encouraged Maudling, Heath, and Macleod to try to emerge, and it was probably not his fault that none of them managed to. (See Macleod, *op. cit.*) By the summer of 1963 he almost certainly wished the choice to lie with Hailsham. Later he turned to Home. Macmillan's actions during the October crisis will be discussed below. At all stages, of course, his personal desires were greatly influenced by his assessment of the party situation.

28. On Butler, see Ralph Harris, *Politics Without Prejudice, A Political Appreciation of R. A. Butler* (London, Staples, 1956); and, especially, Francis Boyd, *Richard Austen Butler* (London, Rockliff, 1956). For a highly impressionistic analysis of Butler's impact on

rank-and-file Conservatives, see the present writer's review article "The Man Who Thinks too Much" in *New Society,* January 23, 1964.

29. It ought to be emphasized at this point that, by contrast with American presidential candidates who are chosen for the purpose of fighting a single election, British party Leaders are chosen for the indefinite future. For example, an unsuccessful American candidate has no more than a moral claim on the nomination four years later, whereas a British Leader carries on indefinitely until he either retires or is deposed. British parties may be saddled with their mistakes for protracted periods. For this reason, they are likely to exhibit considerable (perhaps excessive) caution when picking their Leaders.

30. *Op. cit.,* p. 54. On the method of formal election, and on the whole question of the emergence of Conservative Leaders, see McKenzie, Chapter II.

31. McKenzie, *op. cit.,* pp. 586-92; cf. Churchill, *op. cit.,* p. 126.

32. See Finer, Berrington, and Bartholomew, *op. cit.,* Chapter III.

33. *Op. cit.,* pp. 125-128. References to Churchill below are all taken from Chapters IX and X. The Macleod references are all from his *Spectator* article, *op. cit.*

34. They may in fact not have committed themselves. The statement that they did comes from Churchill and is not directly contradicted by Macleod. But Paul Johnson, a journalist writing some months later, commented: "Mr. Churchill tells us that the cabinet approved the paper, but this is not precisely the impression of some of its members." Johnson goes on to say: "In any case, if the procedure itself was to be invested with the weight of cabinet authority, had not the cabinet an equal right to be shown, and to check, its findings before they were presented to the Queen?" See "Was the Palace to Blame?," *New Statesman,* January 24, 1964. On the role of the Queen, see below, pp. 59-60.

35. For Redmayne's remarks, see the *Listener,* December 19, 1963. Macleod adds, in discussing Redmayne's version of events: "If the recording of opinions approached the confusion known to have been engendered by the method of sounding the Cabinet the margins of error must have been enormous."

36. Macleod, Maudling, and Powell all attended less aristocratic public (i.e., private) or grammar schools; Boyle attended Eton, as did Hailsham, who was about to join the anti-Home cabal. Class lines in Britain are generally conceived of as dividing the Conservatives from the Labour party, but the extent of class divisions within the two parties should not be underestimated. Charles Hill (now Lord Hill of Luton), one of the ministers sacked by Macmillan in July 1962, records in his memoirs how, as a Conservative from a humble background, he was welcomed into the camaraderie of the House of Commons, but how "I sensed that within the larger community of the Commons, as outside, there was the smaller community bound together by strong if invisible ties of birth and background and public

school to which I did not and could never belong." *Both Sides of the Hill* (London, Heinemann, 1964), p. 11. Cf. p. 244; also Finer, Berrington, and Bartholomew, *op. cit.*

37. Why he did so must remain something of a mystery. His friends said that Butler was too proud a man to fight for something he believed should have been his by right. His detractors said his behavior merely demonstrated that—as they put it—"he had always lacked the last six inches of steel."

38. The proprieties of the British constitution prevented these mutterings from ever being voiced publicly, but traces of them can be found in print. For example, Eldon Griffiths, a sometime *Newsweek* columnist, later an M.P., who acted as the Prime Minister's speechwriter during part of 1964, wrote: "Not all of the Prime Minister's colleagues appreciate his lightness of tone. Some still complain he is an 'amateur,' others that he is 'dangerously simple.' " See *Peaceful Change, a Selection of Speeches by Sir Alec Douglas-Home,* edited by Eldon Griffiths (London, Arthur Barker, 1964), p. 15.

39. See above, pp. 31-32.

40. These questions in turn raise the more general question of the ways in which political reputations are generated and communicated through political systems. For a brief discussion of this problem in an entirely different setting, see Richard E. Neustadt: *Presidential Power* (New York, Wiley, 1960) especially Chapters IV and V.

41. See "Premier ready for selection study," *Daily Telegraph,* January 21, 1964; "Opposition exploit Tory leadership row," *Times,* January 22; and Gerald Kaufman's article "Choosing a Tory Leader," *New Statesman,* November 20.

42. See Paul Johnson, "Was the Palace to Blame?," *New Statesman,* January 24, 1964, and the correspondence in succeeding issues; Nora Beloff, "The Queen and the Tories," *Observer,* January 26; McKenzie, *op. cit.,* pp. 594g-h.

43. This section is based largely on Butler and King, *British General Election of 1964.*

44. His efforts in this regard were not particularly successful. Studies of British voting behavior, however, indicate that British electors tend to identify themselves more with the parties themselves than with their leaders. The fact that Sir Alec was relatively unpopular while Wilson was relatively popular undoubtedly made a difference —but not as great a difference as it would have made in an American presidential election. The term "whistle-stop" is an importation from the United States: there are no whistle-stops in Britain.

45. The election could, by law, have been held in any month of the year, but some months were ruled out for various practical reasons, e.g., the summer holidays. The precise election date was not revealed until mid-September. On Sir Alec's decision, see Butler and King, *op. cit.,* pp. 80-83.

46. A variation of this last contention may be nearest the truth.

It may be that many voters who were predisposed in the Conservatives' favor had nevertheless been deflected previously by the Government's continuous run of misfortune and mismanagement. Once things stopped going wrong, they returned to their former allegiance. Light should be thrown on this and many other subjects by a study of electoral behavior—the first nationwide study in Britain—now being completed by David Butler of Nuffield College, Oxford, and Donald E. Stokes of the University of Michigan Survey Research Center. The results of the study will be published in 1966.

47. These comments on the election campaign do not record merely the present writer's subjective impressions. Many opinion polls testified to a general lack of public interest. For example, the Gallup poll consistently found voters less interested in the 1964 election than they had been in 1959. Television viewers in large numbers switched off the parties' broadcasts.

48. Greenwood in 1960 had withdrawn in favor of Wilson; see above, p. 25. Wilson clearly hoped that, by including a number of prominent left-wing figures in his Government, he could effectively neutralize them and reduce the danger of mutinies on the Labour back benches.

49. The absence of regional variation in the past is, of course, in marked contrast to what is found in the United States, where individual districts and states and, occasionally, whole regions defy the national trend. But in Britain in 1955, for example, only one parliamentary constituency changed hands in the face of the nationwide movement towards the Conservatives—even though the national swing was minute, a mere 1.8 per cent.

50. The most prominent Labour M.P. defeated was Patrick Gordon Walker, the member for Smethwick and "shadow" Foreign Secretary. Despite his defeat, Wilson appointed him to the Foreign Office, but only on the usual condition that he soon find another seat in the House of Commons. In January 1965, Gordon Walker contested a by-election in the Leyton division of London, only to be defeated again (possibly also as the result of anti-immigrant agitation). He subsequently resigned from the Government and was replaced as Foreign Secretary by Michael Stewart. On this subject, see A. W. Singham, "Immigration and the Election," Butler and King, *op. cit.*, pp. 360-368.

France: The Search for Presidentialism

by William G. Andrews and Stanley Hoffmann

MEANS WHEREBY PEOPLE MAY DESIGNATE THEIR GOVERNMENT through a clear expression of their will are essential to modern democracy. Authentic popular government requires a visible bond of responsibility between the ruled and the ruler, between the electorate and the chief executive.

Parliaments still exist and perform important functions. They ventilate the chief issues of politics in full public view. They are arenas in which Government and Opposition conduct their dialogue. They provide the diverse interests of a society with the means to express views and exert influence within the State machinery. They supply the individual citizen with an agent to whom he can turn for redress of administrative grievances. They survey critically the operations of government. They perform all these vital functions. But, parliaments do not rule. They do not formulate policy. They review, revise, reject, and ratify. They do not implement policy. They scrutinize its implementation.

The executive rules. In the last analysis, the *chief* executive rules. A political system, therefore, which does not provide a means through which the people can designate the chief executive is not a fully equipped democracy. There must be suitable electoral machinery to perform this function. The system of parties and candidates must also facilitate such election. Finally, popular political attitudes must inspire appropriate electoral behavior.

The United States, Great Britain, and West Germany in recent years have all operated political systems that fulfilled these requirements. The Fourth French Republic, however, was defective.

The French voter had no mechanism through which he could insure that his preference in the choice of chief executive would be known and heeded. Parliament intervened too actively and with too much independent discretion. For instance, the Radical Socialist party and its allies ranked fifth in the number of popular votes in the November 1946 elections with about 12.4 per cent of the total, yet they supplied the chief executive during 49.7 per cent of the following legislative term, far more than any other party. Because popular will was filtered through and distorted by parliament, the people lacked the means to pick their chief executive.

The establishment of the Fifth Republic radically altered the situation. No longer could the chamber intrude between the people and the ruler. It was replaced by a weird electoral college that was unlikely to work successfully. The 1958 system has been modified by practice, by constitutional amendment, and by changes in the political situation.

This essay will examine the system and its evolution to see if it now meets the elementary standards presented above. It will argue that there were two distinct and contradictory interpretations of the original regime; that President de Gaulle's presidential interpretation came in practice to prevail over Prime Minister Debré's parliamentary interpretation; that this interpretation was ratified by the electoral consultations of Autumn 1962; that a democratic electoral system was installed; and that political activity since then has largely been a struggle to develop the party system, array of candidates, and popular attitudes necessary to make the regime work effectively and democratically. The presidential elections of 1965, the campaign preceding them, and the reaction to them are seen as very influential, perhaps decisive, in determining whether the French political system finally will become a fully equipped democratic structure resting on an authentically democratic foundation.

I. THE DUAL PATERNITY OF THE FIFTH REPUBLIC

The French Constitution of 1958 was drafted under the inspiration of General Charles de Gaulle and the direction of Michel Debré. It was implemented by Debré serving General de Gaulle. However faithful was his discipleship, however, Debré's political experience, constitutional views, temperament, style, and functions were not identical with those of the master. Neither was his conception of the regime.

Debré is one of General de Gaulle's most loyal, intelligent, and long-suffering disciples. He became a leader in the Gaullist underground organization in 1942. His public support for the general has never wavered since then. When de Gaulle refused to sanction a separate Gaullist party after the Liberation, Debré promoted Gaullism within the Radical Socialist party. When de Gaulle formed the *Rassemblement du peuple français* (Rally of the French People) in 1947, Debré left the Radicals and became one of its leaders. When the RPF collapsed in 1952, Debré remained among the hardy faithful. In the Council of the Republic he was an unrelenting and acid critic of those who prevented the return of his chief. When the Fourth Republic was on its deathbed, Debré actively conspired to hasten its demise and ensure that de Gaulle became its heir. He served in de Gaulle's government from its formation on June 4, 1958, until April 1962. Neither de Gaulle's "abandonment" of Algeria, which had driven many stalwart Gaullists into bitter opposition, nor the General's alacrity in accepting his resignation drove Debré from Gaullism. He stood as a Gaullist in the 1962 parliamentary elections and, when defeated, contested successfully a 1963 by-election in the distant Indian Ocean island of Réunion. Since then, he has consistently supported de Gaulle's program in the National Assembly. When he took his seat, it was generally expected that he would serve as the nearest French equivalent of a majority leader. In fact, it was not until late 1964 that he began to perform such a role, but his fidelity never wavered.

Unswerving loyalty to de Gaulle was not the only qualification that Debré brought to the preparation of the 1958 constitution. He had also established himself as perhaps the leading Gaullist specialist on constitutional doctrine. He had been the principal author of the first Gaullist constitutional project as early as 1943. After the war he promoted de Gaulle's views while the Constituent Assemblies were meeting. During de Gaulle's long passage in the wilderness, he wrote a spate of highly polemical tracts and edited a political magazine. In both he laid heavy stress on constitutional questions.

One might expect that their long, unbroken, intimate association in the development of Gaullist constitutional doctrine would have produced by 1958 an identity of views between the chief and his leading constitutional adviser. It was hardly surprising, therefore, that Debré became de Gaulle's chief constitution-maker after his return to power. He headed the task force of civil servants that prepared the first draft of the 1958 constitution. He guided it through review by de Gaulle, an interministerial committee, the cabinet, a consultative commission, and the Council of State. Debré was chief author and chief manager of de Gaulle's constitution.

An expectation of consistency in the document is further supported by evidence that de Gaulle himself took a direct part in the drafting process. Not only did he instruct Debré in advance, confer with him several times while the document was being prepared, and preside over meetings that reviewed it, but he also addressed a meeting of the consultative commission and closely reviewed the document at more than one point in its preparation. Indeed, the wording of some articles (Article 16, for instance) is obviously de Gaulle's own.

Other forces, however, were working to produce divergence and inconsistency. Debré's background was parliamentary and legalistic; de Gaulle's was executive and authoritarian.

Debré had studied law and political science at a time when parliamentarianism was held in high esteem. He had been particularly influenced by a law school professor who advocated a "rationalized" parliamentary system very similar to that in Britain. He believed that restraints on parliamentary excesses had developed through custom and political circumstances in Britain. He wanted to impose them by constitutional stricture in France. They would be mainly internal parliamentary restraints, such as procedural regulations. A balanced regime would result, one that would be representative yet authoritative.

Furthermore, Debré had spent 10 years in the Council of the Republic, a parliamentary chamber in a regime dominated by parliament. While he never ceased his trenchant criticism of the institutions, his perspective was necessarily that of a parliamentarian. He was naturally inclined to seek remedies to the defects he saw. Those defects were largely ones of executive subservience to an aggressive and powerful parliament. The solution he saw was essentially negative: to deprive parliament of its capacity to render the executive powerless by "rationalizing" parliament.

Finally, Debré's life was built on law. He studied law and was a career civil servant, serving in that supreme repository of French legalism, the *Conseil d'état*. It is not surprising that he should seek legalistic solutions to political and constitutional problems, that he should seek to bind the parliamentary leviathan with restrictive constitutional provisions, again a negative approach.

De Gaulle

On the other hand, de Gaulle's family and professional background led him to see the problem in the dynamic, positive, power-oriented terms of *command*. He was reared in a monarchist, devoutly Catholic home. He was trained in the military academy of St. Cyr and had served 30 years on active duty by 1940. Monarchy, Catholicism, the French Army are all highly hierarchical in their organizational structure. Power and authority flow downward in pyramidal form. Parliamentary-type bodies are nonexistent in the army and, at best, useful adjuncts in a traditional monarchy and the Church.

De Gaulle had come to believe in the 1930's, however, that the traditional bases of authority were being undermined. Formal designation to a place in the hierarchy no longer conferred power automatically; the pyramid of authority still existed, but the man at the top had to demonstrate personal qualities in order to receive respect, obedience, and *power*. Thus, de Gaulle's conception of authority was more unified, more hierarchical, more personal, more dynamic, and less legalistic than Debré's.

Also, General de Gaulle, as a junior minister, had been more closely and personally involved than Debré in the defeat of 1940. That catastrophe had so deeply impressed itself in de Gaulle's mind that he has constantly striven since then to establish a political regime that could not be forced to abdicate power as had the Third Republic. His own direct contributions to the phrasing of the constitution seem entirely intended to accomplish this purpose: to prevent the debacle of 1940.

De Gaulle has never served in parliament. He has always regarded it from outside. It had collapsed beneath him in 1940. It had driven him from office in 1946. It had rebuffed his efforts to reform the regime during the Fourth Republic. Only when the Fourth Republic parliament knew it had no choice except de Gaulle or an army junta did it accept his leadership in 1958. Parliament had never benefited de Gaulle. He had little reason to believe that a parliamentary regime—even "rationalized"—would serve his purposes.

As Debré's background and temperament led him to reform parliamentarism, de Gaulle's led him to replace it. As Debré's role as constitutional law theorist and constitution framer led him to introduce his reforms by constitutional stricture, de Gaulle's role as commander in chief and chief executive in a quasi-wartime situation led him to introduce his reforms by direct, executive action.

De Gaulle was not inclined to review Debré's constitution with great thoroughness. To the extent that he did, he may not have perceived all its implications. Even if it did, he has not shown notable fastidiousness with regard to constitutional observances. His *coup* of 1940 was clearly unconstitutional. He observed constitutional forms in 1958 only for anticonstitutional purposes. Where the constitution in his mind and heart diverged from the one on Debré's parchment, he could not be expected to show excessive regard for the parchment.

Another possible explanation is that de Gaulle regarded Debré's parliamentary constitution as merely a point of departure. He had expressed the view that the very divisions of public opinion which had paralyzed parliamentary government would make a presidential system impossible too: France had too little consensus and its parties were still too divided and numerous for a popular election of the President to assure him the large majority without which his authority would be impaired. Also, de Gaulle wanted to appease the parties which had brought him back to power and which were all opposed to so drastic a repudiation of France's parliamentary tradition.

Thus, there existed from the outset a fundamental divergence between the Constitution on Debré's parchment and the one in de Gaulle's mind, between the one approved by the voters who said *"oui"* to the text on September 28, 1958, and the one ratified by those who said *"oui"* to de Gaulle in that same referendum.

In Debré's new Constitution the principle of cabinet government was preserved: the cabinet was responsible to the National Assembly. But given the chaotic situation of French parties, a whole series of measures was taken to insure cabinet stability and efficiency despite the probable absence of a coherent and lasting majority in the Assembly. Cabinets could still be overthrown by the National Assembly, but this was much less likely than before, because the new Constitution shortened the Assembly's sessions and regulated quite stringently the conditions in which it could force the cabinet to resign. Also, although Parliament kept the power to vote laws, its legislative powers shrank: the Constitution defined restrictively the domain of legislation (all other matters being left to regulation by the cabinet), established cabinet predominance in the legislative procedure itself, and set up a Constitutional Council to judge whether Parliament's Rules and Regulations and those laws that may be referred to it accord with the Constitution. In other words, in the absence of the "organic" conditions for an effective parliamentary system, the Constitution resorted to "mechanics"—that is, to "legal engineering" provisions designed to protect the cabinet.

Although the Constitution mainly reflected Debré's parliamentary interpretation, a few provisions that apparently came directly from de Gaulle's own pen and his direction of its implementation pointed toward a Presidential system. De Gaulle called for "a national arbiter far removed from political struggles"—that is, a man who would combine in his own person the advantages of executive authority and the virtue of being representative: for he was to be chosen by a broad electoral college, and he was to ensure "the regular functioning of the governmental authorities, as well as the continuance of the state," "national independence, the integrity of the territory, respect for . . . treaties." In order to carry out his task, he received the power to turn to the people as the final judge, through dissolution of the Assembly and (in somewhat more restricted circumstances) resort to referendums on bills "relative to the organization of the governmental authority." He also received important emergency powers under Article 16.

Now, it is clear that the conception on which the Presidency is based is totally different from that which inspired the provisions dealing with the government and its relations to Parliament. The latter try to reach stability *through* the classical parliamentary system which makes the popularly elected Assembly the effective source of political power. The Gaullist conception of the Presidency, on the contrary, tries to *short-circuit* the traditional representative channels. As far back as 1946 de Gaulle had called for "an executive power which does not originate from Parliament," because the "rivalry of parties" would reduce any other executive to impotence. De Gaulle's Presidency was a step on the road to the selection by the people directly of an Executive leader who has the power to appeal to the people. This process curtails the role of the representatives in two ways: first, in depriving them of the power to overthrow the Executive; second, in increasing the role of the electorate beyond the mere election of representatives. In the Constitution of 1958, the President's *powers* exceeded even those of an American President (that is, dissolution of the Assembly, referendums, emergency powers), but he was not *elected* directly by the people.

There was something unfinished about this part of the construction. It was gradually filled out by the President's behavior over the next four years, and the evolution was ratified by the electorate in the referendum of October 1962.

II. THE REGIME IN OPERATION: PRESIDENTIAL PREDOMINANCE

In November 1958 the French elected the first National Assembly of the Fifth Republic. The elections showed the wide extent of popular dissatisfaction with the parties of the Fourth Republic: out of 546 deputies, only 131 had been members of the previous Assembly. The beneficiary of this wave of revulsion was a new party, the Union for the New Republic (UNR), rapidly organized by de Gaulle's supporters. It differed from the late RPF in that de Gaulle was not its titular head: the General had "insisted categorically that his name, even in the form of an adjective, not be used by any group or candidate." But almost all the important figures of the RPF were to be found in the UNR, which captured 17.6 per cent of the votes on the first ballot, 26.4 per cent on the second, and 206 seats in the Assembly. This was some 70 seats short of a majority, but the UNR parliamentary group was by far the largest in the Assembly. The first cabinet of the new regime was headed by M. Michel Debré, a leader of the

UNR, and obtained from the Assembly a vote of approval of 453 against 56. The majority included the UNR, French deputies from Algeria, and the bulk of the deputies of two of the old parties: the Christian Democrats (MRP), who represented a largely conservative electorate although the party's ideology was socially progressive, and the much more deeply conservative Independents.

Prime Minister Debré's majority shrank over the following years, but his cabinet's life was never imperiled. Even though the Constitution stated that "the Government shall determine and direct the policy of the nation," and although Parliament did not greatly complicate the Prime Minister's task, it was the President of the Republic who became the dominant power in the Executive and in the regime. De Gaulle interpreted his role in the most sweeping way, thus insuring the predominance of the "presidential" over the "parliamentary" interpretation of the regime.

He did it in the first place by reducing the importance of the cabinet. All important issues of policy were decided, not at the Hôtel Matignon, the seat of the Prime Minister's office, but at the Elysée Palace. The President of the Assembly, UNR leader Jacques Chaban-Delmas, once referred to this practice as the creation of "reserved domains," off limits to all the "parliamentary" organs—the cabinet as well as the Houses. Thus, foreign policy, military affairs, and the handling of the Algerian war became de Gaulle's preserve: the Prime Minister (and the other ministers) could only execute de Gaulle's decisions, or try to inflect their execution. De Gaulle pushed his conception very far indeed; on May 15, 1962, in one of his stately press conferences, he described his European policy in such terms that the five Christian Democratic ministers of the cabinet, who had not been informed in advance of de Gaulle's words, resigned a few hours after having listened to him. The cabinet was left free to handle primarily economic and social affairs—and thus to serve as the collector of unpopularity, while the President dealt with the loftier issues of State. There never was any doubt that the cabinet, although theoretically dependent on Parliament's support, was actually at the service of the President; it was the President's agency functioning with the Assembly's support, not the Assembly's executive body functioning with the President's toleration. The increasing number of civil servants and decreasing number of parliamentarians who were appointed ministers showed it graphically.

The other branch of the parliamentary machinery, Parliament itself, also suffered from the President's conception of his role. As guardian of the Constitution, the General took it upon himself to interpret it, and his interpretation always went against Parliament's claims. When a majority of the deputies asked de Gaulle in accordance with the text to summon a special session of Parliament to deal with unrest among France's farmers, in March 1960, the General refused. In April 1961, when a military putsch in Algiers threatened the safety of the State, General de Gaulle used his emergency powers, kept them until the fall, and interpreted them in such a way that Parliament, although "meeting by right" during the emergency, could neither legislate nor introduce motions of censure against the government.

Thirdly, the President, having thus reduced the role of the parliamentary organs, bolstered his own position by addressing himself constantly to the people over the heads of ministers and parliamentarians alike. This appeal to the people took two forms: presidential tours of French provinces, and referendums in which the people were asked, formally, to approve bills concerning the fate of Algeria and, quite explicitly, to endorse General de Gaulle in person (January 8, 1961, and April 8, 1962). This was, for the General, both a way of bypassing Parliament and a way of consolidating his predominance over the Cabinet (for although Article 11 says that referendums are called by the President "on proposal of the Government," there was no doubt that the Government proposed what de Gaulle had already decided). It also was a way of demonstrating the spectacular efficiency of de Gaulle's conception of government by a leader who leans directly on the people, unencumbered by any "intermediaries." On April 6, 1962, two days before the referendum on self-determination in Algeria, de Gaulle celebrated the referendum as the institution thanks to which decisive political changes had been made possible: "It adds something essential to the legislative work of Parliament" and would be used again in the future "on matters of vital importance for the country."

Why did the Presidency become the motor of the new regime, instead of being merely its spare tire or its emergency brake?

There were three reasons, of unequal importance. The first was the personality of General de Gaulle. No man in France enjoyed anything near his prestige and his authority. These he owed in part to the role he had played as leader of the French resistance and organizer of France's liberation during World War II; in part to the fact that so many of his prophecies had come true (be it the prediction of the decisive importance of mechanized warfare in the 1930's when he was merely a colonel in the French army, or his warnings against the defects of the Fourth Republic); in part to his extraordinary strength of character, to a statesmanship composed of foresight, obstinacy, cunning and an almost deadly sense of timing; and finally to a literary and oratorical style which makes his war memoirs and speeches comparable to Churchill's. De Gaulle had always been convinced that government means action, that action is the realm of one man, and that assemblies can only deliberate, not act. He thought that French assemblies in particular, given the depth of their divisions and their refusal to accept rules of behavior that would subordinate factional interests to the common good, were indeed major obstacles to action. He also believed that whereas French "intermediaries," deputies, representatives of interest groups, or intellectuals, had been corrupted by long years of fights and splits, the mass of the people preserved a nostalgia for the common good, and would support a leader who could show them where the national interest lay.

A second determining factor was the Algerian war. France's political parties had been unable to end it, and were rescued from a military putsch only by de Gaulle's intervention in May 1958. Only de Gaulle could handle the French army, which was still convinced that military victory was possible. Certainly no other political figure in France had any chance of performing the tightrope walking act that consisted of bringing the army and the settlers to the point of accepting (even bitterly and with rage) the independence of Algeria, while bringing the Algerian nationalist rebellion to the point of accepting (even temporarily) important advantages for France in the military and economic areas. It took de Gaulle four years to succeed. Twice his regime was threatened by putsches in Algiers (January 1960 and April 1961); the last months of the war and the months that preceded the proclamation of Algerian independence in July 1962 were marked by extensive terrorism. Such circumstances imposed one-man rule and a suspension of parliamentary politics, just as winning World War I had temporarily imposed the iron rule of Clemenceau in 1917-1918.

Finally, the behavior of the Prime Minister and of the Gaullist party in Parliament reinforced de Gaulle's position. Debré had been a vitriolic defender of French Algeria under the Fourth Republic; but his loyalty to de Gaulle was absolute, and when de Gaulle, whose Algerian policy had been highly ambiguous at first, gradually switched toward a liberal solution, Debré followed his leader, sadly but faithfully. The UNR deputies had been elected on a platform which combined reverence for de Gaulle and support for French Algeria. Many observers predicted that the party would explode if those two dogmas came into conflict. Actually, only a handful of Gaullist deputies deserted the UNR when de Gaulle's policy moved away from French Algeria: most of them owed their election not to their personalities and ideas, but to the fact that they were the General's men. Consequently, de Gaulle's freedom of maneuver—limited by the army's, the settlers', and the Algerian rebels' grievances—was at least unimpaired in this respect.

The Failure of "Reformed Parliamentarism"

Perhaps the formidable development of the Presidential part of the Constitution would not have sufficed to shape the future of France's institutions if the other part had not failed to exhibit the signs of political health and vigor that Debré had hoped for. "Reformed parliamentarism" proved too fragile for comfort.

As long as the Algerian war lasted, Parliament's docility remained on the whole assured. Nevertheless, despite the existence of a majority behind Debré, Parliament frequently showed its impatience with the restrictions imposed by the Constitution on both its legislative and its political powers. As for the latter, both Houses tried in their Rules to resurrect some of the methods of "interpellation," used under the two previous Republics to harass or even to destroy cabinets, and now abolished by the Constitution. This attempt was beaten down by the Constitutional Council. Also, Debré was obliged four times to stake the life of his cabinet on a bill (three times, it concerned France's nuclear striking force) in order to obtain its passage by Parliament. As for the legislative powers, parliamentary impatience came into the open when all parties except the UNR walked out of the Assembly during the emergency session of 1961, because the Assembly was being prevented from passing bills. Furthermore, Debré had to resort to all the engineering tricks of the Constitution in order to get bills (particularly budgetary ones) adopted without too many amendments, and especially without too many changes designed to accommodate pressure groups.

If Debré had hoped for orderly and trusting cooperation between a chastened Parliament, respectful of Constitutional limitations, and the cabinet, he was disappointed. Even during the Algerian emergency, parliamentary discontent boiled so strongly that the cabinet had to clamp down the lid tightly. In particular, the Senate, in which the old parties had a predominant majority and which had Constitutional powers that were aimed at allowing the Executive to lean on it should the National Assembly become unruly, behaved instead as an opposition chamber, which had to be overridden by the Assembly at the request of the cabinet.

Things got much worse when the war in Algeria ended. Parliament was in its fourth year; under France's electoral law, new elections would have to take place before the fall of 1963. Michel Debré wanted de Gaulle to dissolve the National Assembly right away so that new elections would take place at a time when the General's prestige was particularly high. De Gaulle rejected his advice and replaced him in April 1964 by Georges Pompidou, a personal adviser of de Gaulle, former high school teacher, general director of the Rothschild bank, who had never been a member of Parliament or of a party. His appointment was resented by the Assembly, which saw in it—quite rightly—one more step toward the complete victory of de Gaulle's conception of the regime. Debré, for all his loyalty to de Gaulle and stern rejection of parliamentary encroachments, had at least been a "member of the club," a sincere believer in parliamentary government, and not merely an amiable reflection of the General's ideas. Immediately, a climate of opposition developed—not strong enough to threaten the new cabinet, since few deputies wanted to provoke de Gaulle into dissolving the Assembly just at the time of the Algerian settlement, but vigorous enough to reduce Pompidou's majority, on April 27, to 259 votes against 128, with 119 abstentions. The subsequent resignation of the MRP ministers made matters worse. It provided the opposition with a theme: European integration; it was clear that there was a majority in Parliament for a policy of supranational integration, rejected only by the UNR and the handful of Communist deputies. According to the Constitution, the cabinet was, after all, responsible to the National Assembly. When it came to European policy, however, the cabinet was caught between de Gaulle's implacable hostility to supranationality, and the majority of the deputies. Two incidents in the summer of 1964 clearly demonstrated the difficulties of "rationalized parliamentarism": On June 13, 296 deputies, i.e., a clear majority, having signed a motion for European integration, walked out of a foreign policy debate. But on July 16 only 206 voted for a motion of censure when Pompidou staked his cabinet's life on a budgetary bill. Parliament was no longer docile, but precisely because the dominant organ had become the Presidency, not the cabinet, the Assembly did not dare to challenge de Gaulle openly yet.

Why did the experiment in reformed cabinet government fail? Responsibility here is also divided. In great part, the attempt failed—despite the good conditions in which the existence of a fairly stable coalition had allowed it to evolve—because de Gaulle never really gave it a good chance. Convinced that the old parties were nuisances, he treated them as such, thus giving them no incentive whatever to resign themselves and adjust to the new constitutional order. In part, again, the circumstances were responsible. Often before, France had known emergencies in which popular leaders exerted a sort of Roman dictatorship temporarily, and each time, after the end of the emergency, the political system returned to what de Gaulle had once called the "games, poisons and delights" of parliamentary supremacy.

Moreover, there was the attitude of the old parties: watchful waiting for such a return, rather than active attempts at reform and rejuvenation. They had remained as numerous as ever (indeed, a small new party, the PSU, had appeared in between the Socialists and the Communists); they had made no effort at merging or at changing either their structure or their outlook. When the settlement of the Algerian war was achieved, two of the parties that had supported de Gaulle as long as the war lasted abandoned him. The MRP did so over the issue of Europe, and with reluctance; but it could stomach neither de Gaulle's foreign policy nor his extension of the Presidency's role, and some of its deputies signed the motion of censure on July 11. The Independents also criticized de Gaulle's constitutional and foreign policies, but the main reason for their disaffection was their resentment of Algerian independence: de Gaulle and his Prime Minister succeeded in "selling" this policy to the Independent ministers in the cabinet, but not to the deputies in Parliament. Thus, these two forces joined in the opposition the three parties that were already there: the Communists, bitterly opposed to de Gaulle ever since 1945 and isolated from all other parties ever since 1947; the Socialists, who had hesitatingly (but decisively) rallied to de Gaulle in the troubled days of May 1958, but who criticized de Gaulle for all of his policies except with respect to the now resolved issue of Algeria; and the Radicals, France's main party and "vital center" under the Third Republic, ideologically left-wing and anticlerical but socially moderate, badly weakened by endless splits under the Fourth, crushed at the polls in November 1958, but still influential in the Senate and in some parts of France. As for the UNR, the old parties expected it to remain a passing fad, whose popularity would fade with the end of the de Gaulle era just as the old RPF had vanished. The fact that the UNR had failed to give itself a strong organization or a program going beyond endorsement of de Gaulle, and behaved as a "mass of brute votes" at the disposal of the Executive rather than as a genuine political force inspiring the government, seemed to justify such calculations.

Finally, the Constitution itself fed the hopes of many of the old political leaders: after de Gaulle, a President elected by a relatively sedate electoral college in which small villages and small towns were overrepresented might well be a cipher who would fail to use the powers of the Presidency to the hilt: this had indeed happened already under the Third Republic. If the Presidency should thus wither on the vine, the paper obstacles designed to save the lion tamer, the cabinet, from the lions, Parliament, would not last long—similar obstacles (less drastic, to be sure, but just as artificial) had already failed to stop Parliament under the Fourth Republic.

Awaiting the Test

During the summer of 1962, the main actors in the coming drama seemed to be playing a strange waiting game. On the one hand, the old parties were increasingly unhappy about the regime, yet reluctant to strike out against it right away. The return to peace after 24 years of war, in Europe and overseas, and the successful visit of Chancellor Adenauer to France early in July made the party leaders think twice about acting too fast. Summer months are never good for political initiative. Consequently, Parliament in the last days of its session in July resorted to harassment rather than open rebellion. However, the battle was merely postponed. To provoke de Gaulle into dissolving the Assembly now would have been a mistake; to provoke him at a time when the new elections that must follow a dissolution would be likely to give to the old parties their revenge was another matter. First, in 1877, there was the precedent of Marshal MacMahon, the President of the new Third Republic, who—like de Gaulle—considered that the cabinet had to reflect his views, and who dissolved the House when it overthrew the cabinet he had appointed. His supporters were defeated at the elections for a new House. This led first to his submission, later to his resignation, and finally to the emasculation of the Presidency in particular (the right of dissolution was never used again) and of the Executive in general. De Gaulle too could perhaps be forced to "give in or get out" in this way. Secondly, there was the precedent of de Gaulle himself in 1945-1946: the Provisional Premier of France, who considered himself to be above parties, was faced in November 1945 with a Constituent Assembly which resented his presence and whose constitutional conceptions he did not accept. Disgusted by the parties' tendency to return to what he deemed old errors, convinced that they would not succeed, and unwilling to take against them a public stand which would have tarnished his image as a national symbol, he resigned suddenly in January 1946. In a country where history tends to repeat itself, could the same story not happen again? Maybe de Gaulle had made a serious mistake after all in failing to dissolve the Assembly right after the Algerian settlement, when his popularity was highest.

The other main actor was precisely General de Gaulle. If he

had ever hoped that the combination of a strong Presidency and a chastened parliamentary system, resulting in Executive stability and strength, would suffice to "cure" France's old parties without any need for shock treatment (such as an abrupt switch to a presidential regime), the restiveness of the parties in the Spring and Fall of 1962 would have ridden him of that hope. With the parties unchanged, would not de Gaulle's own Constitution pave the way to a return to the lamentable ways of the Fourth Republic? Should the next National Assembly have a majority hostile to the General, the deputies could make it impossible for him to form any cabinet and oblige him to choose between resignation, capitulation to the wishes of the majority (that is, the end of his conception of government), and the use of his emergency powers (quasi-dictatorship). For in the first year of a new Parliament elected after a dissolution, he could not dissolve the Assembly again. Should he resign, or give in, or die, what guarantee was there that his successor, elected by the college of notables, would be strong enough to maintain de Gaulle's conception of the Presidency and buck the parliamentary tide?

Given these possibilities, it appeared to many observers that there were only two ways of safeguarding Executive authority after de Gaulle. Both required Constitutional changes. One, which had the support of France's Premier of 1940, veteran conservative deputy Paul Reynaud, now in his eighties, was the idea of "a single government for each legislature": should this government be overthrown, new elections would have to be held. Automatic dissolution would thus serve as a kind of deterrent against parliament's appetites. This was a method for reinforcing the Executive while maintaining (or rather restoring) the preponderance of the parliamentary interpretation of the regime, as against the presidential one; for the cabinet's Premier would not have been elected directly by the people, he would be taken from Parliament. The other way, which was advocated by some of France's leading specialists of public law, such as Professor Maurice Duverger, was the adoption of a Presidential system, more or less fashioned after that of the United States; the President would be elected for a fixed term by the people. This would have marked the preponderance of the Presidential element of the regime, although Duverger and his supporters carefully pointed out that in a truly balanced presidential system Parliament ought to recuperate some of the powers it had lost, and the Presidency lose some of the powers it had gained under the Fifth Republic.

De Gaulle himself had hinted at the need for reform. The change he suggested was, as could be expected, in the second direction. He was not concerned with asserting the cabinet's power as opposed to Parliament's, but with asserting the President's power over both. Thus he mentioned, in his press conference of April 11, 1961, that "one could envisage" the election of the President by universal suffrage so as to reinforce his personal authority. He, de Gaulle, had not needed such an election in order to benefit from "a national and popular mandate." Although technically elected only by the notables, he had obtained such a mandate "through exceptional events which will not necessarily be repeated after me"—that is, history and popular endorsement at the various referendums. He warned that "should I have the time and the opportunity, I could, at the right moment put this most important item on the agenda." This warning could hardly be well received by the old parties. Should such a change occur, it could dash the hopes of those who thought that a weakening of the Presidency after de Gaulle might prepare a return to parliamentarism undiluted. Moreover, such a reform, by reducing even further the importance of the cabinet vis-à-vis the President, would leave side by side a Parliament and a President, both elected by universal suffrage, but with decisive advantages for the latter; for whereas the Parliament could only hit at the Premier, but not at the President, the President could always bypass Parliament through referendums, intimidate Parliament through the threat of dissolution, and get whatever legislation he needed by having the cabinet resort to all the devices of the Constitution. In other words, he could do things no American President could do; he would combine the assets of the presidential type of Executive —popular election and stability—with the assets given to the cabinet in Debré's scheme of "reformed parliamentarism." Thus one can understand why the old parties now felt like clinging to the Constitution of 1958 as it was.

If they wanted to reverse the trend, they had to act before de Gaulle had succeeded in reforming the Constitution. In his press conference of May 15, 1962, the General had given them hope by saying that his reform was "not for the time being." On June 8, however, in a speech devoted to Algeria, he once again celebrated the virtues of "universal suffrage" as the decisive political force (not a word was said about Parliament), and he added, ominously, that "in the same way, when the time comes, we will have to ensure that in the future, beyond passing men, the Republic remains strong, orderly and uninterrupted." The battle for succession was clearly outlined, but it had not opened yet.

III. THE REFERENDUM AND ELECTIONS OF OCTOBER 1962

As French politics began to stir again after the usual August hiatus in 1962, it became clear that de Gaulle's presidential regime was about to face its crucial test. There was considerable speculation in political Paris in late summer and early fall that the parties would pass a motion of censure against de Gaulle's government on some issue such as European integration or the nuclear striking force on which they expected to have the support of the French people. De Gaulle would then be forced to dissolve Parliament or admit defeat. The resultant general elections would be fought in circumstances as favorable as possible for the anti-Gaullists. They would have the benefit of long-existent party organizations at the local level, unlike the rootless UNR. The campaign would focus on the issues where de Gaulle was least popular.

The President stole the march on his adversaries. On September 12 he announced that he would submit for approval by popular referendum a constitutional amendment providing for direct election of the President of the Republic by universal suffrage. As the amendment title of the Constitution stipulated parliamentary involvement in all methods of amendment, this was widely regarded as another violation of the Debré Constitution to the detriment of Parliament.

The Assembly had a clear challenge to censure the government. If it did not, the opposition parties could oppose the amendment only on the grounds that it was an undesirable change. This would hardly be a strong position. The people were not likely to take kindly to the argument that they were incompetent to elect the Chief of State. If it accepted the challenge, the opposition could criticize the unconstitutional amending procedure as well. However, censure was certain to be followed by dissolution and parliamentary elections in which the Common Market and nuclear defense would not be overriding issues. This would not be a strong position either, but at least it would be more consistent than acquiescence in the referendum procedure and subsequent opposition. As few vices are more reprehensible to the Frenchmen than inconsistency, the deputies really had no choice. They censured.

As dawn broke over Paris on October 5, the deputies trooped to the Assembly's tribune, weary after a 10-hour debate, and passed by a margin of 39 votes the first successful motion of censure in this century. All or virtually all of the Communist, Socialist, MRP, Radical, Independent, and right-wing deputies voted with the majority. Only the bulk of the UNR and a scattering of other deputies demurred.

As expected, de Gaulle dissolved the Assembly. He also instructed Pompidou and the other members of the cabinet to remain in office until after the elections. (The Constitution requires the Prime Minister to submit his resignation if censured, but does not require the President to accept it.) The French people now made three trips to the polls within a month. On October 28, they passed judgment on de Gaulle's constitutional amendment by referendum. On November 18 they voted for parliamentary candidates, and a week later, in most constituencies, they voted in parliamentary run-off elections.[1]

The referendum battle was the more sharply drawn in that de Gaulle was opposed by all the political parties except the UNR, by the major trade union federations, by every national daily newspaper except the official UNR organ (which had a paid circulation of only about 7,000), and by virtually every prominent political figure who did not owe his career to the general. His action was regarded as unconstitutional by the National Assembly, the Senate, the Constitutional Council, the Council of State, and most leading constitutional lawyers. In previous referendums, de Gaulle had had the support of important non-Gaullist political forces. Now he stood alone. Before, he had shared victory. Now, if he won, he won alone.

The power struggle was sharply drawn, but the issue was not. The form of consultation and the substance of campaign debate confused it. De Gaulle asked the voters if they wished that the

President of the Republic be elected by universal suffrage. His opponents replied by asking the voters if they approved of the "unconstitutional" amending procedure. Finally, in a series of television broadcasts de Gaulle asked the French people if they wanted him to continue in office: "If your reply is 'no' . . . or even if the majority of 'yes' is weak, mediocre, or uncertain, it is quite obvious that my task would be terminated at once and without return." To those three questions, the French voter could give but one reply.

The third question came to dominate the consultation. Observers agreed that most Frenchmen disapproved of the amending procedure but favored the amendment and de Gaulle's continuance in office. Once de Gaulle succeeded in making the referendum a vote of confidence, the outcome was virtually foreordained. The French were given a choice between de Gaulle and they-knew-not-what. The opposition was placed in the impossible political position of trying to beat somebody with nobody.

As shown in Table 1, de Gaulle was supported by 62.3 per cent

TABLE 1. *Results of Referendum of October 28, 1962*

Registered voters	28,185,478
Abstentions	6,490,915
Total ballots cast	21,694,563
Yes	13,150,516
No	7,974,538
Blank or spoiled	569,509

of the valid votes and 46.7 per cent of the registered voters. It being impossible to measure separately support for the man and support for his constitutional conception, approval of both had to be assumed. In any case, that was the practical consequence. The constitutional interpretation which de Gaulle had been implementing for four years now had formal popular ratification. "Rationalized parliamentarism" was decisively discarded. Thenceforth, the Fifth Republic was a presidential system in practice, in letter, in popular image.

The decision of October 28 was reiterated in the November parliamentary elections. The French voters heeded de Gaulle's plea to be consistent, which was combined with another resignation threat. They picked an Assembly with 249 Gaullists[2] in a total membership of 465. For the first time in history, Republican France elected a homogeneous parliamentary majority. The Gaullist delegation increased by 14 seats when the Assembly convened. One additional deputy joined the UNR-UDT group and 13 joined the Independent Republicans. This was a big jump from the 193 seats held by the Gaullist group in the retiring Assembly.

There was, however, an opposition majority of popular votes. The Gaullist parties won only 36.3 per cent in the first round and 42.1 per cent in the second round. Ninety-six deputies, including 58 candidates of the Gaullist parties, won seats on the first round. Voters in those 96 constituencies are not represented in the second-round results. The Gaullist parties won 42.6 per cent of their votes, so the total Gaullist vote in the decisive round was 42.3 per cent. Symbolically, the "rationalized parliamentary" system was also defeated in the person of Debré, who contested unsuccessfully a seat in Indre-et-Loire, the department he had represented as a Senator in the Fourth Republic. The national results are summarized in Table 2.

The "presidential" view of the Fifth Republic, which had obtained in practice and had been ratified by the referendum, was now firmly installed in the Assembly. However, the details of the electoral system were not yet spelled out, and the people and the political élite had not yet developed the political behavior that would give presidentialism life and durability.

IV. CONSTITUTIONAL AND LEGAL ELECTORAL FRAMEWORK

The present presidential electoral system was set up by the constitutional revision of October 28, 1962, the organic law of November 6, 1962, and the decrees of January 25 and March 14, 1964. It replaces the system established by the original provisions of the Constitution of October 4, 1958.

Initially, the President of the Republic was chosen for a seven-year term by an electoral college of about 80,000 members, including the members of Parliament and members or representatives of the municipal and departmental councils. As one-third of the members of the Senate and of the municipal and departmental councils were picked at each triennial election, many members of

TABLE 2. *Results of Parliamentary Elections, November 1962*

	First Round			Second Round				
	Votes	(1)	(2)	Votes	(1)	(2)	(3)	(4)
REGISTERED VOTERS	27,535,019			21,957,468				
ABSTENTIONS	8,603,286			6,132,478				
TOTAL VOTES CAST	18,934,733			15,208,101				
Blank or void	601,747			616,889				
Ext. Right, others	159,682	0.9	—	16,943	0.1	—	—	−11
Ind. Repubs.	798,092	4.4	12	241,853	1.6	8	20	−8
UNR-UDT	5,847,403	31.9	46	6,165,929	40.5	183	229	+34
CNI, Repub. Center	1,742,523	9.5	6	1,177,152	7.8	23	29	−78
MRP	1,635,452	8.9	14	806,908	5.3	22	36	−20
Rads. Left center	1,384,998	6.6	8	1,068,101	4.2	34	42	+1
SFIO	2,319,662	12.7	1	2,304,330	15.2	64	65	+24
Other Left	449,743	2.5	—	183,844	1.2	2	2	+2
Communists	3,992,431	21.8	9	3,243,041	21.3	32	41	+31

(1) Percentage of valid ballots, (2) seats won, (3) total seats won, (4) seats gained or lost from previous assembly.

Sources: All data from *Année politique* 1962, p. 129, except registered voters, abstentions, and Extreme Right vote on second round, which are drawn from François Goguel, "Le referendum du 28 octobre et les elections des 18-25 novembre 1962," *Revue française de science politique*, June 1963, p. 303.

the 1958 electoral college had acquired their mandates as early as 1955, and fewer than 600 had been popularly elected since the new Constitution had been adopted. Furthermore, the electors were chosen mainly to perform other governmental functions than electing a President. This system gave the French people no direct means of expressing their preference for President. Yet, it was the device that supposedly provided de Gaulle with his constitutional authority after his designation by it in December 1958.

The 1962 revision provided for direct election of the President by universal suffrage. The presidential term of seven years was left unchanged. The provision on timing was revised to stipulate that the election "shall take place not less than 20 days nor more than 35 days before the expiration of the term." President de Gaulle had assumed office January 8, 1959, after having been elected December 21, 1958. Therefore, elections were normally due between December 4 and 19, 1965. However, if the office falls vacant for any reason or the Constitutional Council rules, on petition of the government, that the President is incapacitated permanently, elections may be held early. They must then take place not less than 20 days nor more than 35 days after the vacancy has occurred or the President has been declared permanently incapacitated.

If no candidate wins an absolute majority of the valid ballots in the first balloting, a run-off election shall be held two weeks later. Only those two candidates "who, after withdrawals, if any, of better placed candidates, are found to have received the largest number of votes" in the first round shall be candidates in the second round.

The candidates can be nominated only by petition of 100 members of Parliament, of the Economic and Social Council, of General (Departmental) Councils, or elective mayors. At least 10 different departments or overseas territories must be represented among the petitioners for a candidate. No person may endorse the nomination of more than one candidate. No nominee may withdraw before the first round of balloting. A deposit of 10,000 francs ($2,000) must accompany each nomination. It is refunded to all candidates who win as much as 5 per cent of the vote.

A very short campaign is prescribed. It may begin as late as 16 days before the first round of balloting. As nominations may be made as late as midnight of the 19th day before the first polling day, the campaign must begin 18, 17, or 16 days before the election. It ends at midnight on the Friday preceding the election. All French elections are held on Sunday. This means that the campaign must be from 15 to 17 days long. If there is a second round, the campaign begins the day the Constitutional Council publishes the names of the two eligible candidates. This may be as late as midnight of the Thursday following the first polling day. Again, campaigning ends on midnight of the Friday preceding polling day. Thus, the second-round campaign may be as long as 11 days or as short as 8 days and is more likely to be 8 than 11.

The State provides certain propaganda facilities to the candidates. During the campaign, all candidates are guaranteed equal exposure in news broadcasts over the state radio and television system. Each candidate is entitled to two hours of propaganda time on radio and two hours on television during the campaign preceding each polling day. This amount of time may be reduced during the first-round campaign if there is a large number of candidates. By its silence, the decree seems to permit ministers to appear on radio and television during the campaign to defend the government in addition to the time allotted to the government's candidate.

Official billboards are available to all candidates in all municipalities. Not more than two propaganda posters and two meeting announcements of stipulated size may be printed at the candidate's request and the government's expense, distributed by the government to the municipalities, and posted by them on the official billboards. Also, each candidate may have one election broadside printed and distributed through the mails to all the voters at government expense. In addition, the government reimburses 100,000 francs ($20,000) of the campaign expenses of each candidate receiving at least 5 per cent of the vote.

A National Electoral Campaign Control Commission composed of five high civil servants is charged with insuring that the campaign regulations are properly observed. Local control commissions under its direction perform the same functions in each department.

These rules on campaign propaganda prevail, however, only during the official campaign period. Otherwise, candidates are free to promote their causes in any way they see fit, except that access to the state radio-television (RTF) programs is limited by governmental decisions. Shortly after M. Gaston Defferre announced his candidacy for the Presidency in December 1963 the government instructed the RTF to forbid the mention on its programs of anyone in his capacity as presidential candidate. Mayors of cities (Defferre is Mayor of Marseilles) could be shown only on regional programs, only in connection with ceremonies of regional interest, and only if no statements regarding their candidacy were made. In any broadcast of parliamentary proceedings, time had to be given equally to the government, the majority, and the opposition. Broadcast reports of party national congresses could be no longer than 1½ minutes for each day of the congress. No other political meetings could be reported. However, an unlimited amount of time could be devoted to activities and pronouncements of the President of the Republic or of members of the government.

An example of the way these rules were applied occurred on January 31, 1964, when President de Gaulle's press conference was broadcast in its entirety twice for a total of three hours. An SFIO national congress on the following two days which endorsed the Defferre candidacy was reported in three one-minute announcements. Three hours for de Gaulle, three minutes for the Socialists, including about one minute for Defferre, his principal adversary. In addition, the most insignificant statements and official activities of ministers were given extensive coverage.

In a modern mass democracy, campaigns for national office are not confined to a two- or three-week official period no matter what the theory may be. For instance, the campaign preceding the 1964 British general elections began, in fact, in the spring of 1963 when an early summer or autumn election was expected, and it did not stop until election day, October 15, 1964, although the official campaign did not begin until September 25, 1964. It is unrealistic to believe that the decisions of the French voters are made on the basis of the propaganda to which they are exposed during a two-week campaign. The 1965 campaign began, in fact, in September 1963 when a national weekly newspaper launched Defferre's candidacy; de Gaulle was as obviously a candidate as he. The complete effacement of Defferre from broadcasts and the great attention given de Gaulle could have had no other purpose or effect than to favor the latter's candidacy at the former's expense. Indeed, the government admitted as much unofficially in justifying the policy on the grounds that virtually every newspaper in the country was anti-Gaullist and that Gaullist broadcasting was necessary to redress the balance. Its silence, however, could not be regarded as motivated entirely by a desire for propaganda equity. After all, the anti-Gaullist newspapers had given full coverage to M. de Gaulle's activities. The newspaper reader could subscribe to the UNR's *La Nation* if he found his usual newspaper insufficiently sympathetic to de Gaulle, though fewer than 10,000 had done so. The anti-Gaullist television viewer had no analogous solution, for the State network had a complete monopoly in most of the country. The radio listener could escape more easily, as there were commercial radio stations in small countries peripheral to France (Luxembourg, Monaco, and Andorra) that reported the existence of candidate Defferre. In fact, their news broadcasts were so far superior in reputation to those of the government that a public opinion survey conducted by the Ministry of Information showed that three times as many listeners trusted them as trusted the government's transmissions. In any case, every news medium of significance in the world considered the Defferre candidacy newsworthy, except the French state broadcasting, which is controlled by his leading rival.

On the other hand, no allegations of governmental favoritism were made against the state-owned *Agence France Presse,* the French equivalent of Associated Press. Opposition candidates did not have the same opportunities to publicize their efforts as did the official candidate, but their means were sufficient to win the necessary support if that which they offered was attractive to the electorate.

The electoral system as revised in 1962 was suitable to enable the French people to choose clearly their chief executive. It does this, in part, because it narrows the field of candidates to two on the decisive round. A voter cannot foresee the effect of his vote if there are more than two serious candidates. Take, for instance, a plurality election in which three candidates win the following vote:

Communist	18,000
SFIO	28,000
UNR	29,000

Most Communist voters, let us assume, would have preferred the Socialist to the Gaullist candidate. Not being able to foresee the number of votes each candidate would receive, however, they voted their first preference. Their votes had an effect opposite to that intended. They intended to defeat the UNR candidate, yet, by withholding their votes from the SFIO candidate, they helped elect the Gaullist.

Let us suppose, now, that a runoff is provided (as in the case in the French presidential system) in which only two candidates are permitted. The result would now be:

SFIO	46,000
UNR	29,000

Every voter was able to cast his vote with full knowledge of the effect it would have. It would help SFIO and hurt UNR, or help UNR and hurt SFIO.

By requiring an absolute majority for first-round election and by providing that there be only two candidates in the runoff election, therefore, the French system guaranteed that the voters would be presented with a clear choice in the decisive balloting.

If the politics which activated the mechanism, however, were not appropriate to that purpose, the political system might still be defective. Much of French political activity in the years immediately following adoption of the 1962 amendments revolved around efforts to reconstruct French political life in conformity with the constitutional changes.

V. PRESIDENTIAL ELECTORAL POLITICS

Attempts at Party Regroupment

The first presidential elections by universal suffrage were scheduled to take place no later than December 1965. Opposition politicians continued to discuss the inequities of de Gaulle's presidentialism and the need to abolish it, but, even more earnestly, they began preparations to play the game according to his rules. Eventually, they might try to overturn his regime, but their immediate aim was to capture it.

They had learned the hard way that they could not beat de Gaulle with nobody. During the referendum campaign, the main democratic opposition parties (SFIO, Radicals, MRP, Independents) had organized the *"Cartel des nons"* coalition, with agreement on a minimum alternative program. It had failed and was abandoned for the parliamentary elections. "Something" had not sufficed.

"Somebodies" would not work either. This could be seen with mathematical precision. No single non-Communist party in the 1962 elections had polled more than about one-third as many votes as the Gaullists. No two ideologically adjacent parties had polled even 60 per cent as many votes as the Gaullists. Only a candidate supported by all the non-Communist opposition voters or by all the Marxist voters (Socialists, PSU, and Communists) would have a chance of defeating a Gaullist. The democratic opposition parties had won 43 per cent of the 1962 vote, the Marxist parties 36.7 per cent, and the Gaullists 36.3 per cent. A non-Communist opposition candidate could be expected to finish ahead of a Communist and win a place on the second-round ballot only if he had the support of at least three adjacent parties. If a non-Communist went forward to the second ballot by virtue of the withdrawal of a better placed Communist or because the Communists withheld their candidate from the first round in his favor, he would be discredited in the eyes of many voters and his chances of defeating a Gaullist would be reduced. Furthermore, such an arrangement would give the Communist Party an effective veto over their choice of candidates and a claim to a share of the power they sought. The rewards for united action among the democratic opposition parties, therefore, seemed very high, and the costs of failure very great.

Whether their unity would come organizationally or electorally or both or neither depended upon the success of leaders and voters in adopting new political attitudes and behavior suitable to presidential politics. In particular, they had to feel that it was more important to select a chief executive, thereby passing judgment on the incumbent's performance, than to express their views by ballot on a variety of policy issues. That is, they had to prefer managerial to ideological politics. Without such an attitude, the campaign and elections might be conducted with such confusion that there would be serious doubts about the authenticity of the popular will apparently expressed. If the party organizations reached agreement that was not accepted by the voters, the effort would abort. If the parties failed to agree, but the voters rallied to one candidate in sufficient numbers, the parties would be dealt a heavy, perhaps fatal, blow.

The need for regroupment was not newly discovered as a result of the elections. It had become apparent as soon as a substantial opposition to de Gaulle had developed. As early as late 1958 a public opinion survey had show that 97 per cent of Frenchmen believed that there were too many political parties.[3] There had been incessant talk of the need for common action ever since. Apart from the *Cartel des nons,* however, no concrete steps were taken until the Assembly reconvened in December 1962. At that time, 7 of the anti-Gaullist Independent deputies joined with the 41 MRP deputies and 7 other centrists to form a single parliamentary group, the *Centre Démocratique* (Democratic Center). An effort was made to bring the *Rassemblement Démocratique* (Democratic Rally) deputies, most of whom were Radicals, and the Socialists into the same union. This attempt failed because the Radicals would not join without the Socialists, the Socialists would not join unless the parties outside parliament were also merged and a common program adopted, and the other parties would not accept the Socialists' conditions. Even an effort to form an opposition steering committee foundered because the MRP refused to commit itself to systematic opposition.

Another try at regroupment began in January 1963 with the formation of a Study and Liaison Committee of French Democrats by leaders of the Independents, MRP, and Radicals on an extra-parliamentary plane and was continued in December 1964 with the organization of a "parliamentary union" by the same elements. Bertrand Motte, Jean Lecanuet, and Maurice Faure were its principal animators. Once again, however, the Socialists refused to participate on the grounds that it had too right-wing an orientation. In the absence of the Socialists, the Radicals were unwilling to transform the Committee from what was essentially a study group into a genuine union. The project languished.

After those two attempts, little progress was made during 1963. No major groups agreed on any formula for common action. Late in the year, however, an event occurred that transformed the situation entirely. This was the appearance of a serious, declared opposition candidate for the presidency. It became possible that the voters might be regrouped by the candidate over the heads of their titular leaders or that his presence and activities might stimulate and accelerate the process. Some observers believed that this development was the most important political event in recent French history.

The Defferre Candidacy

One day in September 1963 a group of staff members on the weekly Paris news magazine *L'Express* discussed ways they might influence French politics while boosting the magazine's circulation. The fruit of their conversation was "Monsieur X," candidate for the Presidency of the Republic. In a series of articles they described the political qualities of the "ideal" opponent of President de Gaulle in the 1965 elections. It soon became clear to the Paris political elite that *L'Express* was describing Gaston Defferre, wealthy Socialist mayor of Marseilles. Thus launched, he at once took possession of the center of the stage among present and potential opposition candidates.

Defferre had many qualities to commend his candidacy. As mayor of Marseilles since 1953 he was the second ranking chief executive in France.[4] As chairman of the SFIO in the National Assembly, he was the head of the largest opposition group in parliament. As chairman of the Socialist federation in Marseilles, he controlled the largest departmental organization of the largest non-Communist political party organization. His record as mayor had been highly creditable. Marseilles had never had so little corruption or inefficiency. His unblemished anti-Communism made him more acceptable to conservatives than certain less intransigent leftists. Yet, his liberal positions on colonial, Algerian, economic, and social questions made him acceptable to the non-Communist left. His nondogmatic approach to Socialist doctrine and the clerical question had also stood him in good stead winning support from diverse sources.

He had substantial ministerial experience, having served in ministerial office four times during the Fourth Republic for a total of 35 months. Yet, he was not popularly associated with the discredited regime, for his conduct of the Ministry of Colonies was one of its bright spots and he was forced out of office because of his liberal views on Algeria. The *loi-cadre* (framework law) that bears his name made possible the only peaceful resolution of a colonial problem in postwar French history, the "spinning off" of the French possessions in tropical Africa. He had a record of success at the polls, winning all but one of the eight elections in which he had been a candidate.

Born in 1910, he was young enough to be a vigorous adversary of de Gaulle yet old enough to have compiled a substantial record as Resistance activist during World War II, parliamentarian, and administrator. As a Protestant, he was moderate in his position on the clerical question without being suspected of hidden clericalism.

As a successful lawyer, owner of a prosperous provincial newspaper, and husband of the heiress to a shipping fortune, he had the personal financial resources and social respectability to support his campaign. He had voted against de Gaulle's investiture as Premier in 1958 and had opposed many of his policies, especially his economic policies and his nationalism in foreign and defense affairs. Yet, he had favored the new regime from the beginning and had been instrumental in obtaining for it the endorsement of his party in 1958.

WINNING SFIO ENDORSEMENT. Defferre's first task after announcing his candidacy in December 1963 was to win endorsement by the SFIO. This was necessary in order to enhance his attractiveness to Socialist voters who comprise the largest single element in the non-Communist opposition. On the other hand, it could backfire if it were done in such a way as to jeopardize his chances of winning votes from the backers of other parties. In particular, he needed his party's endorsement without having it impose upon him a program unacceptable to other major parties, especially the Radicals and the MRP.

Defferre's efforts to woo the SFIO were seriously complicated by several factors. First, there had long been considerable personal antagonism between the two most powerful SFIO leaders, Mollet and Defferre. Mollet's identification with the Fourth Republic and the debacle in Algeria made him an unattractive candidate to the mass of the French electorate. The colonialist, repressive policies of his 16-month government and his repeated and extensive compromises with the Right during that time made him unattractive to the Left. His leadership in arranging the "Popular Front" alliances with Communists in the 1962 elections made him unacceptable to the Right. But, though Mollet probably realized that his candidacy was not a realistic possibility, he was reluctant to see the honor go to his greatest rival. His hold over the party machinery and two of its three largest federations enabled him to raise serious impediments to Defferre's candidacy.

Second, the manner in which Defferre's candidacy was launched affronted his party. The Socialists have always placed a very high value on party loyalty. The use of a non-Socialist newspaper to establish a Socialist's claim to the party's endorsement seemed designed to take the decision out of the party's hands by bringing to bear upon it great public pressure. This was not regarded as loyal Socialist behavior.

Third, one of the party's principal justifications for its opposition to de Gaulle was the extent to which he had "personalized" power. Many in the party feared that the Defferre candidacy was "Gaullism without de Gaulle." Defferre's campaign seemed to be giving priority to personality over both party and program. Furthermore, this personalization ran counter to long-established and deeply-held Socialist canons of political legitimacy.

Fourth, there was disagreement within the party on the future of the regime. A "parliamentary" faction felt that de Gaulle's departure should lead to abolition of the regime and the restoration of a reformed and rationalized parliamentary system. Others believed that the regime should be transformed into an authentic Presidential system in which parliament would recover some of its authority and independence without again subordinating the executive. The issue of presidential candidacy was subsidiary to that of the regime. The "parliamentary" faction logically required a candidate hostile to the regime or advocacy of an election boycott. A candidate favorable to the system minus its "abuses" was necessary to the "presidential" faction. Defferre suited the second set of requirements, but not the first.

Finally, there was disagreement over the party's choice of allies. A "Popular Front" element led by Mollet urged that priority be given to serious efforts for reconciliation with the Communists. This group, less interested in the presidential than the parliamentary elections, advocated a long-term program to restore the party's revolutionary Marxist character. An opposing group favored a "Labor" or "Democratic" alliance in which the SFIO would subordinate doctrinaire Marxism to a pragmatic reformist vocation and work with parties and other political groups similarly inclined. This faction favored Defferre. The disagreement on alliance orientation was made more difficult to resolve by the fact that, on the basis of the 1962 election returns, it could be argued that either a Marxist or a non-Communist opposition alliance would rest on electoral support broader than the Gaullists.

The lines of division within the party coincided closely on the various issues. The Molletists, party loyalists, antipersonalists, "parliamentarians," and "Popular Frontists" were usually the same people. So were the Defferrists, those less fastidious about loyalty or personalization of power, the presidentialists, and the "democrats."

In retrospect, it may be seen that his campaign, at that time covert, first impinged on national party affairs at the May 1963 congress when Defferre and his friends persuaded the party to defer all major decisions on presidential electoral tactics until the next congress. On the other hand, some policy decisions were taken that seemed to move the party to the left, that is, in the direction desired by Mollet. The extension of the nationalized sector was reaffirmed as a party objective, with the commercial banks specifically mentioned. Mollet may have anticipated the Defferre candidacy and believed it could be prevented or vitiated by committing the party to a program unacceptable to the centrist supporters. Defferre had to win. However, no connection between program and presidential electoral tactics was made by the Congress. When the party next met, it was too late. Defferre had forced its hand.

The *"Monsieur X"* campaign was opened by *L'Express* September 19 and attracted much attention from the outset. On December 13 the Socialist group in the National Assembly, of which Defferre was chairman, urged the party to endorse him for the presidency. On December 18, the party's steering committee summoned a special party congress for February 2, 1964, to consider his candidacy.

It was still possible for the party to accept the inevitability of Defferre's candidacy, yet impose conditions that would destroy it. Defferre removed that possibility by declaring before the congress of his local federation that he required a personal endorsement from the party and must be free to work out his platform in consultation with other parties and potential supporters. At the same time, he committed himself to certain standard Socialist policies—European unification, abandonment of the independent French nuclear striking force, economic planning, educational reforms and expansion.

The Mollet group attempted to head off the Defferre juggernaut in January by opening a newspaper dialogue with the Communists intended to show the likelihood that the Reds would accept Socialist terms for a rapprochement. Instead, it showed that the two parties were still far apart. By the time the special congress met, the Mollet group had a choice only between graceful submission or open defeat. After preliminary skirmishing in a half-hearted attempt to save some of its marbles, the Mollet faction yielded. It extracted no more than a few purely verbal changes in the resolution before joining in the unanimity of the endorsement. For the first time since he won control of the party in 1946, Mollet had been defeated in a party congress.

The grudging submission of the previous majority faction did not assure Defferre the enthusiastic support of a united party. Mollet and the party machine could be forced to swallow Defferre's candidacy. They could not be forced to like the taste. They continued to grumble about the disadvantages and dangers involved, to direct attention away from Defferre and the presidential elections, and to withhold from him their warm support for his provincial campaigning. The Mollet group also tried to keep alive the possibility of an opening to the Left. There was another newspaper dialogue between the SFIO and the Communists in Autumn 1964. An attempt was also made to bring the PSU back into the fold through a series of "Socialist Colloquiums." Four such meetings of SFIO, PSU, trade union, and political club representatives were held between December 1963 and June 1964. They produced little more than an awareness that the obstacles in the way of reunification were formidable.

The failure of those efforts at Marxist rapprochement left Defferre's hold on the party's endorsement unshaken. He was the party's official candidate, but in full control of his campaign. In late Spring 1965, he lost that control when he was lured into attempting to form a permanent "Democratic Socialist Federation," but the fact that his candidacy was created outside and almost in spite of his party is one of the most hopeful signs that French politics may escape the grasp of the narrow, sectarian, ideological parties which monopolized them so long. His candidacy had become so much more significant than Socialist dogma that he could extract the party's endorsement without permitting it to prescribe his platform. The SFIO needed Defferre more than Defferre needed the SFIO.

DEFFERRE'S CAMPAIGN ACTIVITIES. Once Defferre had obtained the endorsement of the SFIO, he carried his campaign openly to the people. He began the week following the SFIO endorsement with a speech to the Association of Parliamentary Journalists in Paris. His campaign consisted of four principal types of activities:

1. He made five provincial tours before the 1964 summer holidays and resumed a similar schedule in the autumn. In February 1964 he visited Bordeaux and its environs and the department of Aude at the eastern end of the Pyrenees. In April he toured Brittany and the department of Eure-et-Loir southwest of Paris. He went to Lyons in May and to the Alpine southeast in June. He closed his spring campaign with a visit to the Phalempin Fair held annually by the two powerful Socialist federations in the most northerly corner of France, Pas-de-Calais and Nord. His 1964-1965 campaign was inaugurated with an October visit to Clermont-Ferrand in central France and a December tour of Alsace. Early in 1965 he visited Mayenne and Sarthe.

2. In late March 1964 he spent eight days in Washington and New York meeting and conferring with American political and governmental leaders, including President Johnson; Secretaries Rusk, McNamara, and Dillon; Attorney General Kennedy; Senators Humphrey, Mansfield, and Fulbright; Ambassador Stevenson; and Mayor Wagner. He also spoke to the National Press Club and met with the Council on Foreign Relations and editors at Time-Life. In April 1964 he went to London at the invitation of a Labour Party faction favorable to British entry into the Common Market. He was received by Prime Minister Home and Labour Party leader Wilson. Defferre, in turn, was host to West German Social Democratic leader Willy Brandt in March.

3. "Horizon 80" committees[5] were established in 17 provincial cities and nationally to provide an instrument for the organization of his campaign apart from the SFIO. The first was organized in Marseilles in February 1964. The national committee was set up in May 1964 with 60 members. Included among them were members of the Socialist, Radical, and UDSR parties, the Christian democratic and Socialist trade unions, political clubs, and nonpartisan university professors. The membership list was not made public. In August 1964 four national subcommittees were formed and a headquarters was established in Paris. There was a full time director, and Defferre was present three days a week. A newsletter was issued and $1 monthly dues were solicited. According to

L'Express the establishment of the national office evoked a deluge of 10,000 letters containing tens of thousands of dollars.[6]

4. His sympathizers in the non-Communist opposition sought to obtain for him their parties' endorsements.

DEFFERRE'S POLICY POSITIONS. Defferre developed two main points in his campaign pronouncements:

1. The performance of the de Gaulle government was unsatisfactory;
2. Defferre government would do better.

He very largely avoided questions of personality or ideology. On the first point, his criticism ranged widely across the spectrum of governmental activity, but hit hardest on de Gaulle's policies toward European integration and NATO and the de Gaulle government's "failures" in the social services. In most cases, however, his position was not radically different from that of the General.

He opposed de Gaulle's long-forgotten proposal of a Franco-Anglo-American directorate of NATO, but believed the alliance had to be reorganized. He charged de Gaulle with hostility to European integration and deplored the manner in which he had dealt with Britain and with France's European partners, but did not commit himself clearly to British entry into the Common Market. He regretted the diversion of resources into the French nuclear striking force, but refused to say what he would do about it until he had examined all the relevant documents.

He was particularly critical of the government's performance in housing, educational, economic expansion, prices and wages policy, and, of course, the management of the broadcasting system. Although Defferre accepted the form of the present regime, he accused de Gaulle of exercising his office in an authoritarian and undemocratic manner, of "continuous dupery . . . ruses and duplicity." He believed the President's term should be made to coincide with that of the National Assembly, that governmental authority should be less highly centralized in Paris, and that the Senate should be transformed into an Economic Chamber whose main function would be the preparation of the economic plan.

Defferre argued that his government would differ from the present one by preparing and implementing a long-term economic and social program. He promised to present a program—a "National Progress Contract"—to the voters at the time of the election. If elected, he would obtain approval of the program by parliament and would charge his government with the elaboration during its first year of a detailed plan for its implementation over a 15-year period. Both prior and subsequent to the parliamentary ratification he would involve "intermediary bodies," especially trade unions, closely in the preparation of the policies. His program would have four main objectives:

1. High rate of expansion;
2. Continuous rate of expansion;
3. Stable prices and currency;
4. Equitably distributed national income.

The program would enable the government to reform and expand education and increase the rate of housing construction, for instance.

Of greater significance than Defferre's criticism were the areas of silence. In particular, his acceptance of the regime was a major event in French politics. The de Gaulle-Defferre dialogue has been carried on within constitutional consensus. It is also notable, however, that most of his policy positions differed only in degree from de Gaulle's and that the dialogue turned mainly on questions of performance.

CAMPAIGN STRATEGY. Defferre's strategy seemed to be to dissociate himself from both the frailties of the Fourth Republic and the authoritarian flavor of the Fifth, from doctrinaire and partisan Socialism, but not from the progressive humanism which he believes it represents. He sought to associate the leaders and organizations of the Center and Left parties in his enterprise without yielding to them control over his platform, but if this failed he wanted to remain free to go over their heads and appeal directly to their partisans. If he were to draw under his banner most of the Communist, Socialist, and Radical voters of 1962, he could expect to poll somewhat more votes on the first round than there were Gaullist votes in 1962 while an MRP-Independent candidate would run a poor third.

As Defferre sought to break with the ideological parochialism that had been one of the most characteristic features of French politics for many decades, so also did he strive to escape its geographic parochialism. None of the political leaders of the Fourth Republic had attempted to establish a nationwide popular political base. Election campaigns had been highly localized. Political leaders did not campaign outside their own constituencies, even to aid party colleagues. De Gaulle had departed dramatically from that tradition with his radio-television addresses and his provincial tours. Now, Defferre followed the de Gaulle lead with a nationwide campaign—provincial tours, foreign trips, a national network of committees.

The changes in French politics from ideological toward pragmatic or managerial politics and from local to national focus had already been evident during the 1962 campaigns. The readiness with which the French people accepted the propriety of Defferre's activities was evidence that the changes were continuing. Acceptance of the propriety of his activity was not, however, evidence of support. To win enough backing to keep his campaign going, he had to win popularity as well as legitimacy. This proved to be a much more difficult task.

POPULAR REACTION. The first purpose of Defferre's campaign activities was to draw attention to his candidacy. The provincial tours sometimes attracted quite sizable audiences. Ten thousand heard him speak publicly in Bordeaux; there were 5000 at Narbonne, 3000 in Lyons (the largest crowd to attend a meeting at the *Bourse du travail* since 1936, according to *Le Monde*), 1800 in the town of Sisteron, and 3000 in Clermont-Ferrand. Both the provincial and the foreign tours, however, were pitched mainly to the national newspaper audience to which they were widely reported. The silence of the broadcasting systems—somewhat relaxed as the campaign proceeded—was a grotesque effort to limit his audience, an effort that would be unthinkable in any other civilized country professing democracy. In spite of that, the number of Frenchmen who recognized Defferre's name increased from 30 per cent to 80 per cent in the year preceding September 1964.[7]

His endeavor to attract support as well as attention was less successful. His campaign, at least initially, did not affect adversely the General's popularity. An average of about 10 per cent more Frenchmen expressed satisfaction with President de Gaulle's conduct of the office during the first half of 1964 than in 1963 (55 per cent compared to 45 per cent). In May 1964, 50 per cent wanted to see him run for re-election and 27 per cent did not. This compared to 37 per cent for each response in June 1963. In May 1964, 45 per cent wanted him re-elected and 32 per cent did not, compared to 39 and 34 per cent 11 months earlier. That his campaign had relatively little impact is further shown by responses to questions asking for the expression of a preference between the two candidates:[8]

	Oct. 1963	Feb. 1964	May 1964
De Gaulle	43	42	46
Defferre	22	24	25
No answer	35	34	29

The susceptibility of Defferre's candidacy to Communist competition was shown when other choices were made available to the respondents in May and June 1964:

	May	June
De Gaulle	43	42
Defferre	23	13
A Communist*	-	10
Tixier-Vignancour	5	4
Cornu	2	2
No reply	27	29

* Included only in the June survey.

However, with de Gaulle replaced by Pompidou and no Communist, the distribution was quite different: Defferre 29 per cent, Pompidou 21 per cent, Tixier-Vignancour 7 per cent, Cornu 4 per cent, no reply 39 per cent.

The May 1964 survey showed that the strength of support for Defferre was directly proportionate to the ideological distance of

Party preference	De Gaulle	Defferre	No Reply
Communist	6	66	28
Socialist	17	67	16
Radical	30	42	28
MRP	62	18	20
Independents	54	15	31
UNR	94	2	4
No party	31	10	59

the voter from the right end of the political spectrum. The Communists gave him an even greater advantage over de Gaulle than did his own Socialists, and the Radicals were the only other party that gave him as much as one-third the support given to de Gaulle.

The partisan distribution of these preferences goes far to explain the positions assumed by the party organizations. Parties should, perhaps, lead, but they cannot lead where their supporters will not follow. This consideration no doubt had a great influence on their reactions to the Defferre candidacy and, more generally, to the problem of regroupment.

The Political Parties React

Although the traditional political parties had lost much of their credit and prestige since their failures in the Fourth Republic, they remained important influences on French political behavior. In the presidential race, as we shall see, a candidate might not be wholly dependent on their favor, but it remained sufficiently valuable to be solicited. An examination of their reactions to the presidential contest, and especially to the Defferre candidacy, is therefore necessary to an understanding of contemporary French politics. Equally important for such an understanding is a review of their behavior in face of the efforts for regroupment. None of the parties has wholly resolved, to its satisfaction and that of its popular following, either of those problems. None has shed fully its parliamentary robes and donned those of presidentialism.

THE FRENCH COMMUNIST PARTY. In recent years the Communists had made great efforts to end their political isolation. This consideration governed their maneuvers with regard to regroupment and the Presidential elections. The natural object of their wooing was the Socialist party (SFIO). But they were so eager to end their quarantine that they affirmed their willingness to cooperate with any anti-Gaullists except the extremist Right.

The UNR's absorption of virtually all the conservative and centrist electorate in many constituencies had given the Communists' appeal new force, especially in parliamentary and local politics. If the Gaullist candidate's vote exceeded that of either the Socilaist or the Communist in a parliamentary election, he won the seat even if the combined Marxist vote were greater. But a joint Marxist candidate entered in such conditions would win.

Defferre's own Marseilles constituency in 1958 is a case in point. The second-round result was:

Marchetti, UNR	18,749
Defferre, SFIO	18,535
Guizard, Communist	10,825

Marchetti was elected. If the Communist had withdrawn after the first round, enough more of his votes would certainly have gone to Defferre on the second round than to Marchetti to have elected him. Meanwhile, in the second district of the department of Aisne the second-round outcome was:

Bricout, UNR	26,393
Renard, Communist	15,767
Bloch, SFIO	14,544

If the Socialist had withdrawn, it is likely that enough of his votes would have gone to the Communist to have elected him. Both Defferre and Renard had led the Left on the first round. Thus, a general agreement between the two parties to withdraw in favor of a better placed leftist candidate would probably have gained one seat for the SFIO and one for the Communists, both at the expense of the UNR. Because of superior Communist party discipline, such an agreement probably would have benefited the Socialists more than the Communists. Therefore, the Communists had something to offer the Socialists in return for easing their isolation.

The value of mutual withdrawals became still clearer at the 1962 elections. Thirty of the 65 SFIO seats were won with the aid of such desistments.[9] So were 22 of the 41 Communist seats. Three other Communist candidates won because of withdrawals by splinter group candidates of socialist orientation, and a fourth could not have succeeded had not both a dissident Socialist and a Socialist candidate stood down.

Both Socialists and Communists profited from mutual desistments in 1962. This was possible because of the multiplicity of parliamentary seats. Reciprocal benefits of this type are not possible in a Presidential election. Only one president is elected. Therefore, the presidential election placed the Communist party in a dilemma. It could not refuse its support to the leading anti-Gaullist candidate without reducing greatly his prospects for success. This would run counter to its overriding purpose of defeating Gaullism. Yet, it could not grant such support without some form of reciprocity. To do so would have been to admit lack of influence over political events, and also would have cost it a chance to end its isolation.

The Communists sought to resolve this dilemma by exacting as the price of their support an agreement that the parties backing the opposition candidate draw up a common program. Presumably, one of the points in the program would denounce the character of the regime. The party repeatedly threatened to nominate its own candidate unless agreement were reached. Its candidate would not win, but his presence would seriously impair the opposition's chance of success.

The principal obstacle to the Communist efforts was the profound distrust in which they were held by the parties. It was the largest, in both members and voters, and best organized French opposition party. The other parties feared that it would control any alliance and would maneuver them into taking action disadvantageous to them. These fears were, of course, increased by the Communists' traditional unwillingness to play the game according to the rules, to regard themselves as visitors in an enemy camp.

Therefore, in recent years the party has exploited every opportunity to increase its respectability. During the 1962 campaign every lead headline on *L'Humanité* but one was designed to encourage rapprochement with the Socialists. In January 1964 the party revised its statutes to provide secret balloting for all party committees except the Political Bureau of the national organization. At the same time, it made doctrinal changes that brought its ideology more closely in line with that of the Socialists. It declared that a single-party regime was not necessary "for the passage to Socialism" and that a peaceful transition to Socialism was now likely. It also sought to show that it was independent of Moscow. When Nikita Khrushchev proposed a world Communist conference probably to expel Red China from the bloc, the French Communists were notoriously slow to fall in line, apparently to show their independence from dictation by Moscow and, when Khrushchev was deposed, they exasperated the Muscovites with their insistence on knowing all the details of the coup.

In parliament, also, the Communists were on their best behavior. They did not cease their intransigent opposition, but neither did they engage in the systematic harassment and dilatoriness that marked their Fourth Republic career. Furthermore, on occasion they supported moves by the non-Communist opposition rather than pursue parallel action.

The Communist strategy, then, was designed to favor the closest possible cooperation with the other opposition parties, especially the Socialists, but not to endorse a non-Communist candidate without having been given some recognition of their acceptability. They many times expressed their hostility to the Defferre candidacy, charging him, especially, with insufficiently intransigent opposition to de Gaulle and his regime and with having too personal an approach to politics, but their real complaint was that he refused to negotiate his program with them.

UNIFIED SOCIALIST PARTY (PSU). Despite its impressive name the PSU was a group of splinters ceaselessly resplintering. Some of its members had drifted in from the SFIO, some had come from the Communist party, others had been left-wing Radicals, a few were refugees from the MRP, still others had never previously found themselves comfortable in a large political movement and had joined like-minded individualists in one or another of the many left-wing ideological cliques that are usually composed of about one-quarter Indians and three-quarters chiefs. Not surprisingly, they continued their sectarian ways under a common label. The second PSU congress (1963) was very nearly its last, as seven different factions emerged and resisted all efforts at compromise.

It was said that whenever 10 members of the PSU met to discuss a question, they would take at least a dozen conflicting approaches. Nevertheless, there was one point of common agreement, and it had special relevance for presidential electoral politics. All believed that the party should serve as a means to effect reunification of the French Marxist Left. Especially, they sought to persuade the SFIO to cooperate with them and with the Communists. Their task was quite seriously complicated by the belief among SFIO leaders that the principal purpose of the PSU was to destroy the SFIO. As the Communists obviously did not expect the PSU to succeed, they preferred to ignore the PSU than be cozy with it and jeopardize their efforts at rapprochement with the SFIO.

The PSU campaign for common action in the presidential contest was based on the same argument for measures rather than men that the Communists use. It wanted the Marxist Left to elaborate a common program as a prerequisite to support for a joint candidate who would necessarily be an SFIO Socialist. Likewise, the PSU was very scornful of the Defferre candidacy on grounds almost identical to those of the Communists.

RADICAL-SOCIALISTS. The Radical movement was the most complete Janus in French politics. The classic descriptions still fit well: heart on the Left, billfold on the Right; like a radish—red on the outside, white within, best taken with a grain of salt. Because of the Radicals' traditional vocation as a managerial party during the Third and Fourth Republics—always ready to join a government whether the coalition be Right, Left, or Center—the party could not afford clear, unequivocal identification with either side of the Great Political Divide. These habits continued into the Fifth Republic although the UNR replaced it as manager. Its vocation now was that of bridge between the main elements of the opposition.

Like all bridges, it had a vital interest in seeing that the breach it spanned did not widen. Hence, it naturally favored efforts toward formation of an opposition coalition. Neither can a bridge bind itself exclusively to only one of its abutments. Thus, the Radicals resisted either a "Popular Front" alliance with the Socialists and Communists or a Center-Right coalition binding them only to the MRP and Independents. The former would have weakened its parliamentary candidates in those areas where its principal non-Gaullist adversaries were on the Right. The latter would have weakened it in other areas where its main rivals were Leftists. The principal purpose of the alliance might be presidential, but the party could hardly prevent its parliamentary politics being affected.

The Radicals, therefore, issued their appeals for common opposition to the broadest possible audience. "The other democratic formations," "all free men," "the widest possible regroupment of democrats" are typical of the terms they used.

Before the Radicals could talk persuasively of a broad coalition of parties, however, they had to put their own house in order. Successive splits, principally resulting from Mendès-France's effort to give the party a clear left-wing orientation, led to the existence of several parties in the Radical family: the original Radical-Socialists, the Democratic Center, the Union of Democratic Forces, the Rally of the Republican Left, the European Liberal Party, the Democratic and Socialist Union of the Resistance (UDSR), the Democratic Left (in the Senate), and the "Moricien" Radicals. Under the leadership of M. Maurice Faure, the president of the Radical-Socialists, this collection had moved slowly toward reunification in recent years. The "mendèsist" Union of Democratic Forces still fluttered fitfully in the shadow of the PSU. The European Liberal Party of Jean-Paul David remained apart. All the others had returned to the parent party or joined with it in the *Rassemblement Démocratique* (Democratic Rally) that holds its annual congresses in conjunction with the congresses of the Radical-Socialists, serves as the designation of the radical-type group in the Assembly, and generally acts as a political holding company of which the Radical-Socialists are the parent corporation.

The relative unity that the Radicals had recovered organizationally was not reflected in their views on common action with other parties. Some leaders such as Maurice Faure and Félix Gaillard favored amalgamation with other parties, but they disagreed on which. Gaillard wanted fusion with the Socialists and believed the party should wait until the Socialists were ready before wooing other partners. Faure agreed that union with the Socialists was desirable, but doubted its present feasibility. He preferred combination with the MRP and the Independents pending a change in the Socialist position. François Mitterrand and his friends in the UDSR would join forces only with "progressive Leftists," presumably not the MRP or Independents. André Morice and Bernard Lafay of the Republican Center wanted a union from the Socialists to the Independents. Other leaders, such as Maurice Bourgès-Maunoury and Emile Hugues, believed it was necessary to strengthen the party before seeking mergers. None openly advocated alliance with the Communists. Thus, the Socialists wanted to join the Communists, but not only the Communists, while the Radicals, their closest non-Communist partners, resisted any grouping that included the Communists and any that did not include the Socialists. The Communists advocated any form of regroupment, the Socialists wanted alliance but not fusion, while the Radicals were undecided on the form that regroupment should take.

On the matter of Defferre's candidacy, there was more agreement in the party. A motion adopted unanimously at the Radical-Socialist Congress in September 1964 endorsed him; the UDSR was even more emphatic at the same time. Several speakers at the congress expressed the hope that Pierre Mendès-France would return to the party, implicitly suggesting his suitability as a presidential candidate. No other candidates were mentioned seriously.

The Defferre endorsements were made without conditions. They were the first he obtained outside his own party.

POPULAR REPUBLICAN MOVEMENT (MRP). Another centrist party, the Christian democratic MRP, had problems similar to those of the Radicals. These problems were compounded by the gnawing fear among its leaders that most of its parliamentary electorate was Gaullist. Not only, then, was it torn among various alternative opposition coalitions, but it also had to decide whether it was opposition or Gaullist. Throughout the Fourth Republic the party had been plagued by a serious divergence between the reformist orientation of its leadership and the conservatism of its electorate. Now, this divergence had been overlaid by a split between the anti-Gaullism of most of its leaders and the Gaullism of a majority of its electorate.

Despite these difficulties, the party took early and unequivocally two stands that have caused the other parties great perplexity:

1. It decided at its congress in May 1963 that it would gladly submerge completely its identity in a new opposition party with a majority vocation (that is, designed to acquire majority support) and was equally clear in its opposition to an alliance among existing parties.

2. It was certain that there would be no room for the Communist Party in such a fusion.

No new party could have a "majority vocation" of any credibility if it were formed only by the Independents and MRP, for they won a combined total of only 18.5 per cent of the 1962 votes. Indeed, the MRP leaders expressly excluded such a narrow alliance. Therefore, the presence of at least the Radicals was also necessary. The Radicals refused to join unless the Socialists did too, the Socialists would not join without the Communists, and the MRP and Independents would not accept the Communists. Furthermore, the Radicals were reluctant to abandon their corporate identity, and the Socialists were certain they would not. Finally, Mollet of the SFIO went out of his way to make clear that he would bend every effort to prevent compromise on the clerical question, precisely the most sensitive issue for the MRP.

Though the party settled quickly and with deceptive ease its attitude toward regroupment, it acted less rapidly on the Defferre candidacy. The party's Congress in May 1964, the first after Defferre had begun his campaign, said nothing of Defferre in its resolutions. None of the orators endorsed his candidacy clearly. Those who mentioned him at all were skeptical of his staying power and reluctant to commit themselves to such a risky venture. Later, some of its leaders, including Lecanuet, expressly disavowed him.

MODERATES. The conservative National Center of Independents and Peasants (CNI) had even less cohesion than most French parties. Not until nearly 10 years after its formation in 1948 did it acquire sufficient unity that it dared hold a national congress. Soon thereafter it split asunder, one group going into various anti-Gaullist extremist movements, a second forming in 1962 the Gaullist Independent Republicans, and a third remaining anti-Gaullist but constitutional. The third group, retaining the CNI label, was even less sure than the MRP of being able to bring its electorate along in an anti-Gaullist presidential campaign. The party, therefore, hesitated long before taking a stand on the main issues regarding the Presidential elections.

When it finally broke its silence in April 1964, these points were clear:

1. It favored a centrist coalition, but did not specify the nature of the relationship it believed should exist among the component elements. Such a grouping should be anti-Gaullist and should include neither Socialists nor Communists.

2. It opposed Defferre's candidacy. Some leaders urged that Antoine Pinay's name be put forward. Others favored giving support to Lecanuet, president of the MRP.

Some party leaders argued that there was not one center but "centers" in French politics, implying that more than one presidential electoral alliance might be formed in the political arena between the Gaullists and the Communists. As the CNI was differentiated from the Independent Republicans only by its anti-Gaullism, it would have had no reason to exist if it had joined with the Gaullists. On the other hand, it was on the far right of the opposition spectrum, so it had no real choice in making alliances. It was the captive of the MRP, its nearest neighbor on the left, and any parties with which the MRP might be allied. Its only alternative was isolation, in which case it would have lost its electorate, partly to the Gaullists and the rest to any centrist or leftist grouping that appeared better placed to beat the Gaullists.

CONCLUSION. The foregoing analysis shows the extent of the continued disarray among the traditional French political parties. They were limited by their organizational interests and ideologies from coalescing in order to strengthen the opposition or from giving freely the broad support a joint candidate required. Only the Socialists and the Radicals (both half-heartedly) had endorsed Defferre during the first year of his candidacy.

Despite the tergiversations of the parties, the presidential elections approached ominously and continued to loom in the popular mind as *the* chief impending political event. However much they might wish, the parties could not distract the voters from that interest. We must look elsewhere, therefore, in search of forces to bring politics in line with the shape of the regime and the expectations of the public. One possible alternative force was the political club, an institution of considerable prominence in Fifth Republic politics.

Political Clubs

Some 120 political clubs grouping perhaps 15,000 to 20,000 members had conducted a lively, running public discussion of political questions since the beginning of the Fifth Republic. They had attracted much attention and had a certain influence, especially on the opposition and on presidential politics. Some of them, such as the *Groupes "Esprit,"* a left-wing Christian democratic group that dates from 1932, were organizations of subscribers to political journals whose principal activity was the group discussion of questions presented in the journals. Most of them, however, were formed of men with similar political views, but not necessarily in the same political parties, as means to give their views effect outside the framework of the traditional parties and traditional political activities.

They fell into two main groups. One was concerned only with discussion and political education. The other believed that discussion should be followed by action to influence political affairs more directly, though not by nominating candidates for election. Both groups felt that the parties had failed to deal effectively with French political problems and sought to infuse them with new vitality. For this reason, they had been labeled the "new strata" or the "live forces" of contemporary French politics. The clubs tended to be hostile to Gaullism, but also opposed to parliamentarism of the Fourth Republic variety.

Most of their members were under 40 years old. They tended to be intellectuals: teachers, professors, lawyers, technicians, middle and higher civil servants. Few came from commerce, fewer still from clerical-type vocations, virtually none from industrial labor or farming. With the exception of *Patrie et progrès,* they were oriented toward the non-Communist Left.

The oldest of them was the *Club des jacobins,* 1500 members, which was founded in 1951 to rejuvenate the left wing of the Radical Socialist party. When Pierre Mendès-France became the principal spokesman of that wing, the club championed his cause. During the time he controlled the party it suspended activities, its members devoting their energies to assisting him in retaining control. When he was forced out in 1957, it resumed activity and became one of the most vigorous and influential clubs. Its founder and president was Charles Hernu, who was also the chief animator of various joint activities conducted by the club movement.

Most of the clubs were founded during the troubled days of late spring and early summer 1958 when it was widely believed that French democracy was on the verge of collapse under the impact of the Algerian nationalist insurrection, military defiance of civilian authority, Communist appeals for armed resistance, and the conspicuous incapacity of the political parties to deal with the dangers. The Club Jean-Moulin (named for a civil servant martyr of Resistance to the Nazi occupation), for instance, was founded on May 25, 1958, by Daniel Cordier as a clandestine network composed mostly of civil servants with the purpose of organizing resistance if France should fall under the rule of a tyrannical regime. It restricted its membership to about 600.

The largest of the clubs was probably "Citoyens 60," which

claimed 3500 members in about 100 local committees. It was another of the 1958 "panic" creations. So was the Cercle Tocqueville of Lyons (about 1000 members), the most notable of the provincial clubs, and Groupes Rencontres (about 1000 members), which was founded by three survivors of Buchenwald to promote contacts between military servicemen and civil servants.

Those and other clubs engaged in a variety of activities. They held regular meetings at which public figures representing a wide range of views and responsibilities were invited to debate leading political questions of the day. They published political newsletters and journals and contributed special pages, columns, and letters to the daily and weekly press. The Club Jean Moulin published several books that circulated widely. Some of the clubs sponsored public lectures, courses in politics and citizenship, conferences, and special interest groups.

The activities that attracted widest attention were several large, public conferences. A number of colloquia were held by various clubs individually. Three joint ventures had special importance. The first of these was a "Banquet of 1000" held at Saint Honoré-les-Bains southeast of Paris on September 15, 1963. It was modeled on the "banquets of a thousand" that had been used to crystallize the opposition to the monarchy of Louis Philippe in 1847-1848 and had played a major role in precipitating the revolution that overthrew it. Under the leadership of the Club des Jacobins, several clubs sponsored the 1963 version. Prominent members of the Radical and Socialist parties and a few Communists were also among the 1200 participants.

The "reflective" group of about 50 clubs held a convocation of about 1000 members at Vichy on April 25-26, 1964. The 11 sponsoring clubs, including the Club Jean Moulin and Citoyens 60 of Paris, Cercle Tocqueville of Lyons, Démocratie Nouvelle of Marseilles, and Positions of Moulins, exchanged views on a wide range of policy questions, but carefully avoided presidential politics, despite the urging of "Démocratie Nouvelle."

The "engagé" group of another 50 clubs under the leadership of the Club des Jacobins met six weeks later at the Palais d'Orsay in Paris in a "Preparatory Convention of Republican Institutions" which 200 delegates attended. The delegates agreed, in their final resolution, on the need to "overturn the present regime," but came to no accord on whether it should be succeeded by a parliamentary or genuinely presidential system. Some orators were critical of the Defferre candidacy; others were favorable; the closing resolution was silent.

On the other hand, several clubs individually supported Defferre's candidacy. These included the Club des Jacobins, the Cercle Tocqueville, Club Démocratie Nouvelle. Also, several of them—notably Club Jean Moulin, Cercle Tocqueville, Citoyens 60, and Démocratie Nouvelle—issued a "manifesto" in mid-December 1963, when Defferre was about to announce his candidacy, describing a desirable candidate who sounded very much like him.

A principal aim of the clubs was to promote "regroupment" and consolidation of the parties. Toward this end, members of the Club Jean Moulin, Club des Jacobins, Démocratie et Socialisme, Citoyens 60, and Gauche européenne participated in the series of "Socialist Colloquia" that are described above, p. 111.

The main constructive impact of the clubs on presidential politics was the initial boost they gave Defferre. It is, however, difficult to say with assurance that the clubs appreciably advanced the Defferre candidacy once it was launched. When, in late Spring, 1965, the still-born "Democratic Socialist Federation" was formed at their instance, they badly overshot the mark (see pp. 137-138 below). As a result, the Defferre candidacy was sacrificed to a regroupment attempt that was decidedly premature and ill-founded. Furthermore, by insisting so strenuously on the importance of program in conventional ideological terms, especially their incessant carping on the need for "socialist" reform, rather than the performance and personal competence issues so necessary for presidential politics they may even be impeding the transformation of French politics.

Other Candidates

Although Defferre's activities dominated party and club consideration of presidential politics, he was not the only announced candidate after April 1964. Furthermore, a number of other hopefuls were believed to be waiting in the wings for an appropriate cue. Finally, there was continuing speculation on the likelihood that de

Gaulle would seek re-election and, if he did not, his probable choice of successor.

While President de Gaulle was in the hospital for his prostate operation in April 1964, two other men anounced that they would seek the Presidency. One was Jean-Louis Tixier-Vignancour, a right-wing extremist. The other was André Cornu, a member of the centrist Radical Socialist movement.

Tixier-Vignancour, born in 1908, was a deputy at the time France fell in 1940. He threw in his lot with the wartime collaborationist regime of Marshal Pétain, serving in his government, but later broke with it and wound up in a Vichy prison. Since the war, he has been prominent in a succession of right-wing organizations and has established a reputation as one of the leading French trial lawyers. His defense of General Raoul Salan, for instance, is credited with saving the head of the Algerian terrorist Secret Army Organization from the firing squad. Tixier-Vignancour was a member of the Chamber of Deputies from 1936 until World War II and of the National Assembly from 1956 to 1958.

Tixier-Vignancour launched his campaign as anti-Gaullist of the Right with a series of public meetings during the last nine months of 1964. He drew crowds of six or seven thousand for his opening meeting in Paris in April, 10,000 in Marseilles in May, 3000 in Rouen in October, and eight to ten thousand in Lyons. He also spoke in La Baule, Le Puy, and Toulouse. His Winter-Spring 1964-1965 campaign included three meetings in Paris and others in Arras, Perpignan, Brest, Reims, Metz, Strasbourg, Dijon, Rennes, Bordeaux, and Tours. In Paris he spoke especially on problems of youth and business; in Arras on agriculture. His audiences tended to be larger than Defferre's even though public opinion surveys indicated that his electoral support was much smaller. This was probably partly because he tended to speak in larger cities, but also because his appeal was directed toward a right-wing audience whose anti-Gaullism was more emotional and because of Tixier-Vignancour's reputation as an orator. Often his audience was composed largely of refugees from Algeria.

On November 3, 1964, he followed Defferre's lead by opening campaign headquarters in Paris. At the same time, he announced the formation of a "Comité T.V." that would sponsor his candidacy, and he read a letter of endorsement from Georges Bidault, former MRP leader, Premier, and Foreign Minister early in the Fourth Republic. He claimed that his campaign was being financed by committee dues and by the sale of books and phonograph records at his meetings.

His statements were strongly conservative, even reactionary. He accepted the form of the regime, but believed that the president should not have "reserved domains" in which he alone wielded authority as he alleged de Gaulle to have. He also advocated the establishment of a supreme court. The treason trial of Marshal Pétain should be reviewed and his ashes transferred to a hero's grave. Those imprisoned for terrorism during the Algerian troubles should be amnestied and the refugees from Algeria indemnified for the lost property.

Free enterprise should be encouraged; socialized medicine opposed; agricultural prices pegged to costs; the income tax cut by 11 or 12 per cent; student assistance, school construction expenditures, and teachers' pay increased; and local liberties recovered from an encroaching national government. His foreign policies were marked by militant anti-Communism and pro-Americanism: Strengthen NATO, SEATO, and CENTO. Speed European integration. Withdraw the Franco-German treaty. Discontinue development of nuclear weapons, cut foreign aid, and eliminate "prestige" expenditures. Finally, his principal complaint against both his adversaries seems to have been their "Communism." De Gaulle was a "tool of atheistic Communism," and Defferre would be a good candidate if he were not "seeking support from the Communists."

Although Tixier-Vignancour repeatedly asserted that he was in the race to win, most observers and public opinion surveys concurred in underlining the unlikelihood that he would. He himself on occasion said he was more interested in defeating de Gaulle than in being President of the Republic and estimated his probable vote at 20 per cent. This suggests that his main purpose was to offer a right-wing alternative to de Gaulle that would draw off enough votes to enable another candidate to defeat the General. Also, like Senator Goldwater in 1964 he would rather be a "choice-not-an-echo" loser than a "me-too" winner. One of his most persistent criticisms of Defferre was that he was too Gaullist. As candidates of the extreme Right won less than 1 per cent of the 1962 vote, Tixier-

Vignancour would have to look elsewhere for enough support to succeed with his strategy. Part of the additional electorate might lie in constituencies where there had been no right-wing candidate in 1962. Part could come from voters, especially Algerian refugees, who had not lived in France in 1962. Still others could be activated by Tixier-Vignancour's oratorical talents and the publicity of a nationwide campaign. In any case, it appeared that he was drawing far more support than the extreme Right had won in 1962, but whether it would be sufficient to accomplish his aims still appeared unlikely.

Cornu is much less well known than either Defferre or Tixier-Vignancour. He was born in 1892 and began his career as a civil servant. He served in the Chamber of Deputies from 1932 to 1936 and had been a senator since 1948. His parliamentary career was singularly undistinguished, marked only by service as Secretary of State for Fine Arts from 1951-1954. He was publisher of a weekly auto magazine.

Cornu was much the least active of the candidates. After announcing his ambition in April 1964 his only spring campaign activity was a speech to a banquet of members of his political club, the Republican Circle, in June. In October he made another speech in Paris to the *Ligue des bleus de Normandie*.

He agreed with his adversaries in accepting the main lines of the Fifth Republic and in believing that the role of the Assembly should be increased at the expense of the chief executive and that the emergency powers article of the Constitution should be repealed. He advocated replacement of the French nuclear striking force by a European force and the curtailment of other "prestige" expenditures such as foreign aid. He favored amnesty for the Algerian terrorists and higher agricultural prices.

He said he would seek endorsement by a nominating convention that Jean-Paul David's European Liberal Party planned to hold April 25, 1965. Cornu's candidacy was the least serious of those anounced during 1964. It seemed little more than another manifestation of the same unrealistic ambition that Cornu had shown when he had posed a hopeless candidacy for the presidency of the Fourth Republic in 1953 and had maintained it until the last moment against the most insistent importunities of his political associates.

A number of other names were persistently mentioned as possible candidates. Prominent among them were Senator Jean Lecanuet, national president of the Christian democratic MRP, and Deputy Maurice Faure, his counterpart in the Radical Socialist party. Lecanuet was handicapped by a mediocre electoral record, having won a National Assembly seat in 1951 but lost in 1956 and 1958. Faure had won his first contest for an Assembly seat in 1951 at age 29 and was re-elected in 1956, 1958, and 1962.

There was also speculation that some leaders of the Fourth Republic might attempt political comebacks in the presidential race. Among those mentioned were Antoine Pinay, Pierre Pflimlin, and Pierre Mendès-France.

Pinay was the most imposing leader of the French conservatives during the Fourth Republic, having served as Premier for ten months in 1952. He rallied early to de Gaulle in 1958 and was his first finance minister, but later broke with him and retired from politics except for an occasional speech. His age (73), his identification with the Fourth Republic, and his long retirement diminished his attractiveness, but his prestige remained high among conservative voters. His candidacy would be likely to split the Right, drawing support mainly from voters who would otherwise vote for de Gaulle. In late Spring 1965 he announced that he was not a candidate but did not exclude the possibility that he would become one.

Pflimlin was the last premier before de Gaulle returned to power and also served in his first government. He had represented an Alsatian department in the Assembly since 1946 under the MRP label and is perhaps the best known leader of the party since the death of Robert Schuman and the defection of Georges Bidault. Pflimlin's candidacy would be tarred with the brush of the Fourth Republic and would suffer from the relative electoral weakness of his party. He would probably be attractive to much the same non-Gaullist conservative elements as would Pinay, but his appeal would extend further toward the Left than Pinay's.

Mendès-France's dynamic conduct of the Premiership in 1954 won for him a large personal following, but he was unable to organize or hold it. An unbroken string of setbacks since 1956 and his intransigent opposition to the present constitution have driven him deep into political isolation. He is further handicapped by his lack of affiliation with any party since leaving the Radical-Socialists in 1959 and ceasing activity in the Unified Socialist Party (PSU) in 1962. A Mendès-France candidacy would draw support primarily from the same elements of the non-Communist Left as Defferre.

There were other possible opposition candidates. The Communists might enter the lists with one of their leaders, perhaps Jacques Duclos or Waldeck Rochet. If Defferre were to fade out, another Socialist might take his place. Guy Mollet, the party's secretary-general, was one possibility. Gaston Monnerville, a Radical, might also make the race. He was President of the Senate. Although he supported de Gaulle in 1958, he broke with him on the constitutional revision issue and had been a particular object of de Gaulle's scorn to such an extent that he had become virtually a symbol of anti-Gaullism. No candidate would be more likely to arouse the President's ire. Some suggested a nonpartisan, prestige candidate—Louis Armand, former head of the French railroads, or Jean Monnet, the architect of European integration, for instance. Mollet has proposed—perhaps tongue-in-cheek—the name of Albert Schweitzer.

Despite all the activity of candidates and the efforts toward common action by the parties, however, as the election approached it became increasingly clear that none of the problems that beset the French political elite under the Fourth Republic had truly been solved. There was neither regroupment nor a presidential candidate who inspired enthusiasm. Well before his withdrawal in June 1965, Defferre's campaign lagged seriously and was not making the necessary dent in popular opinion. No other opposition candidate was considered seriously by anyone.

Gaullist Campaigning

Most observers expected President de Gaulle to run for re-election if his health permitted. He had said as much himself. Even if he did not run, the Gaullists were not likely to have difficulty selecting a candidate. The movement was so much the creature of one man that it was logically bound to accept his designated successor. It had become increasingly clear since the 1962 elections that Premier Georges Pomidou was this man. Others whose shoulders might bear the Gaullist mantle include Michel Debré; Jacques Chaban-

Delmas, Mayor of Bordeaux and President of the National Assembly; and Valéry Giscard-d'Estaing, the Minister of Finance. At one time there was even speculation (perhaps not quite serious) that de Gaulle might prefer the Count of Paris, Orleanist pretender to the French throne, as his successor. It was argued that de Gaulle believed he could not be succeeded by a man, only a dynasty. If the Gaullists wished, for whatever reason, to seek their candidate in another party, the MRP's Maurice Schumann, a consistent supporter of de Gaulle, was a likely choice.

Although President de Gaulle, typically, deferred announcing his candidacy as long as possible, he dropped broad hints on several occasions beginning in early 1964 that he would run. As it was often impossible to draw a line between the activities of President de Gaulle and those of Candidate de Gaulle, no attempt will be made here to describe his campaign in detail. Some of his more obvious and important campaign activities will, however, be mentioned briefly.

The most notable of them were his provincial tours; he had undertaken more than 20 in the first seven years of his reign. In each case he spent several days touring villages and towns in two or more adjacent departments. He had visited officially every department by summer 1965. The President also took the opportunity of his frequent television speeches and press conferences to make campaign remarks. For instance, in January 1964 he took a couple of cracks at the "Monsieur X" whose identity had just been revealed. Finally, the rules for the use of political news material by the broadcasting systems were obviously designed to promote his candidacy. In addition to de Gaulle's personal activities it should be mentioned that the UNR's efforts to strengthen its party organization had obvious relevance to the campaign of de Gaulle or any other Gaullist candidate.

The only other Gaullist who behaved at all like a campaigning candidate as the elections approached was Prime Minister Georges Pompidou. He began in the spring of 1964 to play a more conspicuous and independent role than he had previously. He made a few provincial tours of his own and even went to Sweden on an official visit. He was the principal speaker at a national conclave of the UNR even though he was not a member. In his speeches in parliament and on television he began to sound less like a functionary and more like a politician. Everything pointed toward the likelihood that de Gaulle was grooming him as a possible Gaullist candidate in case he himself were unwilling or unable to make the race.

VI. CONCLUSIONS

This account of the evolution of the Fifth French Republic illustrates all too well how much easier it is to enact laws and promulgate constitutions than to transform political attitudes and behavior. The engrossment of Debre's "rationalized" parliamentarism in the Constitution did not prevent de Gaulle from imposing his presidentialism on the regime. The legislation of a presidential electoral system with all its implications of bipartite, managerial politics wracked the opposition leaders with great agony, but precipitated little constructive action and jarred few citizens out of their habitual patterns of ideological, narrowly partisan responses.

The campaigns of 1962 seemed to reflect the beginning of a new style in French politics, less parochial ideologically and geographically, more appropriate to managerial, presidential politics. The Defferre candidacy seemed well suited to develop those incipient tendencies. Probably no one in France was better qualified to rally the opposition. His campaign was marked by few obvious errors of strategy or tactics, yet it met resistance from virtually every side and evoked little enthusiasm. True, he appeared a pygmy beside the awesome figure of de Gaulle, but less shortsighted and narrow reactions on the part of most of the opposition could have enormously increased his stature.

Several reasons may be advanced to explain the difficulties with which the French political public responded to de Gaulle's challenge. In the first place, the continued and, even, increasingly conspicuous existence of a dual executive encouraged the opposition to believe that after de Gaulle it might be possible to restore parliamentarism. The Presidency would be filled by a nonassertive politician willing to permit the National Assembly to control the executive again, and the Premier would become the head of the government in fact as well as in name. This possibility removed much of the incentive for political realignment along presidential lines.

A second reason was simply the old problem of structural inertia. Parties existed with all their accoutrement of officers, staffs, membership lists, headquarters, and newspaper ties. The individuals who had to take the steps toward merger were just the ones who had the strongest attachments and deepest personal interests in the present arrangements. Many of them had built their political careers entirely on a foundation of loyalty to the party. It was difficult for them to shed the habits of a lifetime.

Finally, de Gaulle's presence had a double, and contradictory, impact on the evolution of presidentialism in the opposition parties. It had convinced them that they could not possibly recover power without realignment as long as de Gaulle was active in politics. On the other hand, they suspected that his presence would prevent their success even if they did act jointly. Believing this latter point, each concluded that the most promising long-term tactic was to bide its time, conserving its organization and the loyalty of its followers until de Gaulle disappears in order to have the strongest possible position in the contest for power that will follow.

The situation could change radically in the final stages of the campaign. Voters are reluctant, especially in France, to respond to public opinion surveys concerning hypothetical problems. As the elections drew closer, as the campaign intensified, both party leaders and voters could re-form in new patterns introducing greater order and simplicity into French presidential politics. Even if they did not, irreversible steps might have been taken toward a new and more modern style of politics. The campaign and, even more, the elections might have the necessary impact on the French political spirit.

In any case, France now had the constitutional and legal structure necessary for the clear expression of popular will in the choice of its chief executive. The structural independence of the presidency was established with de Gaulle's implementation of his interpretation of the Constitution. The electoral machinery to provide it with an independent constituent base has been created. The official campaign period is excessively short and the limitations imposed on news reporting by the State broadcasting system unfairly partisan, but those are not crippling defects. The two-round balloting system with the second round restricted to two candidates is probably as suitable as any for the present political forces in France, though a plurality ballot might have accelerated the realignment of parties. This system must now be infused with the spirit of presidential politics for the transformation of French politics to be completed. On the success of that operation depends the future of the regime and of French democracy.

EPILOGUE

As French politics resumed after the sacred August holidays in 1965, the opposition was in more than usual disarray. With the Presidential elections three months away, the Left had no candidate, the Center had a nonentity, and the Right had a carnival huckster.

On June 18—the 150th anniversary of Waterloo and the 25th of de Gaulle's first call for resistance to the German occupation—Gaston Defferre's attempt to create a Democratic Socialist Federation foundered. One week later, because of that failure, he withdrew his candidacy, although he left open the possibility that he would reenter the race later.

The DSF was launched on April 24-25 when a "Convention of Republican Institutions," held by about 50 "engagé" clubs, called for a "democratic federation with a socialist vocation." Buoyed up by his victory in the March municipal elections in Marseilles, Defferre picked up the challenge and announced on May 10 that he would submit to the forthcoming SFIO Congress a proposal that the Socialists take the initiative to form such a federation.

His proposal was endorsed on May 13 by the Lecanuet-Faure Study Committee of Democrats with the Independents dissenting and on May 30 by the MRP Congress. The Socialist Congress followed suit on June 6, although by a narrow margin. Two days later Defferre began negotiations culminating in a nine-hour session, June 17-18, with 16 representatives of the SFIO, Radical Socialists, MRP, UDSR, Democratic Rally, the "engagé" clubs, and Defferre's Horizon 80 committee.

These discussions showed clearly what many already suspected: the MRP and SFIO endorsements were not entirely sincere; each imposed conditions unacceptable to the other. The main issues that destroyed the federation were:

1. The SFIO insisted that no members of the federation promote State subsidies for church schools during a two-year truce. The MRP refused.
2. The MRP insisted that no candidate of the federation be permitted to form an alliance with a Communist. The SFIO required greater flexibility.
3. The SFIO wanted the federation to commit itself to nationalize commercial banks. The MRP refused.
4. The MRP wanted the federation to become operative only after the presidential elections. Defferre reluctantly agreed. The clubs refused.
5. MRP insisted that party amalgamation be immediate. The SFIO wanted it to take place in stages.
6. The clubs, the SFIO, and the UDSR insisted that the name of the federation include the word "socialist." The MRP refused.

In short, Defferre and his associates attempted to use his candidacy to compel a regrouping of parties with policy positions virtually identical to those of the SFIO instead of simply forming an electoral alliance that would agree on little more than support of his candidacy. The ideological vocation of French politics still dominated their thinking and produced its inevitable consequences.

While Defferre was fizzling, Tixier-Vignancour was percolating briskly.

However thin may have been his probable electoral base, he was certainly making himself conspicuous. After a late spring campaign that included an average of two big meetings every week with audiences ranging from 1,000 to nearly 10,000, he launched a caravan tour of resorts in August. With a 3,000-seat, candy-striped circus tent, 10 giant trailer-trucks, and 16 other vehicles, he carried out a series of 27 beachside speeches.

Mr. Cornu did not fare so well. A riding accident prevented his presenting his candidacy to M. Jean-Paul David's "National Liberal Convention" on April 24 and he slipped from sight without formally renouncing his ambitions. The Liberals endorsed Sen. Pierre Marcilhacy, a provincial *notable* whose political orientation was similar to Cornu's. Although he had served in the Senate since 1948, his career was so undistinguished that his principal political asset seemed to be his ability to look down on de Gaulle from a height of 6′7″.

On the Gaullist side, several events gave Pompidou more prominence. He made a state visit to India in February, intervened actively in the March municipal elections, and gave the principal address at the UNR congress, though not a member himself. Also, for the first time he accompanied de Gaulle on a provincial tour and, in July, made one of Brittany alone. Still, de Gaulle was deferring an announcement on his candidacy and most observers expected him to run if his health permitted. Against such a candidate, the opposition needed all the unity it could muster. Failing to amalgamate its organizations, perhaps its only salvation lay in combining, somehow, in one candidate, the Communists' militancy, Defferre's political standing, Pinay's respectability, Tixier-Vignancour's showmanship, and Marcilhacy's physical stature. As the Fall campaign began, no such miracle seemed likely.

NOTES

1. All candidates receiving votes from more than 50 per cent of the voters and more than 25 per cent of the registered voters were elected on the first round. In all other constituencies a second balloting was required, at which a simple plurality sufficed.

2. Of these, 229 bore the UNR-UDT label and 20 were Independent Republicans. A handful of other deputies, mostly MRP, had campaigned as Gaullists.

3. P. E. Converse and G. Dupeux, "Politicization of the Electorate in France and the United States," *Public Opinion Quarterly,* 1962, p. 10.

4. Paris has no mayor.

5. So named because of M. Defferre's announced intention to draw up a 15-year plan for French development, 1965-1980.

6. "Tens of millions of francs," apparently the old francs worth about 500 to the dollar.

7. Public opinion surveys reported in *L'Express,* September 21-27, 1964.

8. All survey data by *Institut français de l'opinion publique* as reported in *France-Soir* and *Sondages.*

9. Philip M. Williams, "De Gaulle's Challenger," *Parliamentary Affairs,* Summer 1964, p. 269.

West Germany:
The Search for Legitimacy

THE ADENAUER LEGACY

by Elmer Plischke

DR. KONRAD ADENAUER'S RETIREMENT FROM THE WEST GERMAN chancellorship on October 15, 1963, ended an important era in modern German history. Unquestionably, he will rank among such great mid-twentieth-century statesmen as Winston Churchill, Charles de Gaulle, and Franklin Delano Roosevelt, bridging the epoch from World War II to the close of the postwar transition period.

Denoting an end to this era, Adenauer's retirement from active leadership coincided with the passing from the scene of political power of such leading figures as John F. Kennedy, Jawaharlal Nehru, and Harold Macmillan (together with the British opposition leader, Hugh Gaitskell), as well as Pope John XXIII. Of the early postwar leaders in the non-Communist world, only de Gaulle remained. Moreover, President Roosevelt, Premier de Gasperi, and Secretary Dulles had died, while Churchill, Eden, Truman, and Eisenhower had been superseded. During his chancellorship a good many of his German political contemporaries also died or passed from positions of leadership, including former President Theodor Heuss, opposition leaders Dr. Kurt Schumacher and Erich Ollenhauer, and Berlin Governing Mayors Ernst Reuter and Otto

Suhr. Yet, and this must have been a bitter draught indeed for Adenauer to swallow, his principal political enemy, East Germany's Walter Ulbricht, survived him.

West German transition from war, defeat, and occupation to the establishment and stabilization of the Federal Republic of Germany was consummated during Adenauer's incumbency and under his active leadership. He reentered public life in 1945, approaching 70 years of age, when most men of public affairs either have left office or are on the verge of retirement. A year earlier the *Gestapo* had told him that his life was virtually at an end. Yet, *der Alte* ("the Aged One"), as he came to be called but which he personally disliked, who had been born a dozen years before Hitler, entered upon another two decades of challenging, dedicated, and redoubtable service to the rebuilding of West Germany, including 14 years in the chancellorship. Even when he ended this arduous career, he could not bring himself to retire completely, remaining both a member of the *Bundestag* and the leader of his political party.

This is not, however, a eulogy. It is, rather, an identification and assessment of the development under his leadership of some of the important policies and institutions of an important country at a critical moment in its history.

West German achievements under Adenauer's leadership are remarkable both quantitatively and qualitatively. Recall the phenomenal problems of rebuilding a destroyed countryside; reconstructing a shattered economy and founding a sound financial system; terminating a foreign occupation; regaining for Germany a place in the society of nations as a welcome participant and ally with the wholesale establishment of diplomatic and treaty relations; joining or rejoining and assuming a responsible role in a host of international organizations, including the United Nations specialized agencies, the Atlantic Alliance, and the European communities; integrating the West German federal structure and its territorial composition; and, by no means least, launching and maintaining a viable and workable governmental system which met both the needs of the German people and, for a time at least, the requirements of foreign occupying powers. To attain these objectives, and at the same time to revive German respectability at home and abroad in the face of the suspicion harbored by Germany's European neighbors, of Allied occupational demands and controls, and of the hostility exhibited by the Soviet Union and her East European satellites, all within the context of a "totally" defeated country that was many times divided—territorially, politically, and ideologically—was no mean feat.

Within that crucible of conditions, forces, and challenges, West Germany under Adenauer's leadership forged a remarkable blend of national tradition, bold innovation, dedicated hope, political and social experimentation, and enlightened statesmanship that, in linking the past with the future, produced the contemporary governmental system of West Germany. That it is not without blemish is understandable; that it has endured and developed as effectively as it has is, perhaps, remarkable. Comprising a complex federal order with a parliamentary central government, led by a powerful but not wholly uncontrolled chancellorship, and safeguarded by a certain amount of judicial review authority, this new system, during the decade and a half of the Adenauer administration, was able to put its constitutional act into efficacious operation, institutionalize the political activity of the West German people, enact the fundamental legislation essential to cope with the problems of modern socio-political life, and undertake a network of diplomatic and treaty relations with the rest of the world.

Few political leaders of this generation have contributed as much leadership in resolving the manifold problems involved in the comprehensive sweep embracing the conception, birth, infancy, and maturation of the government of a significant power with such rapidity and success as has Adenauer. This is not to say, however, that all credit is due one man, or that all his policies and actions were right or successful, or that he resolved happily all major governmental problems, or even that no one else might have done as well. But there were many potential leaders under whom far less would have been accomplished.

It would be presumptuous in these few pages to attempt a review of the total panoply of Adenauer's contribution, which must rather be left to his biographers and the historians. This brief survey, rather, is devoted to an analysis of a few selected areas of governmental policy and action which characterize the Adenauer years. These include the founding of the contemporary government of West Germany, the revival and stabilization of political activity, the reconstitution of German federalism, the crystallization of the territorial composition of the Federal Republic, the systematic and pragmatic integration of West Berlin with West Germany, and the general problem of German reunification. Virtually all major aspects of these questions, except terminating the legal fiction of separateness for West Berlin and reintegrating the two Germanies (together with the consummation of a final peace settlement), were so successfully resolved during this era that Adenauer's successors were bequeathed an order of governance which, though by no means perfect, could scarcely have been imagined possible when he first assumed the chancellorship.

FOUNDING THE FEDERAL GOVERNMENT

A major achievement of the Adenauer era was the devising and practical institution of the constitutional act (*Grundgesetz*) which prescribes the new central system of government in the Federal Republic of Germany. Its development required qualities of imagination, perseverance, and dedication, if not statesmanship, on the part of Adenauer and a good many other German public leaders.

While there has been some criticism of the fashion in which this was accomplished under Chancellor Adenauer, particularly because of his alleged authoritarianism and apparent devotion to the principle of "the indispensable man," as time goes on it is not unlikely that he will be regarded as the father of the Federal Republic. His tenure as head of government, embracing nearly four parliamentary terms, and exceeding even that of Hitler by approximately two years, is in itself surprising when compared with political developments under the Weimar Republic.

As leader of the Christian Democrats, rather than because he then was an acknowledged statesman or because of widespread popular enthusiasm or personal confidence in him, he was elected to the chancellorship in 1949, although by merely a one-vote margin—which some point to as Adenauer's own deciding vote. He was reelected by more comfortable margins following the general parliamentary elections of 1953 and 1957, especially in 1953 when he received 304 of the 487 votes. In 1961, however, only after seven weeks of difficult and protracted negotiations to form a Christian Democrat-Free Democratic coalition, Adenauer, then aged 85, was elected to a fourth term. Among the conditions the Free Democrats demanded for their cooperation in the coalition was his written promise to resign the chancellorship prior to the end of the fourth *Bundestag* in 1965. Even so, he was elected by a majority of only eight votes. In view of earlier German political history, it is more noteworthy that he should have continued in the chancellorship so long than that political opposition to his protracted continuation in the office existed.

During his incumbency as head of government he guided the important process of establishing and stabilizing the principal elements of governance. That is to say, between 1949 and 1963 virtually all constitutionally required agencies of the West German government were brought into existence and forged into an integrated, manageable, and crystallized system.

The *Bundestag* and *Bundesrat,* comprising the parliament, sprang to life, elected their respective officers, established their rules of procedure, regularized their internal structures including the creation of approximately three dozen standing committees in the lower chamber and some dozen in the upper house, resolved many of the problems that arose in the relations between the two chambers throughout the legislative process, and formalized practices for fulfilling the political process within the aegis of parliamentary affairs. Operationally, under the leadership of Adenauer, the parliament carried out its principal responsibilities—creating other constitutionally required or permitted elements of governance, passing essential constitution amendatory proposals, and enacting the legislation and approving the treaties negotiated by the executive which were required to cope with the manifold affairs of a modern, industrialized, and internationally powerful country.

More than 1500 statutes and approximately an equal number of ordinances having the force of law became operative during the Adenauer years. The Chancellor, moreover, obtained parliamentary approval for dozens of treaties and agreements, including among the more important, perhaps, the Petersberg Protocol, the conventions terminating the occupation together with the instruments admitting West Germany into the North Atlantic Alliance and Western European Union, the treaties creating the European Communities and the Council of Europe as well as providing accession to various United Nations specialized agencies, the arrangements returning the Saar to Germany, restitution agreements with half a dozen European countries and Israel, and, late in his administration, the Franco-German and Nuclear Test Ban Treaties.

On many of these matters he led, rather than followed, public opinion. In some he enjoyed widespread support, as in the case of ending the occupation, rapprochement with France (especially the Franco-German Friendship Accord of 1963, approved by the *Bundestag* with only four dissenting votes and four abstentions), and the Nuclear Test Ban Treaty (which was unanimously approved by the *Bundestag*) after he had left the chancellorship. Respecting certain other matters, however, he ran headlong into opposition. Thus, at the very outset, he ran into difficulties when he signed the Petersberg Protocol with the Western occupying powers late in 1949, by which West Germany accepted the control of the International Authority for the Ruhr. In exchange, the Allies stopped dismantling nearly a dozen and a half industrial companies and permitted limited West German diplomatic practices. For this, he was condemned for ignoring parliament, acting in a dictatorial fashion, and "selling out" to the Allies. Dr. Kurt Schumacher went so far as to brand him unfairly "Chancellor of the Allies."

While Chancellor Adenauer, naturally, had his share of difficulties with parliament, during his incumbency the Federal Government was able to avoid a crisis so severe as to produce a *Bundestag* vote of lack of confidence, although this possibility was given serious consideration by certain *Bundestag* groups in 1958 during debate over the Chancellor's attitude toward West Germany's future nuclear role. Nevertheless, Adenauer's forceful and unwavering personal leadership, the strength of his party at the polls, the fashion in which he and his aides wielded political power, and the constitutional prescription requiring a vote of lack of confidence to be accompanied by the election of the incumbent Chancellor's successor—all these contributed to the relative executive-legislative stability of the Adenauer era.

Simultaneous with these legislative developments, by statutory and administrative action the contemporary legal and judicial systems were created. Based to some extent on previous experience, at both the national and *Land* levels, a series of regular courts having civil and criminal jurisdiction were created or revived. They embraced *Amtsgerichte, Landgerichte,* and *Oberlandesgerichte,* as well as a *Bundesgerichtshof* (Federal High Court)—together with several administrative courts, and, an innovation in postwar Germany, the *Bundesverfassungsgericht* (Federal Constitutional Court). The principal constitutional juridical requirement not met during the Adenauer administration was the creation of an *Oberstes Bundesgericht* (Supreme Federal Court), with responsibility to maintain "uniformity of the administration of justice by the higher federal courts" (Article 95). The *Grundgesetz* specifically requires its establishment, but the Government and parliamentary chambers had never agreed on the details of the law to establish it.

With this exception, the Adenauer administration implemented the constitutional prescriptions governing judicial affairs, for the first time providing a separate constitutionally established judiciary with the independent position of the judges protected by the *Grundgesetz* and a separate superior tribunal to deal solely with questions of constitutionality, thereby, at least in theory, rendering the governmental system subservient to the rule of law. While it may be alleged that the Chancellor and others wielded political power to influence adjudication and judicial administration, progress appears to be substantial in providing a coordinate judiciary relieved of many of the executive controls that previously existed and generally weakened the German governmental system.

Naturally, Chancellor Adenauer contributed especially to devising the contemporary Federal Executive in West Germany. He personally guided the creation and development of the office of the chancellorship, the *Bundesregierung* (the Government), the Cabinet, and the ministries. Not without criticism, he placed his immediate office, known as the *Bundeskanzleramt* (Federal Chancellery), under a State Secretary who exercised considerable responsibility subject only to the immediate direction of the Chancellor. The chancellery constituted a single office initially comprised of three main units: an internal affairs section, a press and information office, and a foreign affairs section, the latter handling liaison with the Allied High Commission. Other units of this section dealt with personnel and organization, protocol, and consular affairs. It is interesting to note the care with which Adenauer kept public relations, foreign affairs, and negotiations with the Western Allied High Commissioners within his immediate control, a practice he later pursued with respect to national defense matters.

When a separate Foreign Office with ministerial rank was established in 1951, the immediate office of the Chancellor was reorganized, leaving two major units, the Office of the Chancellor and, attached to it, the Press and Information Office. Even then, however, Adenauer served personally as Foreign Minister until 1955, when the occupation ended. Additional changes in the structuring of the chancellery were made from time to time. For example, after the security treaties of 1954 were signed, an Office for Defense Affairs was appended, again with Adenauer in close control, until the Defense Ministry was created. In this fashion the Chancellor personally handled what he regarded as the vital segments of executive affairs as well as transitional developments entailing the creation of major administrative units in areas of substantial importance which Adenauer did not feel he could entrust to others.

In general, the Ministers enjoyed direct access to both the Chancellor and his deputy for certain administrative, routine, and coordinating purposes. Whereas Adenauer insisted on determining general policy himself, each Minister presumably was expected to conduct the business of his department independently and on his own responsibility. Yet, the Chancellor made various attempts to intervene in the internal operations of the ministries which, naturally, met with resistance. On balance, of course, intimate liaison between the ministries and the chancellery (including the Press Office, inasmuch as executive press relations are centralized in the West German system) was deemed essential.

The Chancellor, together with the Federal Ministers, constitute the *Bundesregierung* (the Government). The Cabinet formed by Adenauer in September 1949 was generally organized according to the proportional strength of the coalition parties in the *Bundestag*. Eight Ministers belonged to Adenauer's Christian Democratic Union, three represented the Free Democratic Party, and two belonged to the German Party. After the election of 1953, in which the Christian Democrats virtually obtained a majority of the seats in the *Bundestag,* Chancellor Adenauer would have been able to restrict party representation in his Cabinet. Nevertheless, he decided to broaden his coalition in order to command the two-thirds parliamentary majority necessary for certain legislative actions (including amending the *Grundgesetz* in order to deal with the ratification of the European Defense Community

Treaty), so that Christian Democrats were assigned only 11 of the 18 ministries. When, on the other hand, the Christian Democratic Union obtained its greatest majority of *Bundestag* seats in the 1957 election, only two ministries were assigned to the coalition German Party. Four years later Adenauer required the aid of the Free Democratic Party to form a coalition Government, and 5 of the 20 portfolios in his Cabinet were ascribed to it. During the 14 years of his incumbency, therefore, Adenauer and his party generally were able to dominate the West German Cabinet, and there appears to have been considerable merit in his ability to form a Government without too broad a partisan coalition.

Initially, Chancellor Adenauer created 13 Cabinet posts. Aside from the areas normally embraced, such as finance, food and agriculture, interior, justice, public health, and transport and communications, there also were Ministries for All-German Affairs, Liaison with the *Bundesrat,* and the Marshall Plan. Subsequently, he added separate Ministries of Foreign Affairs, Defense, Nuclear Power, Family and Youth Affairs, and Nationally-Owned Property, as well as one Minister without portfolio. He also attempted to create a Ministry of Information which, because of strong reaction in both the foreign and domestic press, proved to be abortive.

When Adenauer left the chancellorship, therefore, the Cabinet was composed of 20 Ministers, in addition to himself. Some of the ministries were unique to the West German system. Certain others, however, such as education, home affairs, overseas territories, and public power, which often are found in governments, were not separately included. By the time Adenauer resigned, the *Bundesregierung* had crystallized in both structure and form. No important changes were instituted by Chancellor Erhard when he took over. Although occasional modifications have been made and others are likely to be made in the future, the fundamental patterning of the *Bundesregierung* was established by Adenauer, and all major areas of executive interest and responsibility appear to have been meshed into the politico-administrative organization.

Dr. Adenauer appointed 50 Ministers during his incumbency. By the time he resigned, seven Ministers had died, a good many had been forgotten by the public, and several had moved on to other important positions outside the Government. Significant changes were made when each new Cabinet was formed, and several Ministers left the Cabinet for personal and health reasons. A few, like Gustav Heinemann, resigned because they could no longer work with the Chancellor, while several others, such as Foreign Minister Heinrich von Brentano and Defense Minister Franz-Josef Strauss, were obliged to resign for political reasons. Former Minister of Agriculture Heinrich Luebke was elected Federal President in 1959, and Ludwig Erhard, Minister of Economics since 1949, succeeded to the chancellorship in 1963.

Seven hundred Cabinet meetings, over which Adenauer presided personally, were held in 14 years to discuss governmental policy. The appropriate ministries were expected to carry out Cabinet decisions. Technically, in the Federal Republic the Chancellor conducts Cabinet sessions in accordance with formalized rules of procedure adopted by it and approved by the Federal President in 1951, as subsequently modified. Differences of opinion among the Ministers are expected to be decided by the Cabinet collegially. Disputes concerning the competency or jurisdiction of a Ministry are determined by vote, and if there is a tie, the vote of the Chancellor decides the issue.

At the outset, Chancellor Adenauer was confronted with the difficult task of furnishing leadership in launching a new governmental system and making it function effectively, while at the same time satisfying both a legislature in which his position depended upon a precarious majority and the Allied High Commissioners, the watchdogs of residual Allied authority. Without posing this as justification, it is not difficult to understand his disinclination to deem himself simultaneously responsible also to his Cabinet colleagues. In any case, he pursued the avenue of acting on his own discretion, subject to formal Cabinet approval, rather than adopting a system of genuine collegial decision-making. After he became accustomed to this somewhat authoritarian conception of his office, he was reluctant to change. To have done so would have been contrary to his character. Consequently, because executive control rather than political leadership was involved, he experienced a number of difficulties in his relations with his chief administrative assistants.

To mention only a few of the specific problems he encountered, in 1950 Dr. Gustav Heinemann, first Minister of the Interior, resigned because he differed with the Chancellor on matters of principle respecting German rearmament and participation of the Federal Republic in Western Europe's defense. He claimed that the Chancellor convened the Cabinet to approve an action two days after it had been taken. Whereas the other members of the Cabinet were willing to endorse the Chancellor's performance, Dr. Heinemann disagreed not only with the substance of the action, but also with Adenauer's procedure in dealing with his Cabinet. Genuine policy differences among Cabinet members are bound to arise and resignation over them, if opposing views are based on principle and cannot be accommodated, is to be anticipated, but the Chancellor must act in good faith and with dignity and honor when leading his Cabinet. Resignation prompted by a belief that he has not, as in the case of Dr. Heinemann, is another matter entirely.

Nine years later, the presidential election approached and President Theodor Heuss could not constitutionally serve a third term. Chancellor Adenauer pressed Minister of Economics Erhard, unquestionably one of the most popular and prominent members of the Christian Democratic Union, to stand for the office in order to forestall the possible election of the well-known Social Democratic leader Professor Carlo Schmid. However, Erhard and other party members regarded this as a maneuver by the Chancellor not only to gain the federal presidency for his party, but also to ease the Minister of Economics out of the Cabinet so as to remove him from eventual succession to the chancellorship.

When a split in the Christian Democratic Union over the matter seemed imminent, the Chancellor surprisingly reversed his position and announced that he would run for the presidency himself. He also indicated, however, that he would be more than a ceremonial head of state; he would continue his active leadership in governmental affairs and would control public policy, especially in the field of foreign affairs. This would have modified the established character of the presidency and the chancellorship, as well as the relationship between the two. As a consequence of the party crisis that ensued, apparently recognizing the serious questions of constitutionality involved and realizing that his plan ultimately might weaken both his party leadership and his governmental power, Adenauer sprang a second surprise by declaring that he had changed his mind and would retain the chancellorship. It is not difficult, therefore, to comprehend why, for a time, his relations with his Cabinet and his party were strained considerably.

Following the 1961 election, Adenauer required the support of the Free Democratic Party to form a coalition Government. During the protracted negotiations which ensued, Dr. Heinrich von Brentano, Minister of Foreign Affairs for half a dozen years, was obliged to resign because the Free Democrats regarded him as too weak and too dependent on the Chancellor, and Adenauer promised to give up the chancellorship before the expiration of the fourth *Bundestag* in 1965. As "lame duck" Chancellor, his position in the new Government was weakened.

Later, the "*Spiegel* affair" produced a most serious governmental crisis. The public reacted strongly to what it deemed a critical challenge by the Adenauer administration to the rule of law. Ultimately, his entire Cabinet resigned. Only extensive and delicate coalition negotiations enabled him to appoint, in December 1962, his fifth Cabinet, which included seven new members. Because the crisis particularly centered upon Dr. Franz-Josef Strauss, the Defense Minister and a leader of the Bavarian Christian Social Union, he had to be replaced. The Chancellor, however, was able to weather the storm personally.

In practice, Chancellor Adenauer regarded his Cabinet less as a collective team than as a board of specialists under his personal directorship. Only he could determine general public policy. As a consequence, the Cabinet did not evolve a tradition of collective responsibility. Not only was an individual Minister criticized in the *Bundestag* or in the press, but on occasion the Chancellor did so himself in private or in public, without necessarily expecting his resignation, however. At times, as a matter of fact, individual Ministers voted against the position taken by the Chancellor in the *Bundestag,* also without being required to resign. Such actions would scarcely be countenanced in a genuine system of Cabinet collegialism, but they may have afforded some requisite resilience during the crucial transition period.

On balance, it may be concluded that under the leadership of Chancellor Adenauer the main elements of the Federal government of Germany—legislative, executive, and judicial—were established and progressed from infancy to what appears to be maturity, combined in a workable arrangement. The hand of the Chancellor pervaded all major phases of this process, especially perhaps in the functioning of the *Bundestag* and the *Bundesregierung*. The contrary could scarcely have been expected during an era of Adenauer's type of leadership. Yet, the fashion in which his will often was imposed, producing what many came to call *Kanzler-Demokratie* ("Chancellor democracy"), will long be remembered—and criticized.

While progress admittedly was substantial if not remarkable, the Adenauer leadership was not always correct or successful, nor is all accomplishment attributable to one person. Nevertheless, a major contribution of the Adenauer legacy was a solid basis for a viable and effective system of governance in the Federal Republic of Germany.

WEST GERMAN POLITICAL DEVELOPMENT UNDER ADENAUER

Naturally, significant political developments paralleled the institution of the government of the Federal Republic. Not the least of these were the crystallization of the West German national party structure, the establishment of precedent for mature and responsible political leadership, the reduction of extremist fracturing of the national partisan activity, and the virtual achievement of a national two-party system.

The nature of recent German party politics may be more readily understood if it is remembered that from the time that the German Reich was created in 1871, the political parties generally represented the three obvious general blocs (the Left, the Center, and the Right). Even during the Weimar Republic, when at one time there were some 30 parties, there were only 7 of major consequence. The Communists, the Social Democrats (Socialists), and the liberal-Democrats formed the Left. The Catholic Center Party and its Bavarian counterpart, the Bavarian People's Party, constituted the Center. The German People's Party representing the industrialists, the conservative-minded German Nationals, and the reactionary National Socialists (Nazis) comprised the Right.

Following 12 years of political sterility under the monolithic one-party dictatorship of Hitler's Third Reich, democratic political life in Germany was revived by the occupying powers in the fall of 1945. Beginning on a small scale, West Germany's postwar parties gained experience through participation in competitive elections and developed organizational strength by means of gradual expansion from the community to the county to the *Land* (state) to the occupation zone and eventually through the interzonal to the national level.

Even though the postwar political stratification of West Germany bears some relationship to what existed prior to the Nazi period, it has changed considerably. The Communist Party re-emerged fairly quickly. The Social Democratic Party, which had all but succumbed under Hitler, revived more slowly. The other postwar major parties are new, though some trace elements of policy and leadership to earlier political factions.

The historic grouping of the parties, therefore, has developed in a somewhat modified and diffused fashion in contemporary West Germany. The principal moderate party, which Adenauer helped to build, is the Christian Democratic Union/Christian Social Union (CDU/CSU), the Christian Social Union being the Bavarian element of the party. It has taken over the traditional Center position. The Leftist vote has come to be concentrated in the Social Democratic Party (SPD), while the Communist Party (KPD), initially at best a splinter faction, was rejected at the polls and judicially declared to be unconstitutional. There are no strongly Rightist parties of national prominence, and the extreme reactionaries—the German Rightist Party (DRP), the Socialist Reich Party (SRP), and the German Reich Party (DRP)—have also been adjudged unconstitutional.

The tendency in West Germany during the Adenauer years favored fewer and larger parties, a situation significantly different from the Weimar experience. There were indications of a general movement toward a two-party system, in which the Christian Democrats, with their Christian orientation and federalist leanings, confront the Social Democratic Party, with its Socialist basis and more centralized conception of the state. While the active major parties are essentially moderate, the more "liberal" and "conservative" parties and supporters have not disappeared entirely. As political shifts took place, one or another of these from time to time, as was the case after 1961 with the Free Democratic Party, emerged as a balancing force in the development of West German political activity.

Adenauer's party, the Christian Democratic Union, became the predominant moderate party of postwar West Germany. At first several centers of the new party emerged, in the Rhineland, in Berlin, and in Munich, but Adenauer outlived or outmaneuvered his rivals for leadership. Politically located somewhat to the right of Center, the CDU took over a substantial part of the former Centrist tradition, as well as many elements that formerly supported the conservative Right. It has a religious orientation respecting public affairs, although it is not a clerical party. Membership has been drawn extensively from the Catholic elements of the electorate, especially from Adenauer's Rhineland and South Germany, but effort has been devoted also to attract the Protestants of the northwest and other areas, in order to transmute the party into a genuine nondenominational Christian fusion movement.

As a political "union" the Christian Democrats, under Adenauer's leadership, have been seeking something broader than a party in the customary sense. Their objective was to develop and represent a cross section of various groups and to cater to those problems and interests which are common to the political community as a whole, thereby serving the common cause. As a consequence, its political outlook has not been so circumscribed or inflexible as that of certain other postwar parties, but neither does it necessarily possess their internal cohesion and discipline. Because it is an amalgam, political fissures have sometimes appeared, particularly as between the more Leftist and the more Rightist elements, but thus far it has been able to withstand the strain of internal differences.

Its principal opponent during the Adenauer era was the Social Democratic Party, located somewhat to the left of Center, but nevertheless a moderate party. Its cardinal objective has been the socialization of the means of production and distribution, but its economic program, favoring gradualism and opposing extremism by revolution, disapproves total state planning as well as uncontrolled laissez faire. Unlike the Communists, it holds that the transformation of the economic structure can be accomplished by parliamentary means.

The Christian Democratic Union, led by Adenauer, fought the first postwar "national" parliamentary elections in 1949 with a program that embraced many social welfare measures, which was inevitable under the then existing conditions, but also with a firm commitment to the private enterprise system. It emerged from the elections the strongest, but by no means a majority, party, obtaining some 7.5 million votes and 139 seats in the *Bundestag.* The Social Democrats fared nearly as well, acquiring 131 seats, and the lesser parties shared the remaining 132 seats.

In the following general election in 1953 the Christian Democrats profited from Adenauer's improved public image and his energetic campaigning under the appealing slogan "Without me . . . ," the rapid improvement in economic conditions, the well-timed reduction of taxes on tobacco and coffee, and the tightened restrictions on splinter and regional or local parties. The Christian Democrats won approximately 45 per cent of the vote and 243 or virtually half of the 487 *Bundestag* seats, a feat which had never before been accomplished by a German political party in a free election. Four years later, in part because Adenauer had pushed a major pension reform through parliament, he achieved an even greater political victory. The Christian Democrats won a clear majority of the votes (50.3 per cent) and 270 of the 497 *Bundestag* seats. In the following (1961) election, the Christian Democratic plurality was reduced to 45.4 per cent of the votes and 242 of the 499 seats in the *Bundestag.*

In 1949, when the Christian Democratic Union and the Social Democratic Party obtained a combined 60 per cent of the votes and held 270 of the 402 seats in the *Bundestag,* the time seemed propitious for statesmen to forget their differences and establish a "grand coalition" of the two leading parties. The need for West Germany to stand together to rebuild the country and revive the postwar economy, to move toward reunification with East Germany, and to present a strong unified front in dealing with the Allied occupation authorities should, it seems, have induced the parties to accommodate their disagreements and join their forces in common cause.

Some party leaders, especially of the *Länder* (states), supported such a movement, but there were distinct deterrents. Perhaps most important, both Adenauer and Dr. Kurt Schumacher, then leader of the Social Democrats, believed in the necessity of having a strong and stable parliamentary opposition in order to avert driving dissident elements to the political extremes. Moreover, the two parties differed markedly on fundamental economic and social policy. The Christian Democratic leadership had committed itself to the economic program of Professor Erhard, whereas the Social Democrats insisted that in any grand coalition they would need to have the primary voice—and, therefore, the power—to determine economic and social policy. In addition, as so often happens in politics, the principal leaders of the two parties suffered from an intense personal rivalry and antagonism, and Adenauer could scarcely envision with pleasure having Dr. Schumacher as his Vice-Chancellor. Consequently, Chancellor Adenauer allied the Christian Democrats with the Free Democratic Party (FDP) and the German Party (DP) in his first parliamentary coalition and *Bundesregierung*. This gave him a working majority of 208 of the 402 *Bundestag* votes.

At the time of the second parliamentary election (1953), in which questions of West German rearmament and national security were paramount, the Social Democrats supported what proved to be an unpopular policy position. The formation of a powerful grand coalition (involving 394 of the 487 *Bundestag* votes), therefore, was perhaps even less possible at that time. Nevertheless, the Chancellor, seeking to increase the strength of his Christian Democratic-controlled parliamentary coalition in order to amend the *Grundgesetz* to provide national security authority, added the Refugee Party (GB/BHE) to his Government. This augmented majority, comprising 333 *Bundestag* votes, continued for only a short time, however, until both the Refugee and the Free Democratic Parties split in 1955 and 1956, approximately three-fourths of the former and two-thirds of the latter leaving the parliamentary coalition.

In the *Bundestag* election of 1957 the two main parties acquired more than 80 per cent of the vote and controlled all but 58 (12 per cent) of the *Bundestag* seats. A grand coalition based on such strength might have been very powerful, but the Chancellor needed it less than previously because the Christian Democrats by themselves had achieved an absolute majority (270 of the 497 seats)—the peak of Adenauer's political success. Only four political groupings, called *Fraktionen* (fractions), were organized in the parliamentary chamber, and the Chancellor's coalition was comprised of the Christian Democratic Union and the German Party, which had been embraced within the parliamentary coalition since 1949.

Four years later, in 1961, the two major parties again obtained 80 per cent of the vote and held approximately 87 per cent of the parliamentary seats. Only the two principal parties and the Free

Democrats were able to constitute *Fraktionen.* Although popular support of Adenauer's party declined somewhat in this election, the Christian Democrats still polled the largest number of votes and held 242 of the 499 *Bundestag* seats, but they lost their absolute majority. This gave the Free Democrats, with 67 seats, the balance of power, because both Adenauer and the Social Democrats could have formed a majority coalition with the support of the Free Democratic Party, but neither could do so without such support. By this time the initial reasons for creating a grand coalition with the Social Democrats had disappeared.

It has been suggested that the Christian Democratic success of achieving an absolute majority might have been repeated by Adenauer in 1961 if the Berlin wall had not been erected by the Communists on the eve of the election, or if the Chancellor's reaction to it had been more positive and immediate. Irrespective of the contention that he awaited firm guidance from the Western Allies, his slow and apparently irresolute reaction afforded West Berlin's Governing Mayor, Willy Brandt, the opportunity to capture the political limelight. Brandt was the well-known leader of the Social Democratic Party, not only in Berlin but also in West Germany, and he had assumed a more decisive and popularly appealing stand on the matter.

The reduction of the number of political parties represented on the national level in West Germany during the Adenauer era—from ten parties in the *Bundestag* in 1949, to five (1953), four (1957), and eventually three (1961)—indicates a significant trend toward the two-party system. This trend was produced by several factors, including the elimination of extremist parties under the provisions of the Electoral Law and by court action, the growing strength and appeal of the principal parties, and the obviously temporary nature of such groupings as the Refugee Party (GB/BHE), the Economic Reconstruction Union (WAV), and the alliance of the All-German People's Party (GVP) with the German League. The Electoral Law prescribes the "five per cent rule," according to which a party must acquire 5 per cent of the vote in order to be represented in the *Bundestag,* which tends to eliminate the splinter parties from parliamentary representation. The rule was made more restrictive in 1953, which accounts largely for the 50 per cent reduction in the number of parties in the second *Bundestag.*

The continuation of the march to a full-fledged two-party system in all probability will depend on whether the Christian Democratic Union can in the long run remain intact, as it did under Adenauer, without moderate Protestants achieving control of this party and driving the Catholic element into some other Centrist-Conservative association, or a new appealing nonextreme right-wing party emerging. Naturally, it also depends upon the quality of the leadership of the two leading political factions. Essentially, of course, West Germany may have a two-party system even if some third parties survive, provided either of the major parties is able to control if not constitute a majority of the *Bundestag* and the third parties are really of a minor nature. For bipartism to function effectively, however, it will be necessary for the Christian Democrats and the Social Democrats alike to be genuine national parties, and both their leaders and members will have to maintain political maturity and statesmanship of a high order.

Perhaps the four most important characteristics of political development that became fixed during the Adenaeur era are the achievement of a high degree of voter participation in general elections (amounting to 78 per cent in 1949 and between 86 and 88 per cent subsequently), the delimiting of political splintering, the trend toward bipartism, and the establishment of a combination single-member/proportional representation method of election. As far as the Electoral Law is concerned, in 1949 the proponents of both the single-member district and the proportional representation systems accepted a compromise under which 60 per cent of the *Bundestag* delegates were individually elected by plurality vote and 40 per cent were selected by proportional representation. Four years later, when the second Electoral Law was under consideration, Adenauer's Christian Democrats pressed for converting entirely to the single-member district process. The Social Democrats supported the retention of the existing arrangement. The new law retained the combined majority-plurality and proportional representation systems, but it adopted a 50/50 ratio for the two methods. Despite the fact that the Chancellor failed to have his way in the matter, the Christian Democrats seem to have fared well under the split arrangement.

It may reasonably be concluded that, on the whole, during the Adenauer years the political parties of West Germany came to evidence a considerable degree of stability and maturity. Although they naturally differed on many policy issues and specific legislative proposals, especially with respect to details, the major parties have been in agreement on the promotion of the public weal by constitutional process and the assumption of public responsibility by the government in the affairs of the family of nations. Adenauer must have derived considerable satisfaction not only from his personal political successes and the electoral victories of his party, but also from the policy changes of the political opposition. He saw the Social Democrats abandon their major opposition policies, namely, nationalization of the big industries with extensive state economic planning, and rejection of German rearmament. The latter issue was even carried to the Constitutional Court. Following the election of 1957 the Social Democrats turned to espousing a free competitive economy and somewhat later, realizing that negotiated reunification in the face of Soviet opposition was unlikely, they accepted German rearmament and participation in the North Atlantic Alliance.

In short, the Adenauer legacy embraces legal and political arrangements adopted to provide a workable and stable parliamentary majority, a substantial and thus far reasonable opposition, and a minimum of political splintering, thereby eliminating some of the defects of the Weimar government which enabled the Nazi autocracy to emerge. The principal parties and their leaders are moderate in their policy positions. Extremist factions have been repudiated at the polls and juridically proscribed.

Nevertheless, a number of weaknesses in the political fabric of West Germany became apparent during the Adenauer years. To the impartial observer there appears to be too high a degree of personal leadership, which the Chancellor encouraged and from which he benefited politically. There also is some evidence of a belief in the "indispensable man," which Adenauer felt strongly. On several occasions he is reputed to have said: "*Mein Gott,* what will happen to Germany after I am gone?" While Adenauer's brand of political leadership may have been desirable if not necessary as exercised by responsible party officials during the difficult transition period in postwar West Germany, in the hands of the aggressive chauvinist or demagogue it could be a serious threat to the democratic development of the country.

Moreover, although a certain amount of shift and adjustment has accompanied the birth and demise of various political groupings and electoral alliances, thereby affording a degree of party fluidity, in general West German political leaders—including Adenauer—are inclined to be somewhat rigid if not suspicious and intolerant of their opponents. Politics appears to be taken quite seriously, and at times there is too little good sportsmanship and professional camaraderie among its chief participants. Nevertheless, on balance the political legacy of the Adenauer era is far richer than could have been anticipated when the Chancellor first assumed responsibility.

REVIVAL OF GERMAN FEDERALISM

Federalism is one of the major political principles introduced into the contemporary West German governmental system and made to function during the Adenauer era. This principle is by no means foreign to German political philosophy and practice. The Empire was federal both in origin and in nature. The framers of the Weimar Constitution debated whether the emergent Republic was to be unitary or federal, and the result was a compromise, retaining the states or *Länder,* but reducing their authority. When the Nazis came to power, all vestiges of political autonomy of the territorial components were eliminated, and centralized control reached an intense stage of integration. The trend, thus, had been from federalism toward unitary government.

The Western occupying powers opposed the revival of highly centralized governmental authority in Germany after World War II and, therefore, reversed the trend. There were four principal reasons for adopting this position:

1. Ascribing inherent political authority in the German *Länder* could restrain the power of the central government;

2. The possession of innate authority by the *Länder* might enhance the development of genuine democracy in Germany;

3. Postwar German political institutions, by necessity as much as by design, had as a matter of fact been rebuilt from the bottom up, so that *Länder* and local governments were operating when the new central system of governance was devised; and

4. The German governmental institutions of the bizonal arrangement, established under the Anglo-American Fusion Agree-

ment of December 2, 1946, were federalistic, and many of the basic political principles incorporated into the bizonal system served as precedents for the shaping of the governmental institutions of the Federal Republic.

When the Allies empowered the leaders of the German *Länder* to convene as the Parliamentary Council in 1948 to draft plans for a central government, they required, therefore, that the eventual constitution create "a federal form of government which adequately protects the rights of the respective states, and which at the same time provides for adequate central authority and which guarantees the rights and freedoms of the individual." In a sense, the federal principle thus was imposed from without, but it was neither non-indigenous nor was it generally opposed by the Germans.

The real crux of the matter, of course, was the fashion of implementing the principle so as to accommodate the various forces concerned (i.e., the fundamental German political heritage, the political parties and factions represented in the Parliamentary Council which drafted the *Grundgesetz,* popular appeals ranging from centralization to particularism, and the Western occupants) and, at the same time, to produce a viable system within which both the new central government and its constituent elements could function effectively. As so often is the case with social orders, success depended as much on the leadership that instituted it as on the formal character of the system. To Adenauer, therefore, initially as President of the Parliamentary Council and later as first Chancellor, fell the important task of launching and guiding the federation through its critical introductory phase.

As in the United States, the central government of the Federal Republic of Germany is essentially one of delegated authority. This is a natural consequence of the fact that the West German system is federal both in that it was created by the federal process and that the end product is federal in nature. An important result is a division of powers—the drawing of an identifiable line between central and state governmental authority.

Certain obvious elements of federal-state relations are constitutionally prescribed. For example, the Federal Government is supreme in the field in which the Basic Law specifically authorizes it to act. Thus, "Federal law overrides *Land* law" (Article 31); "The *Länder* have the power to legislate insofar as this Basic Law does not vest legislative powers in the Federation" (Article 70); and "In the field of concurrent legislation, the *Länder* have the power to legislate as long as, and insofar as, the Federation makes no use of its legislative power" (Article 72).

Again, the Federal Government possesses certain obligations with respect to ensuring appropriate *Land* governmental practice. Most important, perhaps, are the following stipulations: "The constitutional order in the *Länder* must conform to the principles of the republican, democratic, and social state based on the rule of law (*Rechtsstaat*) within the meaning of this Basic Law," and "The Federation guarantees that the constitutional order of the *Länder* conforms to the basic rights and provisions . . ." prescribed (Article 28). Finally, it is specified that if a state fails to fulfill its obligations toward the Federation under the Basic Law or any other federal law, the Federal Government may, subject to approval by the *Bundesrat,* "take the necessary measures to enforce such compliance by the *Land* by way of federal compulsion (*Bundeszwang*)" (Article 37).

As far as legislative division of authority is concerned, as in the United States, the Federal Government of Germany has two fundamental types of powers: exclusive and concurrent. The former are specifically delegated to the central regime and denied to the *Länder.* They include such obvious matters as foreign affairs and national defense, citizenship in the Federation, passports, immigration and extradition, currency and coinage, weights and measures, customs and foreign trade, border control, railroads and air traffic, postal services and telecommunications, patents and copyrights, the international prevention and repression of crime, and others. By and large, the basic legislation required to deal with these matters was enacted during the Adenauer administration, and with but few exceptions, this area of legislative jurisdiction caused little trouble.

The field of concurrent legislation, however, has proven to be far more complex and extensive. Illustrations include civil and criminal law, treatment of refugees and expellees, war damage and compensation (*Wiedergutmachung*), rights of aliens, citizenship in the states, various economic and welfare matters, and transportation and communications. Federal exercise of concurrent legislative authority is limited by the *Grundgesetz* (Article 72), which stipulates that the Federation possesses such legislative power only insofar as a need for regulation by federal law exists for one or more of the following reasons: the matter cannot be regulated effectively by the legislation of individual states, the regulation by a state law might prejudice the interests of other states or of the community at large, or the preservation of uniformity of living conditions beyond the territory of an individual state necessitates federal control. These criteria often were liberally interpreted in favor of the Federal Government during the Adenauer years.

Separate provision also is made in the Basic Law for the administration of public financial matters. Thus, the Federation is given exclusive legislative authority regarding customs and fiscal monopolies, and concurrent authority with respect to a number of taxes. These include levies on income, property, inheritance, real estate, and other matters. However, federal legislative authority in these concurrent fields is valid only if the Federal Government claims the taxes in their entirety or in part to cover federal expenditures, or if need for federal law exists as prescribed by Article 72 of the *Grundgesetz.*

On the other hand, the states, as in the American system, possess reserved authority, embracing such areas as education, cultural and religious affairs (including relations between church and state), police, local government, certain intergovernmental relations, and their own internal administration. The *Länder* are free to legislate regarding these matters, while, in the field of concurrent legislation, as indicated, they may legislate only as long as the Federation makes no use of its legislative power.

The task of rendering this complex governmental plan operational devolved upon Chancellor Adenauer and a good many other members of the central and state governments of West Germany commencing late in 1949. This was far from simple and required qualities of statesmanship on the part of many German officials.

The problem was rendered even more difficult by the existence for a time of a double division of powers. When the *Grundgesetz* entered into force, the Western occupying powers released substantial governmental functions and responsibility to the German people and their government, but continued to retain certain authority as specified in the Occupation Statute. The combined effect of the Basic Law, which defined federal-state relations within the German governmental mechanism, and the Occupation Statute, which prescribed Allied-German relations and specified the reserved powers of the occupation authorities, created this double division of authority. The general consequence was to limit the powers of the Federal Government to those specified in the *Grundgesetz* (and, therefore, not reserved to the *Länder*), as further delimited by those temporarily suspended by the Occupation Statute.

During the next few years, usually on the insistence of Chancellor Adenauer, a number of the powers reserved to the Allies were relinquished by them to the German government, as formally acknowledged especially in the Petersberg Protocol (1949) and the First Instrument of Revision of the Occupation Statute (1951). Eventually, when the occupation was terminated in 1955 by agreements negotiated and signed by the Chancellor, virtually all Allied reserved powers were released, ending this strange complex of multiple federalism. Substantial progress, thus, was achieved during the Adenauer years in establishing the confidence of the occupying powers in the postwar German political order and in inducing them to accept West Germany as an equal, in full control of its own governmental system and capable of resolving its complicated internal federal-state relations.

A final major aspect of the problem of federalism in West Germany during these years of initiation and trial is this question: To what extent did original plans respecting the division of national-state authority prove to be uncertain or inadequate and, consequently, require clarification or modification? Obviously, on the one hand, change in a constitutional arrangement may be brought about by natural growth through interpretation—that is, by legislative enactment, administrative regulation, and judicial decision or advisory judgment. A good deal of such articulation and refinement occurred during the Adenauer years.

Alternatively, of course, the division of powers also may be redefined or modified by formal constitutional amendment which, because it tends to involve the more important aspects of the juxtaposition of federal-state authority, may be more difficult to achieve. In West Germany, an amendatory proposal must be embodied in a law expressly identified as modifying or amplifying the text of the *Grundgesetz,* and it requires the approval of two-thirds of the *Bundestag* members as well as two-thirds of the *Bundesrat* votes

(Article 79). Whereas some two dozen constitutional amendments were enacted while Adenauer was Chancellor, of which half changed the existing text of the *Grundgesetz* and the remaining half were in the nature of supplementary articles, not all were concerned with federalism.

Clearly the most important illustration of formal change in the division of authority achieved under Adenauer's leadership involved the treatment of the defense function. Responsibility for providing national security was not initially ascribed to the Federal Government by the *Grundgesetz*. During the Cold War various alternatives were considered whereby West Germany could contribute to Western defense. The Chancellor was then unable to command sufficient parliamentary support to amend the Basic Law, but his international negotiations on the Plevin Plan culminated in 1952 in a number of treaties designed to enable a West German contingent to become a part of the supranational European Defense Community (EDC) forces. Constitutional modification thus would have been achieved by the treaty process, to which the West German parliament consented, but the instruments concerned were not ratified by the French government.

The complex of treaties and agreements, therefore, was revised two years later, providing for the admission of West Germany into the North Atlantic Treaty Organization (NATO). This meant that a West German national military establishment would be created, which then was rendered internally possible because, Adenauer having strengthened his parliamentary position in the meantime, a resolution formally to amend the *Grundgesetz* was approved in 1954 and became effective the following year. Thus, the division of authority was modified in a vital respect by formal amendatory process. Somewhat reminiscent of United States constitutional practice, this development also illustrates that, in certain respects, the division of power may perhaps be affected or changed via the treaty process.

Certain constitutional safeguards were created, however, as in the American system, to render it legally impossible for the Federal Government to dissolve arbitrarily the federal structure or to disestablish the principle of the division of authority. For example, the *Grundgesetz* specifies that a constitutional amendment affecting the nature of the Republic as a "federal state," "the organization of the

Federation into *Länder*," "the basic participation of the *Länder* in legislation," and certain other provisions of the Basic Law "is inadmissible" (Articles 20 and 79).

Obviously, it is politically possible to amend the *Grundgesetz,* but Chancellor Adenauer's experience with the European Defense Community Treaty indicates that, when the leadership of the Federal Government initiates such a proposal, it must have adequate support in both parliamentary chambers and in the state governments. It took his administration several years and the mounting of substantial political power that resulted from the parliamentary election of 1953 to render this particular change possible.

To conclude, the West German Republic, like the United States, is a federation in three respects. Inasmuch as the *Länder* antedated the Federal Republic, the latter came into being by the federative process, the constituent states participating in devising the *Grundgesetz* and enjoying ratification authority. Furthermore, institutionally the end-product is a federal system with a division of authority between the central and constituent governing units. In addition, in keeping with Professor Carl J. Friedrich's theory on the subject, federalism—that is, the process by which the constituent elements work out solutions, adopt mutual policies, and make joint decisions on common problems—is continuously at work in West Germany.

Whether the particular brand of federalism which was established in West Germany has become firmly entrenched remains to be seen. Aside from the standard theoretical arguments against federalism, there are a number of factors which are peculiar to West Germany. First, there is the contention that the federal principle was imposed by the Western Allies and, therefore, was not a genuine postwar German determination. Second, while there was a good deal of federalism in German history, since the days of Bismarck there has been a tendency toward centralization, and Germany's periods of prominence have been characterized by centralized rule. Third, most of the West German states have been regarded as too synthetic to have deep-rooted traditions of their own. Finally, the mass influx of German refugees and expellees from the East has retarded the development of state pride and cohesion.

It also is argued, on the other hand, that the existing *Länder* have come to value the legal and political role they play in the West German order, and that, if all of Germany were to be united and federated, Prussia could not dominate as it did in the past. Of greater consequence, perhaps, has been the averment that the preservation of federalism is essential because it might be the vehicle through which national reunification may be achieved. Furthermore, an effective federal, decentralized system might be the best bar to a Communist takeover of the whole country following reunification. By retaining substantial governmental authority in the *Länder,* single parties, especially if they are in the minority and of the extreme Left or Right, would find it more difficult to usurp authority than generally is possible under a centralized system. The closer authority is to the people themselves, this line of reasoning continues, the more difficult it is for a minority party to acquire control.

Finally, of course, is the procedural argument that if federalism is to be replaced by a unitary system, the *Grundgesetz* would need to be overhauled completely or replaced. This action, presumably, would necessitate a new constitutional convention, with all the problems it would entail. The very thought of enduring this to replace one "temporary" mechanism of government with another—pending reunification—is sufficient, it appears, to deter the critics of the present system.

Moreover, under Adenauer, federalism proved to be workable, if not in many ways desirable. Although the Social Democrats have favored a more centralized political system, it is questionable whether, were they in power, they would attempt to convert to a unitary government. While some ask whether the Adenauer legacy is truly federal, disquisitions on the subject fail to resolve the practical issues faced during the difficult years of transition. To be sure, the Adenauer government found sufficient flexibility in the *Grundgesetz* to resolve important national questions of public policy. As a matter of fact, it may have been better able to satisfy many of the needs of the masses not in spite of, but by virtue of, the federal order.

COMPOSITION OF THE FEDERAL REPUBLIC

The major problems of the internal territorial composition of West Germany—which, as they pertain to contemporary German federalism, are far more important than may be immediately apparent—generally were resolved during the Adenauer administration. These problems quite naturally were regarded as most serious political issues, and some of them, as in the case of the Saar, were imbued with important international implications.

To supersede the territorial structuring into 32 political districts known as *Gaue* under the Nazis, German territory was reorganized by 1948 into 16 *Länder* more equal in size and population than had previously been the case. Except for the city-state Bremen, each *Land* had a population exceeding a million; most of them ranged between two and six million. All of Germany, except the Saar (which France was seeking to sever from Germany), East Prussia (which had been absorbed by the Soviet Union and Poland), and the eastern borderland (into which Poland had moved) was so organized. Eleven *Länder* were in what later became the Federal Republic, and the remaining five in East Germany.

In this reorganization, traditional boundaries, natural frontiers, and economic and social factors were sometimes compromised by political expedience. Initially, Germans tended to regard the result as a foreign imposition and, thus, fair game for criticism and reform. This situation was intensified by indigenous regional and local particularism, which strongly motivated the political actions of the German people.

The territorial composition of the Federal Republic became an important West German policy consideration, entailing the following major elements: the acceptance initially by Germans of the general Allied delineation of the German *Länder,* specific territorial realignment in the southwestern corner of the Federal Republic, general reconsideration of the entire patterning of the constituent *Länder,* incorporation of additional states into the federal union, and the status of Berlin.

The first of these was considered by the Germans during the process of framing the constitutional system of the Federal Republic. All the rest were seriously reviewed during the Adenauer administration, and several important territorial changes were made. Despite the progress achieved in integrating Berlin into the Federal Republic, only this issue was not fully resolved prior to the Chancellor's retirement.

Fully cognizant of the political implications of Allied realignment of German territory, and to afford the German people the opportunity of reorganizing their boundaries prior to instituting the

Federal Republic, in 1948 the Western Military Governors requested the Ministers President of the *Länder* to present their suggestions for dealing with the matter. Many Germans were unhappy with the situation, and it was debated at length in the Parliamentary Council, which eventually was obliged to admit, however, that it was unable to resolve the problem at the time. Consequently, it was left in abeyance to be dealt with under constitutional warranty after the Federal Republic was established. Any wholesale attempt to reorganize the *Länder* at that time would have seriously impeded progress in drafting the *Grundgesetz*. If the existing arrangement was to be undone before it became inextricably entwined in the fabric of the Federal Republic, therefore, it had to fall to the lot of the Adenauer administration.

The first territorial issue to be resolved by the Federal Republic under Adenauer involved the southwestern states. When the occupying powers divided German territory on a quadripartite basis, in order to afford France a zone of occupation, the two German states of Baden and Württemberg were arbitrarily split into three rather artificial *Länder*—a truncated Baden, a new Württemberg-Baden, and a new Württemberg-Hohenzollern. This resulted in many legal, economic, and cultural difficulties, which were accentuated by the demands of various interest groups.

To rectify this situation, the Parliamentary Council, itself unable to decide the issue, included a stipulation in the Basic Law to the effect that this territorial arrangement could be changed by agreement among the three states concerned. Failing to resolve the problem in this manner, reorganization was to be regulated by federal legislation subject to approval by popular referendum (Article 118).

This territorial reorganization became a bitterly contested political issue. After 15 months of fruitless negotiations by the three *Länder,* the federal parliament took the matter up in the spring of 1951 and, after considering several proposals, enacted a compromise law providing for resolution by popular referendum. In the parliamentary voting the proposal to amalgamate the three states into one new *Land* had the support of the Social Democrats, the Free Democrats and other conservatives, and the extreme Right, but Adenauer's Christian Democratic party was divided on the issue.

As presented to the people, the option was whether the existing three *Länder* should be reorganized into the two original states of Baden and Württemberg or combined in a single new state. The third alternative, of continuing the then existing three *Länder,* was not made available. Only 60 per cent of the electorate participated in the referendum, and the vote favored the creation of the new, amalgamated "Southwest State," given the title "Baden-Württemberg." This is the only major territorial reorganization of the Federal Republic so far. The fact that it took more than three years, two referenda, several legislative proposals, and a Constitutional Court decision illustrates how difficult it is to modify the existing territorial disposition.

The second major issue—the general territorial reorganization which had been deferred—also was considered seriously during the Adenauer era. The framers of the *Grundgesetz* specified that West German territory could be reorganized by federal law, provided that due regard was paid "to regional ties, historical and cultural connection (*Zusammenhänge*), economic expediency, and social structure" (Article 29). It also stipulated that any part of a reorganization law that transferred an area from one state to another must be submitted to popular referendum in that area and approved by simple majority. Furthermore, to protect local interests, it permitted, within one year of the promulgation of the Basic Law, the demand for change by popular initiative. Finally, it required that such general territorial reorganization needed to be concluded within three years.

On approving the *Grundgesetz,* however, the Military Governors of the Western Allies suspended the application of this article, declaring that the boundaries of all *Länder* excepting those in the southwest were to remain fixed until a German peace treaty was signed. Nevertheless, under Adenauer's leadership, this suspension was terminated by the contractual agreements of 1952 and 1954, in which the Chancellor induced the Allied powers to agree that the Federal Republic henceforth possessed "full authority of a sovereign state over its internal and external affairs"—except for authority respecting Berlin and Germany as a whole, including the reunification of the country and a final peace settlement.

In the meantime, the Federal Government appointed a special committee in 1951 to review the entire territorial situation. Its report, thorough and painstaking, published in the fall of 1955, found three territorial issues to be of particular concern, but, with one exception, recommended no changes. It regarded *Land* Schleswig-Holstein as being economically unsound, and *Land* North Rhine-Westphalia as too large and populous, but it counseled against immediate modification. It did propose a number of alternatives respecting the Rhineland-Palatinate, however, because of its lack of historical and economic unity. Yet, because these suggestions either would have further increased the size of *Land* North Rhine-Westphalia, or engaged other states in jurisdictional controversy, it is doubtful whether such reorganization was then feasible or would be in the near future, and no formal change was instituted.

Thus, during the Adenauer administration, West Germans themselves undertook a careful and protracted review of the territorial structuring of the Federal Republic, and the onus as an Allied imposition lost much of its currency. The failure to modify what the occupying powers had established emphasizes the historically recognized difficulty of undoing by legal process the territorial *status quo* of a federal union with any facility. While the allegation of liability for the existing patterning continues to devolve upon the Allies, the responsibility for not changing—and improving—it is attributable to the Adenauer Government.

Another territorial issue, which involved the process of admission to statehood, was resolved during Adenauer's chancellorship. In many respects the "Saar Question," both as an internal West German problem and as an international issue, produced some strange but interesting developments. Small in size and population, this territory, located at the juncture of Germany, France, and Luxembourg, became the center of a Franco-German controversy for several years that ultimately was decided in a fashion contrary to Adenauer's avowed desire.

The French acquired administrative jurisdiction over the area as part of its occupation zone, separated it from the French occupation territory, removed it from the responsibility of the Allied control machinery, and incorporated it into the French economy, while leaving the question of its political status for determination by a future peace treaty with Germany. A Saar government favorable to French interests was established, and a series of bipartite conventions was negotiated to regularize Franco-Saar relations and expedite autonomy, to which the British and United States governments generally acquiesced, subject to the reservation that the matter would not be prejudiced so far as the eventual peace settlement was concerned.

In the meantime, however, beginning in 1948, West Germany began to show increasing concern over the Saar, which unquestionably is ethnically German, and since its existence under the Holy Roman Empire was almost continuously subject to German influence and suzerainty. In the early 1950's, when West Germany and France were seeking European integration, French interest switched from autonomy for the Saar to internationalization. Protracted diplomatic consultations ensued in which Adenauer, espousing a liberal policy regarding the Saar in order to promote Franco-German rapprochement and European union, often was opposed bitterly in the *Bundestag*.

In 1954, negotiations eventuated in a series of treaties, which, while recognizing German sovereignty, continued French economic control and provided for the internationalization of the Saar under a new "Statute." The latter placed the territory under the supervision of the Western European Union (WEU), the seven-power politico-security arrangement devised to take the place of the abortive European Defense Community. Despite severe criticism in the West German parliament, especially by Social Democrats and Free Democrats, and a reluctant *Bundestag* endorsement, both signatory governments ratified these treaties, and implementation generally was taken for granted.

The new Statute, however, had to be approved in a popular plebiscite by the Saarlanders, who not only had grown weary of French influence but, in addition to being influenced by their traditional loyalities, were increasingly attracted by the remarkable economic development of West Germany. As a consequence, despite the avowed support of the Statute by Adenauer's administration, as well as by the governments of France and the Saar, it was rejected by some two-thirds (67.71 per cent) of the people. A new, pro-German government thereupon replaced the pro-French regime in the Saar, new treaties were negotiated between West Germany and France, and on New Year's Day of 1957 the Saar could again call itself German.

Interestingly and quite logically, no provision was made in these agreements for the "return" of the Saar either to Germany as a whole or to the West German Federal Republic, and this had to be separately accommodated. To be sure, the West German Government under Adenauer technically had never recognized the *de jure* separation of the territory from Germany, but neither was it *de jure* a part of the West German Republic under the *Grundgesetz*.

This juridical enigma of being "German-though-not-West-German territory" had to be rectified in order to incorporate it formally into the Federal Republic. Undoing the *de facto* severance from Germany and achieving the *de jure* accession to statehood in West Germany were accomplished by a single legislative enactment—the *Eingliederungsgesetz* (Law of Incorporation)—passed in late 1956. It simply extended the West German *Grundgesetz* and legislation to the Saar, which was renamed the "Saarland," gave the latter the status of a constituent and co-equal *Land* in the Federal Republic, and provided for appropriate representation in the West German parliament.

This unusual saga of the Saar, a territory which for years hovered between French annexation, virtual independence, and internationalization, illustrates how other portions of German territory, which are not now included within the West German Republic, might at least theoretically be incorporated into and become integral elments of the Federation.

It remains for Adenauer and his biographers to reveal whether he surrendered supinely and wholeheartedly to the French in accepting the Saar Statute, as some contend, or whether, by agreeing with the French on internationalization, he unwittingly rendered a great service to German unity in the name of European unification, or whether he realized that the most diplomatic way to retrieve the Saar for West Germany, while not inhibiting Franco-German cooperation to promote European integration, was to induce the French Government to agree to loosen its ties with the territory and permit the Saarlanders to decide their own fate, knowing full well that they would reject any solution other than their return to Germany. In any case, Adenauer may have possessed greater political vision and wisdom than his critics, and both West Germany and the Saarland were beneficiaries of the diplomacy in which he engaged to resolve the Saar problem.

With the exception of the Berlin question, which is discussed in the following section, and, of course, the longer-range matter of the territory in East Germany and the eastern provinces, the major issues pertaining to the territorial composition of the Federal Republic thus were resolved during the Adenauer era, although not always in keeping with his avowed policy or that of his party. Experience was gained and decisions were made with respect to a general review of territorial composition, specific territory was reorganized by federal law subject to local referendum, and former German territory lying outside federal jurisdiction was incorporated into the West German domain and made a constituent element in the Federation by federal law. The most pressing territorial issues that were pragmatically resolvable, consequently, were resolved during the Adenauer era.

This experience evidences constitutional and political flexibility respecting the matter of internal territorial composition, which is important to a healthy and viable federalism. To summarize, West Germany began its postwar independent existence with 12 constitutionally identified *Länder* (*Grundgesetz,* Article 23), but only 11 in actual practice (because of the *de jure* exclusion of Berlin by the Allied Governments). This number was reduced when three amalgamated to form the combined *Land* Baden-Württemberg, and since the admission of the Saar, the Federation has comprised 10 *Länder*. In view of the artificiality of some of their boundaries, compounded by sectional particularism, pressure for territorial realignment is likely to reemerge, but history is replete with accounts of the difficulty of accomplishing realignment equably and equitably. The basic pattern of the territorial composition of the Federal Republic, therefore, can be said to have been stabilized and become an important part of the Adenauer legacy. Future modification of the *status quo* is most unlikely, though not impossible.

INTEGRATING BERLIN AND THE FEDERAL REPUBLIC

As a postwar political entity, Berlin has taken on a number of distinguishable but conflicting guises. Simultaneously, it possesses characteristics of a national capital, a populous metropolitan city, an associated or quasi-integrated element in a federal union, and a political community of considerable international significance. Yet, in each respect, and in all of them conjointly, Berlin is unusual if not unique. The leaders of the Federal Republic under Adenauer, in cooperation with those of Berlin, employed imagination and statesmanship in coping with the "Berlin problem." While a great deal of interest has centered on the international aspects of and crises involving the city, the governments in Bonn and Berlin worked out a network of interrelations to resolve the "internal" aspects of governance that have received far less public attention.

West Germans and West Berliners alike wish to have Berlin regarded as a constituent *Land* and a fully integrated member of the Federal Republic of Germany. Chancellor Adenauer avowedly pursued this policy without deviation. Yet, as a practical matter the knowledgeable appear unwilling at this time to press the concept to the point of terminating the residual legal obligations of the four wartime Allies, which would entail relinquishment of their juxtaposed rights and responsibilities regarding the metropolis and consign the Berlin question to the two Germanies, requiring the Federal Republic to negotiate *de novo* with East Germany.

The juridical relationship of Berlin and the Federal Republic, therefore, poses a particularly thorny problem. The question of its inclusion as an original constituent *Land* was given serious attention at the time the *Grundgesetz* was being prepared. The Parliamentary Council added Berlin as a "twelfth *Land*" in its draft constitutive act. However, the Western Allies took exception to this action, stating that they appreciated the solicitude shown for the metropolis, but in view of the existing international situation, the reference to Berlin needed to be suspended. Nevertheless, it was not deleted from the final version of the *Grundgesetz*. As a consequence, when the Allied Governments gave their approval, they clearly expressed a reservation concerning the inclusion of Berlin in the Federal Republic, and this reservation has not been rescinded.

Similar action was taken in devising the Berlin Constitution of 1950. In giving their approval, the Western Allies specified a number of reservations, stipulating that the paragraphs recognizing Berlin as a constituent *Land* in the federal union and applying the West German *Grundgesetz* and legislative enactments to Berlin were deemed to be "suspended," and "during the transitional period, Berlin shall possess none of the attributes of a twelfth *Land*" in the Federal Republic of Germany.

Thus, the effect of the manner in which the legal aspect of the Berlin territorial integration issue was handled appears to be that, whereas the Western Allies were not willing to insist upon the deletion of the references to the national position of *Land* Berlin from the West German *Grundgesetz* of 1949 and the Berlin Constitution of 1950, nevertheless they temporarily but designedly suspended Berlin's participation as an equal, integral element of the Federal Republic. From the very nature of this action, it is important to note that, as far as the Western Allies are concerned, simply the rescinding of their reservation would in fact effectuate the immediate legal incorporation of Berlin into the Federal Republic of Germany.

While Berlin, therefore, remains outside the Federal Republic in a legal and formal sense, during the Adenauer era—with the cooperation of the governments of West Germany, West Berlin, and the Western Allies—it has virtually been integrated with West Germany in a practical, political, and administrative fashion. This integration has been consummated in a number of ways. Among the more important are the virtually full-fledged participation of the Berlin Government and Berliners as individuals in the government of the Federal Republic, the widespread application of West German legislation and treaties to Berlin, and the establishment of wholesale administrative and financial interrelations—all intended governmentally to coalesce West Berlin as intimately as possible with the Federal Republic.

The interests of Berlin are represented in various ways in the political life and institutions of the West German Government. As a matter of fact, officials of the city participated in the very founding of the government of the Federal Republic. The city sent five delegates to serve on the Parliamentary Council to draft the *Grundgesetz*. Later, while Berlin was limited initially to sending eight delegates to the *Bundestag* "in an advisory capacity," its representation gradually took on more and more the character of that of the West German *Länder*. Early in 1952, for example, the Adenauer Government promulgated legislation to increase Berlin representation to 19, and the following year the number again was augmented, so that, since the 1953 West German election, the metropolis has been represented by 22. Numerically, this equitably represents the population of West Berlin.

Originally, Berlin deputies were to serve simply in an "advisory" role, ostensibly having no voting power in the *Bundestag*. Subsequently, however, this came to be interpreted more and more liberally, so as to accord these delegates all functions in legislative decision-making short of participation in the formal vote on statutory proposals. From the very outset they have enjoyed the right to address plenary sessions and to participate in the important legislative committee work. In addition, they are active members of the parliamentary political factions (*Fraktionen*) which decide party positions respecting legislative policy, they may be elected to office in the *Bundestag* including its presidency, and they vote in the legislative standing committees, thus giving them a status quite different from that presumably contemplated in 1949.

Berlin also has had four delegates in the *Bundesrat,* the upper West German legislative chamber. This number has not changed, because the size of all component *Land* delegations ranges from three to five members, generally reflecting population ratios. The Berlin delegation, elected by the Berlin *Senat* (the collective executive or cabinet, comparable to the *Landesregierung* or the executive of the West German *Land*), invariably embraces the Governing Mayor, the Mayor, the Senator for Federal Affairs, and a fourth member as the *Senat* may decide. The Berlin representatives have the right to vote in committees, and they also vote in plenary sessions, but their vote is merely advisory and is not counted in the official tally. However, in the important Joint Conference Committee (*Vermittlungsausschuss*), which composes differences between the two parliamentary chambers, Berlin representatives of the *Bundesrat* have full voting membership.

During the Adenauer administration other practices further evidenced the integration of Berlin into the government of West Germany. For example, though perhaps largely of symbolic importance, in the last three presidential elections (1954, 1959, and 1964) the *Bundesversammlung,* or Federal Convention, which elects the Federal President, was convened in Berlin, and in 1959, Dr. Eugen Gerstenmaier, President of the *Bundestag,* propounded the remarkable decision that West Berlin possesses full voting rights in electing the President. The Berlin government, then represented in the balloting by 44 delegates or electors, theoretically could have cast the deciding votes in electing Dr. Heinrich

Lübke. In 1964 the Berlin delegation again participated in the balloting, but its votes were not decisive.

By contrast, the Berlin members of the *Bundestag* do not participate in the election of the Federal Chancellor. Apparently they do cast votes, but they deposit their secret ballots in a separate urn, and their votes are not tallied in deciding the outcome. The legal propriety of counting these votes is not the only issue. Because the Berlin delegation is heavily Social Democratic and this party has constituted the principal opposition element in the *Bundestag* since 1949, the Berlin votes could hold the balance of power in a close contest, as in the case of the first election of Adenauer, inasmuch as an absolute majority is required to elect the Chancellor.

In addition to representation and voting in the West German parliamentary chambers, a number of Berliners served in Adenauer's Cabinet, including Jakob Kaiser, Ernst Lemmer, and Dr. Heinrich Krone. Moreover, in accordance with the *Grundgesetz,* Willy Brandt, West Berlin's Governing Mayor, while serving as President of the *Bundesrat,* automatically became Acting President of the Federal Republic during the temporary absence from West Germany of its then President Theodor Heuss—a strange role indeed for the executive of an "unintegrated political entity." In the parliamentary elections of 1961 and 1965 Governing Mayor Brandt also was designated the Social Democratic candidate for the chancellorship, and in view of the ostensible relationship of Berlin and the Federal Republic, his becoming Chancellor would be even more remarkable.

Berlin is also used as the occasional headquarters site of the West German government. The Federal President has a state residence at Bellevue Palace in Berlin. Furthermore, the historic *Reichstag* building, located near the Brandenburg Gate in the center of the city and destroyed by fire during the Nazi era, is under reconstruction; one refurbished wing, dedicated late in 1963, was turned over to the *Bundestag,* and for the time being it is used primarily for meetings of legislative committees. In the meantime, the West German parliamentary chambers sometimes hold sessions in other facilities in the city.

A second major test of the extent to which Berlin has been incorporated into the Federal Republic is the degree to which the city is a part of the federal statutory and treaty complex. Here, too, developments since 1949 under Adenauer have reversed the status of isolation originally required by the Allies. The issue at hand is simply the manner whereby, and the extent to which, arrangements were worked out during the Adenauer administration for West German statutes and treaties to become "the law of the land" in West Berlin. Unilateral action by the Federal Republic rendering its statutory law and treaties automatically binding in Berlin would have controverted the 1945 four-power concept of legal and political separateness of the metropolis. In practice, however, workable systems were instituted by the Adenauer and Berlin governments, with the acquiescence of the Western Allies, which, while paying homage to the legal fiction of non-integration, nevertheless permit West German laws and treaties to become applicable in the metropolis virtually by *pro forma* action on the part of the Berlin government.

The Allies early insisted that the "provisions of any federal law shall apply to Berlin *only after they have been voted upon* by the [Berlin] House of Representatives and *passed as a Berlin law*" (italics added). The intent of this reservation appears to be that, for a statute of the Federal Republic to be applicable in Berlin, it must be separately enacted into law by the Berlin legislature. Automatic application solely by virtue of the action of the West German government is thereby precluded. Although from the very outset the Allies were not opposed to Berlin's having legislation identical with that of West Germany, they held that juridically Berlin could not function under the legislation of the Federal Republic. That is to say, the legislation of West Germany must be both adapted by and overtly adopted by the Berlin government. Consequently, to put it technically, in fact as well as in law it must be Berlin—not West German—legislation.

The essence of this legal condition has continued, but, under pressures applied by both the Adenauer and Berlin governments, the process of dealing with it in practice changed considerably during the Adenauer era. Initially, Berlin was required separately to enact the full text of each West German law it sought to place in effect, but in 1951 the Allies liberalized their procedure substantially. Thereafter, the Berlin legislature was empowered to take over a West German statute simply by means of a *Mantel-*

gesetz or "cover law," provided the stipulations of the federal enactment are otherwise valid in Berlin and reference in the law to any federal agency is construed as referring to the appropriate Berlin authority.

On occasion, as a matter of fact, a West German statute may specify differences in the substance of the law as it is to pertain to Berlin, and these may be inserted in a special "Berlin clause" or in other portions of the federal enactment. Procedurally, of course, the content of the federal law may be influenced by Berlin authorities before it is enacted by the federal parliament, in that the Berlin delegates play an active role in the legislative process of both the *Bundestag* and the *Bundesrat*. Often a *Mantelgesetz* is only a few lines in length, and its three articles respectively stipulate simply that the federal law applies to Berlin, identify the agents or agencies responsible for enforcing it, and specify its date of effectiveness.

A similar, practical process for the application of West German treaties to West Berlin also was perfected during the Adenauer years. Internationally, Berlin has become a part of the West German treaty network, thereby enjoying a *de facto* integrated status in this regard as well as with respect to West German legislation. This was made possible by a Western Allied "Declaration" of 1952, in which the three powers approved the applicability to Berlin of West German treaties, subject to certain conditions. For example, Berlin cannot simply be automatically covered as a part of the federal territory, but must be separately mentioned in the treaty or its ancillary instruments. The effect of such separate identification, apparently, is that the treaty thereby applies theorectically to two territorial entities—West Germany and Berlin. The Declaration adds that, if it is impossible to insert the name of Berlin into the text of the treaty, the Federal Republic, either in its instrument of adherence or in a separate statement issued at the time of signature or ratification, is required to stipulate that the provisions of the treaty apply also to the metropolis.

The procedure whereby such treaty effectuation is consummated for Berlin is relatively simple. West German treaties intended to apply also to the metropolis normally contain a "Berlin clause." This stipulation is inserted in all such treaties except multilateral conventions, in which case Berlin is covered rather by inclusion in supplementing instruments at the time of signature or ratification, and treaties between West Germany and the East European bloc countries, respecting which Berlin is encompassed by indirection where this is possible and desirable.

For a treaty to become legally binding in West Germany, naturally it must be ratified in keeping with established West German constitutional procedures. Additionally, however, to apply to Berlin it also must separately be made part of Berlin law by the overt action of its government. To regularize its procedure, in 1953 the Berlin legislature enacted a law specifying: "Laws on international treaties of the Federal Republic are considered promulgated with effect also for *Land* Berlin upon publication in the *Federal Legal Gazette* [*Bundesgesetzblatt*], as soon as *Land* Berlin, by law, has declared them applicable to Berlin." Such an *Anwendungsgesetz,* as it is called, is a short enactment which simply reads that the federal law approving and/or implementing a treaty "will be applicable to Berlin," with effect on a specified date. At times a single *Anwendungsgesetz* may bring into operation a whole series of West German treaties—as many as some 30 at one time.

The Western Allies rarely object to applying West German treaties to Berlin, and non-Eastern governments, by and large, do not draw any significant legal-political distinction between the Federal Republic and West Berlin for treaty purposes. Both the Adenauer Government and West Berlin were anxious to apply West German treaties liberally to the metropolis, so that the only major types of treaties that normally have excluded Berlin are those, understandably, which deal with military alliance and air traffic, because these functions continue to fall directly within the residual competence of the Allied authorities.

Thus, during the Adenauer era systems were instituted for the application of West German legislation and treaties to Berlin with as little technical difficulty as possible. As a consequence, despite very real problems flowing from Berlin's strange legal status, the Chancellor was able to approximate his goal of pragmatic political coalescence.

The third major aspect of this amalgamation is the nature and extent of administrative integration that was accomplished during Adenauer's administration. The essence of the problem was to work out arrangements which permitted Berlin to be treated administratively in a manner comparable to that employed in ordinary West German federal-state relations, except where privileged treatment was deemed necessary.

In establishing his *Bundesregierung,* Adenauer created a "Ministry for All-German Affairs" (*Ministerium für Gesamtdeutsche Fragen*), and for some years it was headed by Jakob Kaiser and Ernst Lemmer, both Berliners. On the proposal of this ministry, the Chancellor also appointed a "Representative of the Federal Republic in Berlin" (*Bevollmächtigte der Bundes-republik Deutschland in Berlin*), who, as a member of the Federal Executive at a high level, represented Adenauer and the Federal Government to the ranking officials of the Berlin Government. The *Bevollmächtigte* was put in charge of the *Bundesvertretung* or Federal Representative Mission in Berlin, composed of a small agency of the Chancellor (*Bundeskanzleramt*), which he personally heads, and bureaus of a dozen of the federal ministries, having a combined staff of 150 to 200 persons.

The Government of Berlin—not unlike the constituent West German *Länder*—also established important parallel liaison with Adenauer's *Bundesregierung* through its own agencies at Bonn. It is represented by the Senatorial Department of Federal Affairs, headed by the *Senator für Bundesangelegenheiten,* which has functioned both in Berlin and in Bonn. This executive agency is supplemented by the Berlin delegations to the *Bundestag* and the *Bundesrat,* and, because the latter theoretically is in continuous session (meeting biweekly or triweekly), and inasmuch as the Berlin delegation is headed by the Governing Mayor, actually the latter not only promotes the legislative interest of Berlin in the upper West German parliamentary chamber, but he also personally represents the metropolis to the Chancellor and other members of the *Bundesregierung.*

Augmenting these rather comprehensive executive liaison activities in the relations of Berlin and the Federal Republic, during Adenauer's incumbency a broad spectrum of the federal administration was located and active in the metropolis. In some respects West German agencies were empowered directly to exercise federal functions in Berlin (as they do in the federal territory) whereas in the case of others, their national headquarters were housed in the metropolis, and they engaged some 18,000 to 20,000 employees. In part, the Adenauer Government established such heavily staffed federal agencies in the beleaguered city to afford indirect West German economic support and to assist in coping with the local employment problem. All told, while Adenauer was Chancellor, some 65 federal agencies were operating in the metropolis. The breadth of their activities ranged from liaison with the Berlin Government to direct and indirect administration of federal affairs, or simply to headquartering federal administrative functions in the city.

West Berlin also has been incorporated generally into the comprehensive West German financial system. Because of its unique territorial and political situation, naturally it has encountered serious financial difficulties. Following a number of makeshift arrangements, relations were regularized during the Adenauer administration by the *Drittes Überleitungsgesetz* (Federal Transfer Law), which, among other things, applied the West German tax structure to Berlin. This statute prescribes that the Federal Republic will provide a contribution covering the Berlin budget deficit, the amount for which is incorporated in the federal budget, and funds are transferred in monthly installments. The annual amount of this direct subsidy is negotiated by the Berlin *Senat* and the Federal Ministry of Finance. In recent years it has approximated 1.75 million DM per annum, or 40 per cent of the Berlin budget. This contribution rarely evokes serious difficulty in the West German parliament. Usually it is not debated publicly in the federal legislature.

In recent years, according to the Berlin *Senat,* if one includes certain loans for which only token repayment to the Federal Republic is required, the Federal Government has been contributing approximately 4 billion DM annually to the governance of Berlin over the amount it collects in the metropolis. Moreover, this amount does not include the salaries paid to thousands of federal employees located in the city, as well as other indirect financial underwriting, which further subsidize its economy.

In short, during the Adenauer administration both federal and Berlin administrative machinery were made to operate side by side in Berlin, and there is no question that the metropolis was tightly integrated by the Chancellor into the general administration and the monetary and financial systems of the Federal Republic. Yet, because of the difficulties flowing from the city's peculiar international situation, it has been accorded preferential fiscal treatment. As a matter of fact, one may well wonder who would provide such financial assistance if the city were severed from the Federal Republic, and whether, without such generous and willing West German financial support, West Berlin would collapse economically.

To conclude, West Berlin, although formally not an integrated *Land* in the Federal Republic of Germany, nevertheless, under Chancellor Adenauer was made to approximate such status in practice, and has come to be increasingly treated as one of the Federal Republic's constituent *Länder*. Despite the many limitations and problems resulting from this enigmatic *de jure-de facto* dichotomy, a rational and workable relationship was produced, paying homage to the legal fiction of juridical or at least theoretical dissociation of West Berlin from West Germany, while at the same time permitting practices which virtually consummated such incorporation as a matter of practical governmental administration—indeed one of the more remarkable elements of the Adenauer legacy.

REUNIFICATION—ADENAUER'S UNFULFILLED OBJECTIVE

Historically speaking, the major change in the political structuring of Europe resulting from World War II was the territorial partition of Germany. Undoing this—that is to say, reunifying Germany—was one of Adenauer's primary goals, and its lack of realization perhaps his greatest failure.

This does not mean that either the division of Germany, or the inability to reintegrate the country territorially, are solely or even largely the fault of the Chancellor or, for that matter, of the West Germans. All of the leading powers involved in the postwar treatment of Germany bear some of the responsibility—the Soviet Union, the three Western Allies, the Federal Republic, and the East German regime. Each played a significant part in producing the fragmentation, establishing and maintaining two Germanies, and rejecting reunification except on its own conditions. The degree of responsibility naturally varied among them, however, and to accomplish reunification one or another of the powers would have been obliged to compromise significantly on its vital interests in the matter, as it conceived them. Thus far, none has been prepared to make the concessions necessary to produce a formula acceptable to the others.

In general it may be said, therefore, that the West German Government under Adenauer and each of the other powers concerned has favored reunification, but only on its own terms, and the positions taken by East and West basically have been so antithetical as to cause them to reject the preconditions demanded by the opponents. Therefore, whereas the desire to reunify may have been, if not compelling, at least sincere, a negotiable plan has not yet been found.

The issue, of course, is not purely West German, nor is it entirely the concern of only the two Germanies; rather, it is both an international (East-West) and an internal (German) question. Actually, four territorial elements are involved: West Germany (the Federal Republic), East Germany (the German Democratic Republic), Berlin, and the Eastern territories lying beyond the Oder and Neisse rivers. None of these four segments can be completely dissociated from the others in considering reunification, but, at least in principle, amalgamation could be achieved for the first three—the Federal Republic, the Democratic Republic, and Berlin—without necessarily reincorporating the Eastern territories. Inasmuch as none of the major Western Powers has acknowledged the validity of Polish absorption of these Eastern provinces, however, they remain an important factor in any serious consideration of the problem.

Reunification also is closely related to the matter of a final World War II peace settlement with Germany, and this relationship has become a major factor in the argumentation of West and East. The state of war between the wartime Allies and Germany has been terminated *de facto,* but not *de jure,* in that they have not yet signed a peace treaty. After the three Western Allies assisted in establishing the Federal Republic and in regularizing their relations as equals in the family of nations, and the Soviet Government permitted the creation of the German Democratic Republic and instituted diplomatic and treaty relations with its regime, the process of reunification became possible in one of several ways:

1. By agreement among the four wartime Allies without the participation of the present regimes of West and East Germany, which is quite improbable;
2. By agreement between the two Germanies without involving the wartime Allies, which is even less probable;
3. By agreement between the four wartime Allies and the Communist regime in East Germany, which is virtually inconceivable;
4. By agreement of the four wartime Allies and the Federal Republic, which is possible if the Soviet Government were prepared to sacrifice East Germany, and therefore is unlikely;
5. By agreement between the Soviet Union and the two Germanies, which also is unlikely though not impossible; or
6. By agreement among all six powers, which is feasible if an agreeable formula can be produced.

While, on occasion, one or more of the powers has been suspicious of the possibility of resort to such of these alternatives as bypass its direct participation, only the last—agreement among all six powers—has been seriously pursued, although Adenauer presumably would have preferred ignoring the East German communist regime. Nevertheless, a manageable solution, it appears, would need to constitute a "package" embracing an agreement respecting a peace settlement, a proposal for uniting either the two Germanies or the four original occupation zones (together with Berlin), a method of devising an acceptable all-German government, an understanding respecting Germany's position vis-à-vis the North Atlantic and Communist alliances, a prescription for settling the European security question, and a plan for resolving the disposition of the German Eastern territories. It does not require uncommon imagination to appreciate the many complexities entailed in fabricating such an arrangement which could be agreed to by all the parties concerned, nor is it difficult to understand Adenauer's inability readily to produce the elusive solution.

The consummation of a German peace settlement clearly involves the vital interests of the four wartime Allies, although either the three Western Powers or the Soviet Government might very well be disposed to negotiate such a treaty independently with a

German government which it might be willing to accept as validly representing the entire country. This, no doubt, is one of the reasons why the Federal Republic under Adenauer and his successor has contended that it possesses the only legitimate government of Germany and represents the country in its entirety, while at the same time the Constitution of the East German Republic alleges that it pertains to the whole of the country, and why both Germanies oppose the international acknowledgment of each other either as the spokesman for Germany as a whole or as a legitimate participant in the family of nations.

Naturally, the creation of a genuine all-German government would require the acquiescence of the authorities and people of the two Germanies. The Soviet Union, it is true, has threatened to negotiate a separate peace settlement with only the East German Republic as juridically representing all of Germany. Yet, the Soviet-East German convention of 1964 clearly concedes that it is not such a "German peace treaty." Were the Communist powers to pretend otherwise, such a treaty could scarcely be deemed valid except by its signatories and such of their allies as were willing to accept it.

The German question is one of the most troublesome pragmatic issues in the East-West conflict, with West Germany and its interests being accepted and espoused by the Western Allies, and East Germany bearing a similar relation to the Soviet Union and its satellites. A major confusing factor in this international bifurcation is the diplomatic recognition of the Federal Republic by the Soviet Government and the commencement of Soviet-West German diplomatic relations, which Adenauer negotiated during his Moscow visit in 1955, two months after the Geneva East-West summit conference. This action was not imitated by the Western Powers respecting East Germany. In his exchange of letters with the Soviet Government, the Chancellor specifically reserved the matter of the status of German territory to a final peace treaty and restated his position that the Federal Government represents "the German nation."

In view of Soviet recognition of the Federal Republic, it would seem that, while in fact there are two Germanies and the authorities of each wish to be accepted as speaking for the country in its entirety, under Adenauer the Federal Republic came to enjoy wider acceptance in this capacity by the family of nations. However, because neither the Federal Republic nor the East German regime has been universally regarded as representing all of Germany, the twin problems of reunification and a World War II peace settlement remain.

In the context of this cursory review, it remains only to examine briefly two aspects, namely, the nature of West German reunification policy under the leadership of Chancellor Adenauer, and the theoretical feasibility, as an internal political question, of governmental amalgamation within the political system which emerged under his leadership.

In his general governmental policy declaration at the time of the institution of his first Cabinet, on September 20, 1949, Adenauer avowed hope for reunification with the Eastern Zone and Berlin. This goal often was repeated by him and other members of the West German government. The Chancellor specifically alluded to it in his policy pronouncements at the commencement of each new *Bundestag,* as well as in communiqués following summit consultations (as he did at the time of his meeting with President John F. Kennedy in Washington late in 1961) and in a good many public addresses.

There is little doubt, therefore, that reunification has been a primary objective possessing the character of a vital national interest. Adenauer even characterized it as "the *supreme aim* of the policy of the Federal Government" (italics added). Yet, while he and other West German leaders may have sincerely intended this, the course of events relegated it to play a lesser role than other, perhaps more realizable, goals.

Accomplishing the objective of reunification obviously necessitated resolving procedural details. From time to time, Adenauer referred to achieving reunification "in a free and unified Europe," "in peace and freedom," and "on the basis of self-determination." Such illusive qualifying terms were inclined to be subjectively interpreted by both the West and the East, and they intended or implied conditions which, as viewed by the Chancellor and the West, were bound to be unacceptable to the Soviet Union and the East German regime. Entirely aside from the propriety of demanding reunification on such nebulous conditions, it was because of them, at least in part, that the goal remained unrealized.

Another impediment was the position taken on the timing and nature of "free elections." As early as 1950 Adenauer and the Western Allies proposed that, as a first step in the process, all-German free elections be held under the control of a commission consisting of representatives of either the four wartime Allies or the United Nations, in order to elect a national constituent assembly to draft an all-German constitution. In the colloquy that followed, the governments of the two Germanies respectively proposed specific draft election laws for this purpose, and in 1952 a United Nations Commission was dispatched to investigate conditions for the holding of such free elections. This Commission was unable to accomplish its mission, its two reports indicating that East Germany and the Soviet Government refused cooperation.

Three years later, at the Geneva summit conference, the heads of government of the four wartime Allies agreed "that the settlement of the German question and the reunification of Germany *by means of free elections* shall be carried out in conformity with the national interests of the German people and the interests of European security" (italics added), and they instructed their Foreign Ministers to work out the details, but the Soviet Foreign Minister failed to honor this mandate. It is quite evident that free elections, as intended by Chancellor Adenauer and the Western Allies, are not acceptable to the Communist leaders.

There also have been other particulars on which the West and the East have held opposing views. These include the time relationship between reunification and the conclusion of a peace treaty, the German neutrality and rearmament issue, the Eastern territories question, and the concept of confederating the two Germanies on the basis of equality.

In 1952 the East German Democratic Republic and the Soviet Union declared that only the conclusion of a peace treaty could restore German unity, and the Soviet Government presented draft texts to the Western Allies in 1952, 1954, and 1959. Chancellor Adenauer and the Western Powers took issue both with the suggestion that a treaty settlement should precede reunification and with the details of the Soviet proposals.

Neutralization of Germany might have been generally negotiable in the early 1950's, but Adenauer rejected the Communist overture respecting it because West Germany then was negotiating with the Western Allies to terminate the occupation concomitant with a West German contribution to the European Defense Community (later for admission into the North Atlantic Treaty Organization). Once West Germany became a member of the Atlantic Alliance and East Germany joined the Warsaw Pact powers in 1955, the matter of neutralization ceased being negotiable—unless, of course, both Germanies were able to put reunification above other policy goals, including collective security within the alliance arrangements they preferred.

As far as the Eastern provinces are concerned, Adenauer and the Western Allies have insisted that legal determination regarding their disposition must await a final peace settlement, and the Chancellor avoided any semblance of official acquiescence in the acceptance of the status quo either by dereliction or by prescription. Nevertheless, the loss of this territory to an amalgamated Germany is not likely to be reversed in any voluntarily negotiated agreement. The issue, therefore, appears to be important largely as a bargaining factor.

Finally, it needs to be noted that, regardless of the credence attributed to the goal of reunification by the Adenauer administration, the Chancellor participated in consummating a whole series of policies and actions which made the integration of the two Germanies far more difficult, if not impossible. Among the most inhibiting were the rearming of West Germany with a national military establishment (or, for that matter, by means of a contribution to the continental unified military force contemplated by the European Defense Community Treaty, had it come into effect) and the joining of the North Atlantic Alliance, Western European Union, and the European Communities. Under present circumstances it is visionary to expect the Soviet and East German regimes to agree to any plan for general reunification under which the new Germany would continue to be powerfully armed and integrated within both the Western Alliance and the European Six. This is not to suggest that Chancellor Adenauer was unwise or unrealistic in pursuing the objectives he did, but rather that circumstances and the pursuit of these other goals combined to render the realization of reunification increasingly improbable.

Parenthetically it should be noted that still other important goals presumably were also given priority over reunification, such as terminating the occupation and joining the society of nations as a respected member, rebuilding the West German economy and resuming a strong international financial and trade position, resolving other territorial issues (such as the Saar), and pragmatically integrating Berlin into the Federal Republic. To some extent, the fulfillment of each of these also inhibited the process of reunification.

Various formulae have been posed for the governmental system to accompany reunification. These have varied from the nebulous joining of the two Germanies as equal elements in a loose confederation, suggested by East Germany and the Soviet Government, to establishing an entirely new government founded on a new constitution drafted by a constitutional convention comprised of delegates elected directly by the German people in secret elections, as espoused by the Adenaur Government. Both the West and the East have thus far rejected the substance of the other's proposals.

They also have differed on timing, and this is a vital element because it actually could determine the outcome as far as the government and politics of a reunified Germany are concerned. Chancellor Adenauer insisted that free, all-German elections must come first, as noted, to be followed by the drafting of a constitution by a constituent assembly and approved by the people, then the establishment of an all-German government founded on the new constitution, and finally negotiation of the German peace treaty. The East German regime has insisted on the inverse order —namely, first a German treaty, then the establishment of a German government, and finally the holding of elections. Each side naturally has expected to gain the most, or to lose the least, by the sequence it supports.

The alternative procedures for devising a government for a reunified Germany basically are threefold. The most obvious, of course, is the creation of a new government founded on a new constitution, either negotiated by the governments of the two Germanies or drafted by a popularly elected constituent assembly. The second is acceptance by the German people of the West German *Grundgesetz* as the valid constitution for all of Germany, and the formal incorporation into the West German Federation of the East German *Länder* under the accession to statehood process referred to earlier in relation to the Saar. This might be a feasible technique for "unification" if the people of East Germany were able to dispose of the yoke of the East German communist regime. Although it may not have been the only motivation, the possibility of such state admission/accession may have been an important reason why the Communist leaders disestablished the East German *Länder* in 1952. The remaining alternative is for the people of West Germany to dispose of the West German government and become absorbed into a unified Germany under the existing East German Constitution, which, as noted, presumes to apply to all of Germany. These last two alternatives are improbable in the absence of internal revolution, and most likely for this reason they have not been seriously argued. Yet, strictly from an internal point of view, they remain juridical potentialities.

Nevertheless, if reunification is to be accomplished, most likely it will be by means of the first alternative—the creation of a new, all-German government—to which West Germany and the other powers appear to be committed. This brings one full circle to the abortive argumentation and negotiation on the matter during the 14 years of the Adenauer administration.

It is axiomatic that the success or failure of a foreign policy goal is measured by the degree to which it is capable of attainment. On the face of it, it appears that in this context Chancellor Adenauer's pursuance of the objective of reunification was a dismal failure. However, it also is axiomatic that when a series of goals are simultaneously espoused, some of them being intrinsically competitive, success or failure becomes relative rather than absolute. Inability to realize reunification, therefore, needs to be assessed not in and of itself, but in relation to the other policy goals embraced by Adenauer, and the success or failure attending them. On balance, it may be fairly concluded that the consummation of reunification might very well have mitigated seriously against a good many of the other political achievements which comprise the Adenauer legacy, and only history will be able to assess properly the wisdom of his choices.

The Erhard Trusteeship

by William G. Andrews

ON OCTOBER 16, 1963, LUDWIG ERHARD WAS ACCEPTED BY THE Bundestag as Federal Chancellor by 279 votes to 180 with 24 abstentions and one invalid ballot. The following day, he appointed his cabinet. Like its predecessor, it was composed of Christian Democratic and Free Democratic party members. Twelve ministers were CDU, five were FDP, and four were from the CSU. Only three new men joined the cabinet. Kurt Schmuecker, CDU, assumed the post of Economics Minister which had been held by Erhard since the Federal Republic was established. Erich Mende, the FDP chairman, became Vice Chancellor (a designation held by Mr. Erhard since 1957) and Minister of All-German Affairs, taking the latter portfolio from a Christian Democrat. To maintain the party balance, another Christian Democrat, Hans Krueger, became Minister of Refugee Affairs, replacing an FDP member.

The new chancellor set the tone of his administration in his inaugural statement to the Bundestag. He proclaimed his intention to pursue a middle of the road policy and act as chancellor of the whole people. Not surprisingly for one who had played so important a part in his predecessor's government for so long, Erhard announced that he intended to adhere closely to the policies of the Adenauer government. His rather unemphatic pledge of fidelity to the Franco-German Treaty, however, was sandwiched in between a lengthy, unequivocal tribute to NATO and European integration, on the one hand, and a vow to work for British integration into the European Community, on the other. This indicated a cooling off from Adenauer's love affair with the French.

Most comment observed that the new chancellor had taken over his predecessor's policies but had given them, from the outset, his own unmistakable stamp.

His investiture speech was, indeed, an accurate prelude to the policies his government pursued. There were few changes or new initiatives in domestic policies. On the other hand, Erhard's foreign policy developed subtle but important nuances of divergence. His very un-Adenauer-like wrangle with the French over the agricultural Common Market reflected both his less fervent attachment to European integration and his less favorable view of the Franco-German alliance.

In foreign policy, also, the Erhard administration was marked by the increased prominence of Foreign Minister Gerhard Schroeder. Adenauer had held tight control over foreign policy matters to the extent that his two successive foreign ministers had been little more than eminent errand boys. Erhard played the ceremonial role well. He traveled abroad more than any German chancellor in history, visiting the United States, Britain, France, Scandinavia, the Low Countries, and Italy during his first nine months in office. But much more than had ever been the case under Adenauer, the actual management of foreign affairs and its defense before parliament became Schroeder's.

This did not mean, however, that Erhard turned away from the "Chancellor democracy" developed by Adenauer. On the contrary, Erhard's control over the cabinet appeared to be as great as Adenauer's had been, although his style was markedly more flexible. This was true despite the fact that Erhard did not combine the office of CDU party leader with the chancellorship as Adenauer had. Indeed, his control over the cabinet may have been enhanced by his less partisan identification. It enabled him to win less grudging support from the FDP, despite the approach of general elections.

His predecessor had often been criticized for treating parliament with too little regard. Anyone who had expected improvement under Erhard was disappointed. If anything, he involved the Bundestag even less in the important affairs of state. This was largely possible because of the plentiful evidence that his popularity among the people was very high, much higher than that of his party. For instance, in November 1964, 37 per cent of the respondents in a public opinion survey indicated they favored the SPD against only 30 per cent for the CDU and 5 per cent for the FDP. Yet, at the same time, Erhard was preferred over Brandt and Schroeder as chancellor by 71 per cent to 23 per cent and 16 per cent.[1] Another poll indicated that the CDU had overtaken the SPD in popularity. It showed a 35 to 32 per cent CDU lead in November compared to a 32 to 34 lag in October, the first poll "in a long time" to give the CDU the advantage.[2] By April 1964, Erhard had already surpassed Adenauer in public opinion polls as most popular German politician, 27 per cent to 24, with Brandt polling 17 and Schroeder 4 per cent.[3] Furthermore, Erhard had reversed a trend toward the SPD in state elections. In the ten state elections between 1961 and mid-1964, the SPD had won 12.4 million votes compared to 12.0 million for the CDU.[4] As late as two weeks before Adenauer finally accepted the inevitable and Erhard obtained CDU endorsement as his successor, the party had suffered a severe setback in the state elections of Rhineland-Palatinate.[5] However, shortly after his designation, Erhard campaigned in the Lower Saxony state elections where the CDU was expected to lose strength. Instead, the CDU gained 6.9 percentage points, 1.5 more than the SPD gained.[6] The CDU also gained in the Bremen state elections in September 1963 and in those of Baden-Württemberg of April 1964.[7] The latter election was especially significant in that the CDU vote increased 4.7 more percentage points than did that of the SPD, and both Brandt and Erhard campaigned extensively for their parties.

Erhard's aim to detach himself from both the Bundestag and the CDU more than had Adenauer and to rest his authority directly on the people was further aided by his special relationship to the FDP. In the 1961 elections, the FDP had campaigned in favor of continuing the CDU-FDP coalition but replacing Adenauer by Erhard as chancellor. This meant, in effect, that Erhard had been the FDP's chancellor-candidate. Furthermore, Erhard's personality led him to be more respectful of his junior partners in the government than had been his rather arbitrary predecessor. He even went so far as to suggest that the two parties run a joint campaign for the 1965 elections, an offer which the FDP declined. The greater respect accorded to the FDP was symbolized by the designation of Mende, FDP leader, as Vice Chancellor. It was rewarded by a reluctance on the part of the FDP to oppose the chancellor within the coalition, a normal tactic in a pre-election period when the junior partner must distinguish itself sufficiently from the senior partner to be able to make a separate appeal for votes.

The approach of those elections, however, smoothed Erhard's way with his own party. His CDU rivals could ill afford to precipitate a party crisis with elections so near. No sooner had his six-month "honeymoon" ended in April 1964 than the CDU congress was held at which, in effect, the election campaign began.

On the other hand, there were several factors that increased the difficulty of Mr. Erhard's task. First, he had inherited an office that had been occupied during its entire 14-year history by the same man. It had been tailored so much to Adenauer's measure that it had been expected to fit anyone else uncomfortably. The cabinet and parliament that had chafed so much under Adenauer's tight rein was regarded as likely to kick up its heels under more permissive direction.

Second, Adenauer's stubborn opposition to Erhard certainly did not strengthen the chancellor's position. Nor had Erhard's reaction to Adenauer's attacks won him support. His passiveness had been regarded as weakness.

Third, Adenauer's opposition and Erhard's age (65) had encouraged rivals, both from personal ambition and because of policy disagreements. In the latter category belonged those who considered him an insufficiently fervent "European" as well as the "Gaullists." The most prominent of his rivals were Franz Josef Strauss, former Defense Minister and leader of the CSU, and Eugen Gerstenmaier, president of the Brundestag. Nor could the former chancellor be left entirely out of the picture. He remained head of the party and had little success concealing his dissatisfaction with the performance of his successor. He gave several interviews in which he criticized the government, directly or indirectly, and he traveled to Paris in late 1964 in an apparent effort to undercut Erhard's policy vis-à-vis de Gaulle.

Finally, Adenauer had left him some peculiarly difficult policy problems. In at least two vital areas, his predecessor had assumed conflicting commitments which Erhard was compelled to resolve. One of those was agricultural prices: The Adenauer government was committed both to the maintenance of German agricultural prosperity and to the integration of the German agricultural market into the European Economic Community at the lower French price levels. The other was defense: Adenauer's Franco-German treaty conflicted with his commitment to support the American-sponsored multilateral nuclear force (MLF). In effect, he resolved these problems by giving priority to the commitments to Europe and to the MLF.

Even the limited experience of the early post-Adenauer period permits tentative conclusions regarding the likely permanence of some characteristics of German politics during the Adenauer era. In the first place, "Chancellor democracy" in both its electoral and operational aspects is apparently a permanent feature of German politics. The 1965 election appeared to be as fully a contest between Erhard and Brandt as had been the 1961 election between Adenauer and Brandt. Indeed, it was more so, for the FDP was not backing a serious rival to Erhard as it had Erhard against Adenauer in 1961. Operationally, there was no more "collective responsibility" in the Erhard cabinet than there had been in Adenauer's, nor was the chancellor any more subject to day-to-day parliamentary control than Adenauer had been.

Secondly, the trend toward bipartism which had appeared so clearly in the first 12 years of the Republic (but had been halted in the 1961 elections) resumed. The two-party vote, which had been 60 per cent in the 1949 parliamentary elections, had risen to 74 per cent in 1953 and 82 per cent in 1957, but declined slightly to 81.6 per cent in 1961. In state elections between the 1961 federal elections and Erhard's accession the two-party vote averaged about 85 per cent, and in the April 1964 election in Baden Württemberg it was 83.5 per cent, up from 74.8 per cent in the 1960 state elections.[8] Furthermore, the principal reason that the FDP was able to suspend the trend toward bipartism in 1961 had disappeared. That is, in 1961 it had provided a means by which CDU voters could express their dissatisfaction with Adenauer's refusal to retire, yet not help the SPD.

Third, Erhard's conduct of the office was even more pragmatic than that of his predecessor—a stance that was fully supported by the April 1964 CDU congress at Hannover. The SPD's 1959 conversion to pragmatic politics was confirmed for the post-

Adenauer era in the resolutions it adopted at Karlsruhe in November 1964. In particular, for the first time it eliminated appeals to specific classes and strata of society as part of its turn away from ideological, class-based politics.[9]

On the whole, the Adenauer legacy of German politics, radically changed from the Weimar and Nazi period, was carried intact through the "lame-duck" Erhard "trustee" administration. They were increasingly bipartisan, chancellor-oriented, and pragmatic. Whether Erhard could become heir to this legacy in his own right after the 1965 elections, or whether the SPD and Willy Brandt would accede to power and the classical bipartisan pendulum swing of political fortunes would develop in Germany remained to be seen. What seemed beyond doubt, however, was that the legacy would be passed on undiminished and that the heir would be devoted to its preservation.

NOTES

1. Multiple responses were permitted. *Die Welt,* November 21, 1964.
2. *Die Welt,* November 22, 1964.
3. *Die Welt,* April 23, 1964.
4. *Luebecker Nachrichten,* July 19, 1964.
5. New York *Times,* April 1, 1963.
6. *Ibid.,* May 21, 1963.
7. *Ibid.,* September 30, 1963, and April 27, 1964; *Die Zeit,* May 1, 1964.
8. Guenter Triesch in *Die Politische Meinung,* September 1963; New York *Times,* September 30, 1963, and April 27, 1964.
9. *Die Zeit,* November 27, 1964.

Selected Bibliography

Note: The asterisk at the end of an entry indicates that the item contains a bibliography.

Books

Adenauer, Konrad. *World Indivisible*. Trans. by Richard and Clara Winston. New York: Harper, 1955.

Alexander, Edgar. *Adenauer and the New Germany: The Chancellor of the Vanquished*. Trans. by Thomas E. Goldstein. New York: Farrar, Straus, and Cudahy, 1957.

Almond, Gabriel A. (ed). *The Struggle For Democracy in Germany*. Chapel Hill: Univ. of North Carolina Press, 1949.*

Bathurst, M. E., and J. L. Simpson. *Germany and the North Atlantic Community—A Legal Survey*. New York: Praeger, 1956.

Brandt, Karl. *Germany: Key to Peace in Europe*. Claremont, Calif.: Claremont College, 1949.

Brecht, Arnold. *Federalism and Regionalism in Germany: The Division of Prussia*. New York: Oxford Univ. Press, 1945.

Chamberlin, William Henry. *The German Phoenix*. New York: Duell, Sloan, and Pearce, 1963.*

Clay, Lucius D. *Decision in Germany*. Garden City, N. Y.: Doubleday, 1950.

Clay, Lucius D. *Germany and the Fight for Freedom*. Cambridge: Harvard Univ. Press, 1950.

Conant, James Bryant. *Germany and Freedom: A Personal Appraisal*. Cambridge: Harvard Univ. Press, 1958.*

Craig, Gordon A. *From Bismarck to Adenauer: Aspects of German Statecraft*. Baltimore: Johns Hopkins Press, 1958.

Deutsch, Karl W., and Lewis J. Edinger. *Germany Rejoins the Powers*. Stanford: Stanford Univ. Press, 1959.*

Feld, Werner. *Reunification and West German-Soviet Relations*. The Hague: Nijhoff, 1963.*

Freund, Gerald. *Germany Between Two Worlds*. New York: Harcourt, Brace, 1961.

Freymond, Jacques. *The Saar Conflict, 1945-1955*. New York: Praeger, 1960.

Friedrich, Carl J. *The Soviet Zone of Germany*. New Haven: Human Relations Area Files, Inc., 1956.

Golay, John Ford. *The Founding of the Federal Republic of Germany.* Chicago: Univ. of Chicago Press, 1958.*

Grosser, Alfred. *The Federal Republic of Germany: A Concise History*. Trans. by Nelson Aldrich. New York: Praeger, 1964 (French original, 1963).*

Heidenheimer, Arnold J. *Adenauer and the CDU: The Rise of the Leader and the Integration of the Party*. The Hague: Nijhoff, 1960.*

Hiscocks, Richard. *Democracy in Western Germany*. New York: Oxford Univ. Press, 1957.*

Horne, Alistair. *Return to Power: A Report on the New Germany.* New York: Praeger, 1956.

Howley, Frank L. *Berlin Command.* New York: Putnam, 1950.

Keller, John W. *Germany, the Wall, and Berlin: International Politics during an International Crisis.* New York: Vantage, 1964.

King-Hall, Stephen, and Richard K. Ullmann. *German Parliaments: A Study of the Development of Representative Institutions in Germany*. New York: Praeger, 1954.*

Klemperer, Klemens von. *Germany's New Conservatism: Its History and Dilemma in the Twentieth Century*. Princeton: Princeton Univ. Press, 1957.

Kohn, Hans. *The Mind of Germany: The Education of a Nation.* New York: Scribner, 1960.

Lane, John C., and James K. Pollock. *Source Materials on the Government and Politics of Germany*. Ann Arbor: Wahrs, 1964.

Legien, Rudolf Roman. *The Four Power Agreements on Berlin: Alternative Solutions to the Status Quo?* Trans. by Trevor Davies. Berlin: Heymann, 1960.

Lewis, Harold O. *New Constitutions in Occupied Germany*. Washington: Foundation for Foreign Affairs, Pamphlet No. 6, 1948.

Litchfield, Edward H., and Associates. *Governing Postwar Germany.* Ithaca: Cornell Univ. Press, 1953.

McClellan, Grant S. *The Two Germanies*. New York: Wilson, 1959.

McInnis, Edgar, *et al. The Shaping of Postwar Germany*. New York: Praeger, 1960.

Merkl, Peter H. *The Origin of the West German Republic.* New York: Oxford Univ. Press, 1963.*

Morgenthau, Hans J. (ed). *Germany and the Future of Europe*. Chicago: Univ. of Chicago Press, 1951.

Neumann, Franz L. *German Democracy, 1950*. New York: Carnegie Endowment, *International Conciliation,* No. 461, May, 1950.

Office of Military Government (U. S.). *Documents on the Creation of the German Federal Constitution*. Berlin: OMGUS, 1949.

Office of Military Government (U. S.). *Land and Local Government in the United States Zone in Germany*. Frankfurt (Main): OMGUS, 1947.

Pinney, Edward L. *Federalism, Bureaucracy, and Party Politics in Western Germany: The Role of the Bundesrat*. Chapel Hill: Univ. of North Carolina Press, 1963.*

Plischke, Elmer. *The Allied High Commission for Germany*. Bad Godesberg/Mehlem, Germany: HICOG, 1953.

Plischke, Elmer. *Allied High Commission Relations with the West German Government*. Bad Godesberg/Mehlem, Germany: HICOG, 1952.

Plischke, Elmer. *Berlin: Development of Its Government and Administration*. Bad Godesberg/Mehlem, Germany: HICOG, 1952.

Plischke, Elmer. *Contemporary Government of Germany*. Boston: Houghton Mifflin, 1961.*

Plischke, Elmer. *Government and Politics of Contemporary Berlin*. The Hague: Nijhoff, 1963.*

Plischke, Elmer. *Revision of the Occupation Statute for Germany*. Bad Godesberg/Mehlem, Germany: HICOG, 1952.

Plischke, Elmer. *The West German Federal Government*. Bad Godesberg/Mehlem, Germany: HICOG, 1952.*

Pollock, James K., *et al. German Democracy at Work: A Selective Study*. Ann Arbor: Univ. of Michigan Press, 1955.*

Pollock, James K., and Homer Thomas. *Germany in Power and Eclipse: The Background of German Development*. New York: Van Nostrand, 1952.*

Pounds, Norman J. G. *Divided Germany and Berlin*. Princeton: Van Nostrand, 1962.*

Robson, Charles B. (trans. and ed). *Berlin: Pivot of German Destiny*. Chapel Hill: Univ. of North Carolina Press, 1960.

Russell, Frank M. *The Saar: Battleground and Pawn*. Stanford: Stanford Univ. Press, 1951.*

Smith, Bruce L. R. *The Governance of Berlin*. New York: Carnegie Endowment, *International Conciliation,* No. 525, November, 1959.

Speier, Hans, and W. Phillips Davison (eds). *West German Leadership and Foreign Policy*. Evanston: Row, Peterson, 1957.

Stahl, Walter (ed). *The Politics of Postwar Germany*. New York: Praeger for Atlantik Bruecke, 1963.*

Szaz, Zoltan Michael. *Germany's Eastern Frontiers: The Problem of the Oder-Neisse Line*. Chicago: Regnery, 1960.

United States, Department of State. *Germany, 1947-1949: The Story in Documents*. Department of State Publication 3556. Washington: Government Printing Office, 1950.

United States, Senate. *Documents on Germany, 1944-1961*. 87th Cong., 1st Sess. 1961.

Wallenberg, Hans. *Report on Democratic Institutions in Germany*. New York: American Council on Germany, 1956.

Wallich, Henry C. *Mainsprings of the German Revival.* New Haven: Yale Univ. Press, 1955.*

Wells, Roger H. *The States in West German Federalism: A Study in Federal-State Relations, 1949-1960.* New York: Bookmann Associates, 1961.

Weymar, Paul. *Adenauer, His Authorized Biography.* Trans. by Peter de Mendelssohn. New York: Dutton, 1957.

Wighton, Charles. *Adenauer: A Critical Biography.* New York: Coward-McCann, 1963.

Wolfe, James H. *Indivisible Germany: Illusion or Reality?* The Hague: Nijhoff, 1963.*

Articles

Adenauer, Konrad. "The Development of Parliamentary Institutions in Germany Since 1945," 7 *Parliamentary Affairs* (Summer, 1954), pp. 279-286.

"The Adenauer Era: The Chancellor and His Work," from *Die Welt,* embracing 21 installments in *The German Tribune* (Hamburg, Oct. 19, 1963-Mar. 7, 1964).

Bathurst, M. E. "Legislation in the Federal Republic of Germany," 1 *International and Comparative Law Quarterly* (Jan., 1952), pp. 40-53.

Baxter, Craig. "Germany's Christian Democratic Party," 30 *Social Science* (Jan., 1955), pp. 17-22.

Brecht, Arnold. "The New German Constitution," 16 *Social Research* (Dec., 1949), pp. 425-473.

Brecht, Arnold. "Re-establishing German Government," 267 *Annals* (Jan., 1950), pp. 28-42.

Cole, Taylor. "Functional Representation in the German Federal Republic," 2 *Midwest Journal of Political Science* (Aug., 1958), pp. 256-277.

Cole, Taylor. "Three Constitutional Courts: A Comparison," 53 *American Political Science Review* (Dec., 1959), pp. 963-984.

Cole, Taylor. "The West German Federal Constitutional Court: An Evaluation after Six Years," 20 *Journal of Politics* (May, 1958), pp. 278-307.

Dietze, Gottfried. "The Federal Republic of Germany: An Evaluation after Ten Years," 22 *Journal of Politics* (Feb., 1960), pp. 112-147.

Edinger, Lewis J. "Post-Totalitarian Leadership: Elites in the German Federal Republic," 54 *American Political Science Review* (Mar., 1960), pp. 58-82.

Fay, Sidney B. "Leadership at Bonn," 30 *Current History* (Apr., 1956), pp. 217-224.

Fliess, Peter J. "Freedom of the Press in the Bonn Republic," 16 *Journal of Politics* (Nov., 1954), pp. 664-684.

Friedrich, Carl J. "Rebuilding the German Constitution," 43 *American*

Political Science Review (June and Aug., 1949), pp. 461-482, 704-720.

Heidenheimer, Arnold J. "Federalism and the Party System: The Case of West Germany," 52 *American Political Science Review* (Sept., 1958), pp. 809-828.

Hermens, Ferdinand A. "Democracy at Bonn," 9 *Social Order* (May, 1959), pp. 215-220.

Hiscocks, C. R. "The Development of Democracy in Western Germany Since the Second World War," 20 *Canadian Journal of Economics and Political Science* (Nov., 1954), pp. 493-503.

Holborn, Hajo. "Achievements and Prospects of German Democracy," 70 *Political Science Quarterly* (Sept., 1955), pp. 421-433.

Kirchheimer, Otto. "The Composition of the German *Bundestag*, 1950," 3 *Western Political Quarterly* (Dec., 1950), pp. 590-601.

Kirchheimer, Otto. "Notes on the Political Scene in Western Germany," 6 *World Politics* (Apr., 1954), pp. 306-321.

Kirchheimer, Otto. "The Political Scene in West Germany," 9 *World Politics* (Apr., 1957), pp. 433-445.

Loewenberg, Gerhard. "Parliamentarism in Western Germany: The Functioning of the *Bundestag*," 55 *American Political Science Review* (Mar., 1961), pp. 87-102.

Loewenstein, Karl. "Law and the Legislative Process in Occupied Germany," 57 *Yale Law Journal* (Mar.-Apr., 1948), pp. 724-760, 994-1022.

Mason, John Brown. "Federalism—The Bonn Model," in Arnold J. Zurcher, ed., *Constitutions and Constitutional Trends Since World War II* (New York: New York Univ. Press, 2nd ed., 1955), pp. 134-153.

Mehren, Arthur T. von. "The New German Constitutional Court," 1 *American Journal of Comparative Law* (Winter and Spring, 1952), pp. 70-94.

Merkl, Peter H. "Equilibrium, Structure of Interests, and Leadership: Adenauer's Survival as Chancellor," 56 *American Political Science Review* (Sept., 1962), pp. 634-650.

Merkl, Peter H. "Executive-Legislative Federalism in West Germany," 53 *American Political Science Review* (Sept., 1959), pp. 732-741.

Nagel, Heinrich. "Judicial Review in Germany," 3 *American Journal of Comparative Law* (Spring, 1954), pp. 233-241.

Neumann, Robert G. "New Constitutions in Germany," 42 *American Political Science Review* (June, 1948), pp. 448-468.

Neunreither, Karlheinz. "Federalism and West German Bureaucracy," 7 *Political Studies* (Oct., 1959), pp. 233-245.

Neunreither, Karlheinz. "Politics and Bureaucracy in the West German *Bundesrat*," 53 *American Political Science Review* (Sept., 1959), pp. 713-731.

Plischke, Elmer. "Integrating Berlin and the Federal Republic of Germany," 27 *Journal of Politics* (Feb., 1965), pp. 35-65.

Pollock, James K. "The Electoral System of the Federal Republic of Germany—A Study of Representative Government," 46 *American Political Science Review* (Dec., 1952), pp. 1056-1068.

Prittie, Terence. "The Federal German Parliament," 8 *Parliamentary Affairs* (Spring, 1955), pp. 235-239.

Prittie, Terence. "How Far Does the German Parliament Govern?" 10 *Parliamentary Affairs* (Winter, 1956-1957), pp. 57-64.

Reich, Donald R. "Court, Comity, and Federalism in West Germany," 7 *Midwest Journal of Political Science* (Aug., 1963), pp. 197-228.

Roeper, Burkhardt. "The Realization of Democratic Ideals in Germany," 1 *Confluence* (June, 1952), pp. 14-22.

Schneider, Carl J. "Political Parties and the German Basic Law of 1949," 10 *Western Political Quarterly* (Sept., 1957), pp. 527-540.

Schultes, G. Karl. "German Politics and Political Theory," 28 *Political Quarterly* (Jan.-Mar., 1957), pp. 40-48.

Ullmann, Richard K. "The Struggle for Representative Institutions in Germany," *Parliamentary Affairs* (Autumn, 1949, and Spring, 1950), vol. 2, pp. 361-377, and vol. 3, pp. 321-338.

Van Hoek, Kees. "Bonn and Its Parliament," 177 *Contemporary Review* (June, 1950), pp. 332-338.

EPILOGUE

West Germany entered the second half of 1965 in a pre-electoral fever that was radically different from that in France but not unlike the British situation in 1964. The Germans had an authentic contest with an out-party that had high hopes of winning.

Chancellor Erhard's honeymoon had ended. Sharp personal and political antagonisms within the Christian Democratic and coalition leadership were clearly evident behind a brave campaign front. Chancellor Erhard and ex-Chancellor Adenauer debated sharply by open insinuation at the party's Duesseldorf conference in March. Relations between the chancellor and Foreign Minister Gerhard Schroeder, never good, became especially taut during the spring diplomatic crisis in the Near East.

Feelings among the coalition partners notably worsened. The government barely escaped a crisis when FDP Minister of Justice Ewald Buecher resigned in April to protest the extension of the statute of limitations for the prosecution of major wartime crimes. The continued exclusion from the cabinet of ambitious CSU leader Franz Joseph Strauss kept alive the ominous possibility that the two branches of the Christian Democratic movement might split asunder.

The chancellor had as much difficulty in Parliament as in the Cabinet. The extension of the statute of limitations was painfully obtained and he failed to win enactment of a bill granting the executive emergency powers and another distributing shares of the state-owned VEBA firm. Nor could attention be distracted by diplomatic triumphs. Two pillars of postwar German foreign policy were badly shaken. The Hallstein doctrine, implying sanctions against governments recognizing the East German regime, was put to a severe test by the complicated crisis in its Near East relations. The movement toward European unification suffered its worst setback since the French defeated the European Defense Community treaty in 1954 when negotiations on the Common Market broke down.

The difficulties affected public opinion, although as late as July a survey indicated that three times as many people believed the performance of his government to be satisfactory (or better) than thought it unsatisfactory. On the other hand, Erhard's personal popularity sagged. Adenauer was again "most admired" by 22 percent of Germans and Erhard by fewer than four percent. State elections in the Saar gave the CDU a gain since 1960 of only 6.1 percent compared to a 10.7 percent gain by the SPD, both at the expense of the smaller parties.

The Saar elections, in which the two major parties were separated by only two percentage points, seemed to confirm public opinion polls pointing toward the closest election in postwar German history. One poll in April posted the SPD five points over the CDU. Another at the same time gave the SPD one point edge.

All this led the SPD to scent blood. It sought to emulate the British Labour Party in 1964 which had turned out a conservative government with almost as much tenure headed by a Premier whose public image for maladroitness was not greatly unlike Erhard's. It prepared for battle by discarding most of its remaining ideological baggage and by giving a prominent role to its official "shadow cabinet." Upon the success of this effort depended the prospects of Germany quickly completing its establishment of a system of two parties alternating as majority governments similar to that in the United States and Great Britain.

The Soviet Union: The Search for Theory

by Samuel Hendel

SINCE THE OCTOBER REVOLUTION OF 1917, THREE MEN—LENIN, Stalin, Khrushchev—have largely dominated the Soviet scene and to a great extent shaped its history. The ouster of Khrushchev in October 1964, and the assumption of power by Brezhnev and others has led to changes in program, policy, and assuredly in style, but, in my opinion, it would be unwise to assume that the new Soviet leaders are limited only by the exigencies of power and expediency. It would be well to recognize that they, like their predecessors, are, to a considerable extent, prisoners of the Russian and Soviet past with its special and particular conditions, history, traditions, and Marxist-Leninist ideology.

The first sections of this essay will discuss some recent literary-political and economic developments in the U.S.S.R. that may have played a part in the undoing of Khrushchev and certainly pose important problems for the new leadership. The concluding section argues that Marxist theory has had a marked impact on Soviet practice and is likely to operate as one of the principal and continuing limitations on the power of the new Soviet leaders.

I. POLITICS, THE ARTS, AND INTELLECTUAL FERMENT

"Literature," wrote Oscar Wilde, "always anticipates life." Like most all-inclusive generalizations, it is an exaggeration, but one that contains a special insight in relation to the Soviet Union, a doctrinaire society in which literature and politics have been close handmaidens.

Since the death of Stalin, a dedicated corps of writers and artists has led in evincing a determination to broaden the area of creative criticism and freedom—for themselves and for the whole of the society in the U.S.S.R. Expression of this intellectual and cultural ferment is to be found—to cite only a very few recent publications *within the Soviet Union*—in the critical and revealing memoirs of Ilya Ehrenburg, *People, Years, Life*; the understated and thus all the more powerful and moving story of life in a Soviet concentration camp, Alexander Solzhenitsyn's *One Day in the Life of Ivan Denisovich*; Viktor Nekrasov's unusually balanced account of his visit to Italy and the United States, *On Both Sides of the Ocean;* the literary support of A. T. Tvardosky and of Konstantin Paustovsky; and, not least, the poetry of Yevgeny Yevtushenko, Boris Slutsky, and Andrei Voznesenski.[1]

Typical of the hopes and fears of these "liberals" and "anti-dogmatists" is the appealing if unrealistic demand of the poet Alexander Yashin, "Let us be truthful from now on in everything," [2] and of Yevtushenko "To double, to triple the guard . . . so that Stalin may not rise, and, with Stalin, the past. . . . Here I mean by the past the ignoring of the people's welfare, the calumnies, the arrests of the innocent." [3]

But it would be a mistake to think that the trend has been unimpededly in the direction of greater and greater artistic freedom. Khrushchev, in a special meeting with writers and artists in March of 1963, went to special pains to set and define limits. "The press, radio, literature, painting, music, cinema and the theater," he declared, "are a sharp ideological weapon of our Party. And the Party is concerned that its weapon be always in battle readiness and hit the enemy accurately. The Party will allow no one to blunt its edge, to weaken its effect." [4]

Although the New Party Program adopted in October 1961 (the third in the history of the Party) proclaims that the Soviet state has "become a state of the entire people," manifestly this is not intended to interfere with Party dominance. On the contrary, in a comment reminiscent of Rousseau's conception of the general will, Khrushchev affirmed that "The Party's policy expresses the interests of society as a whole and consequently of each separate individual as well." In this spirit, he scathingly attacked some of the "liberal" writers and artists, denounced "modernist" and "abstractionist" art, in general, as "dirty daubs that any donkey could paint with his tail" and, more significantly, as a waste of the people's money, and made some pithy comments about jazz and modern dancing. His sharpest barbs, however, were directed at Ilya Ehrenburg, who, in his memoirs, had stated that many who had known of Stalin's arrests of entirely innocent persons, and other abuses, had seen no alternative but to remain silent and live "with clenched teeth." [5]

The implication that Khrushchev and many other Party officials must have known of the arbitrary persecutions, and either were too implicated or too fearful to intervene, was inescapable and also inadmissible. A heavy barrage was loosed against Ehrenburg.[6] As for Khrushchev, he categorically denied that "the leading cadres" of the Party had known that innocent people were being punished. "They believed Stalin," he insisted, "and did not admit the thought that repression could be applied against honest people devoted to our cause." Quite inconsistently, in the same speech, Khrushchev pointed out that in his last years Stalin was a "profoundly sick man who suffered from suspiciousness and persecution mania" and "created such 'cases' as the 'Leningrad case,' and the 'doctors' case!' " These "cases," he added, "would have been considerably more numerous if everyone who worked beside Stalin had agreed with him in everything." He specifically credited Stalin's cadres (of whom he was one) with saving the Moscow Party organization from "new mass repressions" and the Ukrainian Bolsheviks (with whom he had close ties) with resisting the purge of the Ukrainian intelligentsia.[7]

The attack on Ehrenburg tellingly illustrates the limits of criticism; clearly the writer could not, for example, point up Khrushchev's vulnerability and the glaring inconsistency in his argument. Apart from limits set by the leaders out of concern for their personal safety and power, there is, I think, little reason to doubt that they regard themselves as particular and peculiar guardians of doctrine and fear that the Revolution and its goals would be placed in grave jeopardy if far-reaching political freedom were extended to the Soviet people. There may be a special relevance here in Ehrenburg's pointed quotation that "The misfortune of despotism is not that it does not love people, but that it loves them too much and trusts them too little." [8]

The salient fact, however, is that despite limits on freedom, despite swings of the pendulum between greater latitude and restraint, liberalization, in the sense of widening the scope of permissible dissent, has been real and substantial; and, while it ought not to be exaggerated, neither should it be denied or denigrated. The Party, it is clear, retains its hegemony and the apparatus with which to curb dissent. But reinstitution of systematic and pervasive terror to assure the virtually total outward conformity and uniformity that marked long periods of Communist Party rule seems extremely unlikely.

This appears to be true for several reasons. The Soviet people know the massive, wanton, and often senseless cruelty which so poignantly affected so many of their lives, and are likely to resist its recurrence. What is more, they—and particularly the youth among them—have breathed some of the heady air of greater freedom and developed expectations of greater benefits (material, cultural, and political) which they will not willingly forego. In an important sense, too, the leadership has staked its own future, against internal and external pressures alike, on its anti-Stalinist position. Apart from concern with personal survival, many of these leaders may recoil from the reimposition of the rule of terror, as a matter of principle, but, in any event, at least as inexpedient if the creative energies and initiative of the Soviet people are to be fully released.

Then, too, while the Soviet leaders may be unimpressed with appeals for greater freedom from cold war and ideological opponents, they must concern themselves with neutralist opinion and, even more assuredly, with that of allied Communist parties. A striking illustration is the late Italian Communist leader Palmiro Togliatti's strong suggestion, published in September 1964 (*in the U.S.S.R.* as well as abroad), that "open debates on current problems" in which the leaders take part might be useful, that the "origin of the cult of Stalin and how this became possible" must be considered "in general as unresolved," and that a problem, demanding "greater attention" affecting "as much the Soviet Union" as other Socialist countries, is that of "overcoming the regime of restrictions and suppression of democratic and personal freedom introduced by Stalin." He found particularly difficult to explain the Soviet Union's "slowness and resistance" in a situation in which "there is no longer capitalist encirclement and economic construction has had tremendous successes." [9] Subsequently, in October 1964, the summary dismissal of Khrushchev from all positions of party leadership evoked the comment from Togliatti's successor, Luigi Longo, that "The manner in which this change in the summit of the Soviet party and state occurred leaves us preoccupied and critical." [10] Similarly, the Politburo of the French Communist Party sought "explanations concerning the conditions and the methods under which the changes" were carried out.[11]

It is probable, too, that the new leadership, among whom Leonid Brezhnev as Party Secretary appears to be pre-eminent, will move in the direction of a greater diffusion of power within the Party hierarchy. Professor Zbigniew Brzezinski is probably right when he interprets the dismissal of Khrushchev as a "step in the progressive weakening of personal dictatorial power." [12] It is noteworthy, but not surprising, that the first statement to appear in *Pravda,* after Khrushchev's fall, underscored the virtues of collective leadership and the vices of the "cult of personality." [13] And in his first address as Communist Party Secretary, Brezhnev promised "to develop socialist democracy in every way." [14] It should also be noted that Brezhnev, Podgorny, Kosygin, and most of the new leaders, so far as can be judged from their earlier careers, were not directly implicated or involved in the abuses of the Stalin period and would seem, therefore, to have no *personal* stake in resisting closer scrutiny of those abuses and their implications.

It is possible, of course, that in this instance, as in the past, declarations in support of collective rule will prove only to have been lip service to a frequently dishonored principle and hence only a brief prelude to the emergence of a single peerless leader; but it appears dubious that such a leader could exercise the plenitude of power of a Stalin or even a Khrushchev. For one thing, each ouster, with its revelation of prior abuses, makes it more difficult to cloak the new leader with the necessary charisma and mantle of infallibility. For another, the organized and pervasive terror on which Stalin relied to curb all opposition, real, potential, and imagined, is no longer a viable instrument. In consequence of Stalin's concentration of complete power in his own hands, despite the official myths of a hierarchical scheme of elections within the

Party, collective rule, and democratic centralism, at his death in 1953, no institutionalized procedure existed in the Soviet Union for the orderly transfer of power. For that reason Russia lived in a state of fear and uncertainty in the wake of Stalin's demise, followed by a reported attempt by the head of the secret police, Lavrenti Beria, to seize power. And, in the West, the question was raised whether "a murderous struggle for power" would not take place "each time a transition in leadership is required." [15]

In contrast, in all the subsequent leadership crises, the clearly dominant center of power proved to be the Party central apparatus which, on the two most recent occasions, extended beyond the Party Presidium to include its Central Committee. In 1957, the Central Committee actually reversed the decision of the Presidium to oust Khrushchev. In 1964, it concurred in the decision of the Presidium to dismiss him. On both occasions, the decisions were made in the midst of national calm. This would appear to justify the conclusion that the U.S.S.R. has now demonstrated a capacity to make its central apparatus both the avenue of orderly political succession and a curb upon Napoleonic pretensions.[16]

It must not be overlooked, however, that recent changes in leadership in the Soviet Union, while they may involve some diffusion of power at and near the top of the Party pyramid, do not involve real participation and democratization within the Party or the nation generally. There is no intention to allow open, public presentation of opposing positions or factional organization within the Party. Khrushchev, on his ouster in 1964, for example, was afforded no opportunity to reply to his denunciation in *Pravda*, among others, for allegedly "harebrained scheming, immature conclusions, hasty decisions, actions divorced from reality, bragging, phrase-mongering, and commandism." [17] Of course, this was no worse than the fate meted out by Khrushchev in 1957 to the so-called Anti-Party group, which included Malenkov, Molotov, and Kaganovich, who were subjected to even worse vilification without opportunity to respond.

Certainly, the Party's monopoly of power is not to be broken. On the contrary, *Pravda* affirmed that "The role and significance of the Communist party, as the leading and directing force of Soviet society, is growing. . . ." [18] And Brezhnev quickly added that the Soviet people "fully trust the party" and regard it as "the only force . . . insuring continuous progress of Soviet society." [19]

In all these circumstances, while a return to a prototype of Stalinist totalitarianism and terror seems to be excluded, it would be highly speculative and unwise—for reasons to be more fully developed later—to assume that liberalization must inevitably and inexorably proceed to the realization of political democracy in any thoroughgoing sense.

II. ECONOMIC CHANGE

In the Soviet Union, because of the very nature of its centrally planned economy, there is a close interdependence and interrelationship between economics and politics. It is desirable, therefore, to give some attention to recent developments in the Soviet economy and their implications.

The past few years have witnessed a sharp and significant decline in the Soviet Union's *rate* of economic growth. To understand what has happened, and why, the reader must bear with a few key statistics. According to *official* Soviet sources, in the basic area of *industrial production,* in which the U.S.S.R. consistently claimed increases in growth by 10 to 20 per cent in the late 1940's and the 1950's, the rate of increase reported was 9.1 per cent in 1961, 9.7 per cent in 1962, 8.5 per cent in 1963, and 7.5 per cent for the first six months of 1964.[20] If we take account of other sectors of the Soviet economy, including *agriculture,* with its admittedly poor record in 1962 and 1963, and transmute the figures into terms of gross national product (GNP—a concept used in the West to cover the sum of *all* goods and services produced), the *official* Soviet claim suggests an average over-all growth rate for the period of about 5 per cent.[21]

This figure, however, has been substantially discounted by many Western economists. In 1964, a group of professional experts submitted to the Join Economic Committee of the United States Congress statistical and interpretive materials which, based on independent analyses of key variables in the Soviet economy, concluded that Soviet growth in GNP had declined from 6.5 per cent in 1961 to 2.2 per cent in 1962 and, "if provisional information for 1963 is introduced, an even slower growth than for 1962 appears." [22] Earlier in 1964, the Central Intelligence Agency of the United States, which employs many Soviet specialists, released a summary (without substantiating data) which maintained that the Soviet Union's economic growth for 1962 and 1963 had been less than 2.5 per cent per year.[23]

It must be emphasized that some Western specialists, while agreeing that a sharp decline has in fact occurred, are extremely skeptical of the low Soviet growth figures set in the Joint Economic Committee and C.I.A. reports.[24] What is indisputable, however, is that a drastic decline has taken place. Why? The explanation is complex, and it is possible to suggest here only in summary form some of the relevant factors. Furthermore, to judge their significance, it is necessary to distinguish between those difficulties which may be of temporary duration and those which appear to be more deep-rooted and intractable.

A major element in the poor growth of the Soviet Union in 1962 and 1963 was "two disastrous agricultural years in succession" and, for 1963, what Communist leader N. V. Podgorny called the worst drought in major farm areas of the U.S.S.R. in three-quarters of a century.[25] As a consequence, the U.S.S.R. had to buy 12 million tons of grain abroad and slaughter 40 per cent of its national stock of pigs. The agricultural deficiency, in turn, negatively affected the processed food industry and a number of related branches of light industry.[26] But it must be borne in mind that the agricultural record for 1962 and 1963 was particularly poor and that by September 1964 the evidence was in that the harvest for that year would show substantial improvement over the two previous ones.[27]

It is probable, too, that considerable disorganization affecting the growth rate was caused by the tremendous difficulties involved in getting the new chemical production program under way. In the longer run, therefore, improvement may be anticipated as a result of the planned increase in the use of chemical fertilizers, insecticides, mechanization, and irrigation.[28] Notwithstanding these prospects, a serious question remains as to whether the persistently poor performance of the agricultural segment—which employs 45 per cent of the Soviet labor force to produce the food and fiber to meet the needs of the Soviet people, while the 8 per cent employed in agriculture in the United States oversupplies the American people—can be drastically improved within the framework of the collective farm system.[29]

Another factor of some consequence contributing to the poor growth record of the Soviet Union was the sharp decline in recent years of entrants into the labor force because of the impact of World War II on the Soviet birth rate. But, beginning in 1964, the supply of young workers increased, and for the decade ahead greater numbers of young skilled workers will be entering the Soviet labor force.[30]

Other deficiencies retarding the growth rate of the Soviet economy, however, may prove more difficult and intractable. The collective farm system is only one. The shift in investment emphasis from heavy industry, agriculture, raw materials, and power supply into service areas and, within industry, into chemical technology, has already led, and may continue to lead, to a decline in the productivity (growth intensity) of investment.[31] "It was easier," one CIA analyst commented, "to build more and more steel mills and cement plants and hydroelectric dams than it is to build chemical plants and diversified consumer goods."[32]

Another cardinal difficulty derives from the very nature of a centrally planned and directed economy which threatens to drown Soviet planners in a paper ocean. With the inherent complexity of planning the production of literally millions of items in their multiple interrelationship, the use of computers and of other advanced instruments and techniques, together with a measure of decentralization (within the essential framework of a planned economy), may be expected to mitigate, but not to eliminate, the difficulty.[33]

Other defects of the Soviet system of planning have been the failure to use adequate devices to set rational limits on the amount of capital that enterprises will seek to employ, the inefficient dispersal of capital investments, the lack of a price system which properly measures the real cost of resources, the chronic understatement of production goals to enhance enterprise profit and bonuses, and the pressure to meet set quotas at the expense of quality, diversity, and technical advances. It remains to be seen how extensively the proposals of some leading Soviet economists, such as Professor Yevsei G. Liberman and Academician Vadim A.

Trapeznikov, for a variety of techniques to improve Soviet economic performance will be adopted and, if extensively adopted, how effective they may prove.[34]

To conclude our discussion at this point would be to give a partial and one-sided view of Soviet reality. Its centrally planned economy also has certain strengths and advantages, often neglected in partisan analyses. To begin with, it now seems to be firmly established that the Soviet institutional arrangements are such that its system is not subject to severe depressions or recessions. (It can no longer be argued, as it once was, that this would prove true only in the period of initial and rapid industrialization.) Related to this is the fact that, notwithstanding the inefficiency and waste involved in central planning and in the actual distribution and application of resources, the U.S.S.R. does employ the resources it has developed to full or nearly full capacity. It would be unthinkable, in short, for the U.S.S.R. to have the capacity to produce, let us say, 80 million metric tons of steel and, in the presence of continuing social need, produce only half that amount. Even in agriculture—where the Soviet failure in light of the input of effort has been egregious—a centrally planned economy makes possible extensive and systematic mechanization. Finally, it must be recognized that the nature of that system discourages expenditures for the production of socially useless, or even harmful, products and services.

The long-range implications of these varied considerations affecting the Soviet economy must be left to the judgment of the reader. In more immediate terms, some generalizations may be ventured. In the first place, it may be said that while the rate of economic growth in general—and consumption growth in particular—has slowed down in recent years in the U.S.S.R., as compared with the trend in the 1950's and with the performance of countries like Japan and West Germany, the Soviet Union continued throughout to make progress which, by generally prevailing international standards, is quite respectable.

Secondly, with respect to the living standard of the Soviet people, there has been, particularly in the years since Stalin's death in 1953, a steady improvement, even though the spectacular promises made in the New Party Program adopted in late 1961 are not likely to be realized. According to the Soviet claim (which is probably exaggerated and so must be discounted, but cannot be dismissed), in the past decade, the real income of its working people increased substantially; about 108 million people (almost half the population) moved into new homes or improved their housing; public fund expenditures increased from 15 million to about 34.5 million rubles (the ruble is officially valued at $1.11); and whereas in 1939 about 16 million people had a higher or secondary school education, by the beginning of 1964 there were more than 70 million, or four and a half times as many. The Soviet Union claims, too, that it has one of the best doctor-patient ratios—"one fourth of all the doctors"—and "the lowest death rate in the world." [35]

In summary, it must be recognized that the Soviet Union, under the dictatorship of the Communist Party, continues to impose limits on free expression which are almost intolerable to the free spirit, and suffers from the deficiencies and dissatisfactions engendered by its centrally controlled and planned economy; but it is nonetheless a viable and functional social order, with promising economic and social prospects as well as tensions and disabilities.

III. MARXIST THEORY, SOVIET PRACTICE, AND SOME FALLACIES OF SIMPLISM

I turn now to an investigation of the major aspect of this study—the special and important question of the continuing significance, if any, of Marxist theory for an understanding of the operative Soviet order. The fact is that, although far-reaching changes have occurred in the U.S.S.R. since the death of Stalin, there has been little reconsideration of the conception, long and generally favored in the West, that however variously Soviet history may be explained or appraised, commitment to Marxist theory on the part of Soviet leaders forms little or no relevant part of that explanation or appraisal. For some observers of the Soviet scene, Marxism is constantly being revised or discarded, but never appears to exist or exert influence. For others, like Daniel Bell, the ideology of Marxism has been "exhausted."

Denigration of the impact of Marxist theory on Soviet practice is understandable in light of the wide disparity between myth and reality in the U.S.S.R. It is undeniable that certain ideological goals that found expression in the writings of Marx and Engels, however officially rationalized, have been abandoned, perverted or attenuated. This process was begun by Lenin himself. Time and again, the Soviet leaders subordinated theory as they yielded to other drives and exigencies. Even loyalty to certain Marxist principles was punished as a crime, when they conflicted with the prevalent official orthodoxy.

But time after time, when the complete demise of theory as a guide to practice had been assumed or predicted, it showed a persistence or a renaissance, and a vitality and influence, that cannot reasonably be denied. This has been true not only with respect to policies pursued, but also those debarred. Despite its amazing flexibility, it is probably correct to say, with Isaac Deutscher, that before the Soviet regime could embrace *certain* policies, it "would first have to ban the works of Marx, Engels, and Lenin, that is to say to destroy its own birth certificate and ideological title deeds." [36] It seems to me that some Western writers fall into the fallacy of simplism when they insist that theory has had no continuing impulsion of its own, that it has not interacted with, modified as well as been modified by other compulsions and drives.

Preliminarily, it must be pointed out that, contrary to the focus of much recent discussion, evaluation of the interrelationship of *Marxist* theory and Soviet practice is properly and essentially concerned only with *internal* rather than external policy. There is little that one can glean, even by indirection, from a reading of Marx (as distinguished from Lenin, Stalin, and Khrushchev) about Soviet policies suitable to the "coexistence" of socialist and capitalist countries. Marx expected socialist revolutions to mature more or less simultaneously in advanced industrial countries; but in any event, once revolution had taken hold in any one country, he believed the force of its example and momentum would soon prove overwhelming.[37]

Foreign policy apart then, what evidence and reasoning support the thesis that in significant respects Marxist theory, *qua* theory, played and continues to play an important role in influencing Soviet practice? To deal with this inquiry, it will be useful, first, to give consideration to several leading formulations which, directly or indirectly, have sought to evaluate this interrelationship.

The "Naked Power" Thesis

One of the most influential schools of Soviet analysis maintains that the history of Bolshevism and of the U.S.S.R., from Lenin through Stalin to Khrushchev, may be understood essentially as a struggle for internal and external power—with all other considerations including Marxist theory either subordinated or abandoned to the power drive. A recent illustration is to be found in Nicholas P. Vakar's *The Taproot of Soviet Society*. Vakar tells us that the "practical men" who ruled and rule the U.S.S.R. altered Marxism "to fit their needs." To be sure, they used the language of Marxism, but that language, "long ago emptied of meaning, has become, like any official piety, perfectly adaptable." In short, they respond "to the impulsion of *power* rather than to the compulsion of *ideas*." (Vakar's emphasis.) And this "without the slightest practical regard for the ultimate Marxist future." [38]

The most detailed, systematic, and probably the most influential, formulation of this thesis appeared some years ago in W. W. Rostow's *The Dynamics of Soviet Society* which purported to synthesize much of the available knowledge of Soviet society, and was meant to assist the makers of American policy. Mr. Rostow's central thesis, "the concept of the priority of power," is that whenever conflict arose, the Soviet leaders, beginning with Lenin, chose "the power of their own political group" as against Marxist doctrine, revolutionary goals, the aims and traditions of the progressive movement, or the majority will of the people. While priority of power drew support from elements of Marxist doctrine and from Russian history and geography, "the inner core of consistency in the story of the Russian Communists is the priority they were prepared to give to the maintenance and expansion of their own power. . . ." Specifically, with regard to theory, what remains of Marxism is what has been found useful "to support the maintenance and enlargement of power by the regime at home and abroad." [39] In a more recent study, *The Stages of Economic Growth,* Mr. Rostow postulates that "*the* motive" (my emphasis) of "Communist political economy" is "the maintenance and extension of the elite's power" which exercises its dictatorship over the majority "in terms of its own interests." [40]

Just how the "priority of power" thesis is applied to the U.S.S.R. is often a study in argument by selected instances and flat assertion. These techniques enable Mr. Vakar to draw the sweeping conclusion that "the goal" that the Soviet leaders "talk about exerts no perceptible attractive or compulsive force on them as practical politicians. . . . It points them in no direction they would not otherwise choose." [41] Or consider Mr. Rostow's technique. When Stalin opposed rapid industrialization and collectivization, which were being urged by other Bolsheviks in the mid-1920's, this was essentially because "Stalin was concentrating his attention on the problem of achieving and consolidating his dictatorship, and he used his growing power to restrain accelerated industrialization until his dictatorship was secured." When, on the other hand, in 1928-1929, Stalin embarked on these measures, this was "a decision by a personal ruler, who had fully consolidated his position, to increase his hold over his own domain and to enlarge the strength and power his state might exercise in the world arena." And, when Stalin called a temporary halt, in 1930, to the tempo involved, it was because to maintain power he was "forced" to do so.[42] On this basis, Mr. Rostow simply cannot lose.

What we are offered in the Rostow-Vakar thesis is a version of Soviet history as pervasive, oversimplified, and misleading in its own way as the materialist conception of history is in another. This view enables the Communist Party of the Soviet Union, in its New (1961) Program, to maintain that a bourgeois republic, "however democratic," inevitably constitutes "a machine for the exploitation and suppression of the vast majority of the working people by a handful of capitalists." As for social welfare legislation, and even the welfare state itself, these are no more than devices to preserve the capitalist system and mask its exploiting character. "The vaunted 'welfare,'" we are told, "is welfare for the magnates of finance capital, and torment and suffering for hundreds of millions of working people." [43]

The absurdity of crude Marxist formulations regarding the structure and uses of power in many countries of the West is apparent. What we tend to ignore, however, is that the Western view of the U.S.S.R. also frequently suffers from crude oversimplifications which, turning Marxism upside down, see in the Soviet state exclusively an organ for exploitation and oppression and reduce complex motivations to some monistic explanation such as "the priority of power."

This is not to deny that Soviet history may be explained, *in significant part,* in terms of a personal, dictatorial power drive, however rationalized. Some of its clearest manifestations are found in the destruction of all opposition parties, the tawdry internecine battles among the Bolsheviks, the deliberate rewriting and falsification of Soviet history, and the cynical manipulation of all mass media to glorify and discredit particular leaders and causes. But it seems to me erroneous to elevate the power struggle from its role as an important and necessary part of a complex explanation of Soviet history to the status of virtual self-sufficiency. If one were seeking, for example, to explain the prewar history of Germany, would it be correct to reduce the complex amalgam to the manic propulsions for power that guided Hitler? There is wisdom in Laski's statement that "the impulses of men are never referable to any single source."

Even the "amoral" Machiavelli, who sought to construct a science of power by abstracting politics from ideology (and ethics), necessarily failed because in the real world ends and means are not wholly separable; and because politics is a system of controls inevitably based, in good part, on a system of values. Sidney Hook is, I believe, right when he rejects the notion that the only reason men are Communists is their desire for power or gain and adds, "No one understands the first thing about Communism unless he understands that it is a disease of idealism." [44]

The "End" of Ideology

Perhaps it is unconscious recognition of these considerations that leads some Sovietologists to cast Marxism out the front door only to readmit it, at least a little, through a side door. Thus Robert V. Daniels, for example, categorically asserts that in the U.S.S.R. "Theory does not guide practice, but it is manipulated to justify it after the fact." But in the same piece he says, "From Lenin's time on, the Communist leaders have been active men, not philosophers; they have found in Marx's doctrine a more-or-less comfortable rationalization for what they *wanted to do* or *felt should be done.*" [45] And elsewhere he writes, "Marxism in Russia has from the very beginning neatly fit Marx's own definition of ideology as 'false consciousness'—a set of ideas used without concern for truth or consistency to rationalize the *interests and aims* of a particular social group."[46] (My emphasis.)

Now, there is a palpable ambiguity here. Are the "interests" and "aims" of the leaders and what they "wanted to do" and felt "should be done" all self-consistent and compatible? Would not the "aims" and conceptions of "what should be done" have been moulded, in significant part at least, by the Marxist philosophy in which they have been educated and nurtured? What men "should" do, Professor Robert M. MacIver has said, is always expressive of a myth-complex, that is, a given ideology. To put it more concretely, if the aims of the leaders (consciously and unconsciously influenced by Marxist conceptions) are to achieve Marxist ends (which they may, in any event, genuinely regard as inevitable), may not their "aims" at times conflict with their "interests"? If this is so, how can it be categorically asserted that "theory does not guide practice" at all!

Or consider Daniel Bell's position. He argues, on the one hand, that the old ideologies, and Marxism foremost among them, have been "exhausted," that is, "have lost their 'truth' and their power to persuade." As for the specific merits of communism, "the content of that doctrine has long been forgotten by friends and foes alike."[47] Yet, on the other hand, as Bell himself has recognized in his provocative "Ten Theories in Search of Reality," ideology cannot be disposed of in quite so cavalier a fashion. Thus, he states that "Every society, every social organization, lives for certain goals which in considerable measure are dictated by its ideology." While it is true that he then goes on to argue that with the advent of Khrushchev, practical considerations rather than ideology seem to determine policy in important fields, tellingly he concludes that at some point some essential aspects of the regnant ideology must be maintained, for "without a central belief system with some continuity, disintegrative opinions begin to spread. . . ."[48]

It does not follow from this criticism of the "end of ideology" Sovietologists that the Communist leaders are single-mindedly and consistently committed to Marxist theory. Far from it. Khrushchev's comment that "We Communists attach great importance to revolutionary theory and we are achieving all our successes precisely because we are always guided by Marxist-Leninist teaching" [49] is arrant nonsense.

Continuity and Change

Approached from the historical point of view, a steadily diminishing significance is assigned to Marxist doctrine, *per se,* in the writing of even so scholarly an observer of the Soviet scene as Edward Hallett Carr, who, in his monumental history of the Soviet Union, writes concerning the impact of the Bolshevik revolution: "Never had the heritage of the past been more sharply, more sweepingly or more provocatively rejected; never had the claim to universality been more uncompromisingly asserted; never in any previous revolution had the break in continuity seemed so absolute." However, continues Mr. Carr, "presently tradition begins to unfold its power as an antidote to change," a process which may take a few years or a few generations, but "broadly speaking, the greater the distance in time from the initial impact of the revolution, the more decisively does the principle of continuity reassert itself against the principle of change." [50]

There is considerable truth in this perceptive analysis *if* Soviet society is viewed in the contrasting perspectives of the revolutionary period and a relatively short distance-in-time thereafter. In the aftermath of the Revolution, the forces of tradition and continuity proved increasingly compelling against the revolutionary impetus since, as Carr points out, the Revolution had been made in a specific material environment by men reared in a specific national tradition, transformed from a revolutionary movement into an established government, and forced to adopt a foreign policy which was necessarily governed, in part, by immutable geographical factors and, in part, by economic conditions which could not be changed immediately.[51]

The more grandiose and doctrinaire intentions and aspirations of the Bolsheviks were compelled, too, to confront the realities, *inter alia,* that, contrary to Marx's expectations and predictions, the Revolution had come to a backward, semi-Asiatic country without a developed industrial base and proletariat, and with a long history of despotism; and that it had failed to touch off successful revolutions in some of the advanced industrial countries. What is more, the devastation (physical and human) wrought by the war, civil war, and intervention, compounded by certain doctrinaire policies, made it essential that a breathing space be sought; and this was reflected in such "retreats" as N.E.P. and "socialism in one country."

But *if* the Carr thesis is viewed in the context of a greater distance-in-time, it appears to be based on the enunciation of a historical "law" of dubious validity. May it truly be said that the forces of tradition and continuity have become more pervasive and dominant in the years since the Bolshevik Revolution and that, concomitantly, "change" embodied in the theories of Marx has increasingly been attenuated? Do not recent developments in the U.S.S.R. suggest that a tenable argument can be made, as Isaac Deutscher does, for an opposing conclusion? Writing in 1959, he said "Far from having spent itself, the dynamic of the revolution seems to be growing; and after a period in which it was indeed overlaid by the patterns of Russian tradition, it reasserts itself all the more powerfully—industrialization and mass-education have shattered the very foundations of the old Russian tradition." [52]

The Coming "Triumph" of Ideology

It is one thing, however, to recognize the continuing importance of the revolutionary dynamic; it is quite another to maintain, as Deutscher does, that "Marxism has entered into the very core of national consciousness" and that "whatever its mutations Marxism remains the mainstream of Soviet thought." [53] Guided by this proposition, Deutscher insists that the working class "cannot possibly remain content with the administrative-ideological limitations of the post-Stalinist reform" and is eventually bound "to give a distinctive proletarian meaning and content to the current ideas and slogans of democratization." [54] We are told that "the social and cultural advance tends to make the masses aware of the fact that they are deprived of political liberties and are ruled by an uncontrolled bureaucracy. In coming years this will impel them to seek freedom of expression and association, even if this should bring them into conflict with the ruling bureaucracy." [55] In an earlier study Deutscher had concluded that "the balance of domestic factors favors a democratic regeneration of the regime." [56]

Deutscher appears to have moved to another extreme and permitted his own Marxist determinism to carry him beyond the established facts of industrialization and collectivization, urbanization, mass education, increase in social welfare, and relaxation of the dictatorship to insist that the process of change cannot be halted or aborted (except for temporary setbacks) short of the realization of a democratic socialist society truly in the image of Marx. Liberalization, as suggested earlier, has probably gone so far, gathered so much support, and aroused such expectations as to make it extremely difficult to revert to a form of Stalinist totalitarianism. But the evidence from Soviet experience, in particular, or human experience in general, seems insufficient to warrant Deutscher's far-reaching optimistic prediction.

The Durability of Soviet Despotism

It is noteworthy that Leonard Schapiro, for one, basing himself upon essentially the same developments, found that "the trend of the past few years in the Soviet Union has been in the direction of benevolent despotism rather than towards a free society." Neither greater prosperity nor industrial development, he stated, was likely to affect this pattern so long as the party preserves its monopoly of power. In fact, increased benefits may make the system more acceptable, and thus more durable.[57]

Bertram Wolfe, in even more categorical fashion, insists that "the durability of Soviet despotism" derives from the nature of modern totalitarianism, which is based upon a powerful and self-perpetuating framework enabling it to absorb changes (both intended and forced) so that "they tend to remain *within-system* changes in an enduring system." (Wolfe's emphasis.) To the argument that totalitarianism is incompatible with the complexity of modern industry and advanced technology, he counters that "Germany adopted totalitarianism when it was the paramount country of Europe in industry and technology." [58]

IV. THE ROLE OF IDEOLOGY IN THE U.S.S.R. TODAY

It is, I believe, highly significant that each of these projections —whether based essentially on the priority of power, the force of tradition, the dynamic of Marxism, or the within-system durability of totalitarianism—although arguable, is far from demonstrable. What is even more important, in each case there appears to be substantial evidence and logical bases for alternative and even contradictory theses.

"The function of history," J. B. Bury has written, "is to belie prophets." Thus, history has dealt harshly with the assumption, particularly prevalent after World War I, that liberal democracy, on the Anglo-Saxon pattern, was the final product of enlightenment, a system toward which all societies would naturally tend. This was true, Laski once argued, because "men who have once tasted power will not, without conflict, surrender it." But, authoritarianism in one form or another, as George F. Kennan reminds us, has throughout the ages been the normal lot of mankind.[59] So, also, Marx's confident assumption of the inevitable triumph of socialism in the advanced industrial countries was confounded by his own oversimplified analysis of the nature and "contradictions" of capitalism. It is curious to observe how so many who reject Marxist determinism, as grounded upon inadequate understanding of the complexities of capitalism, substitute a determinism of their own so confidently charting the direction of Soviet society.

There is, I fear, no escape—no matter how appealing and beguiling our quest for simplicity—into a universal formula which either totally accepts the integral relationship of Marxist theory and Soviet practice or totally rejects it. Every attempt to do so, whether by Soviet leaders or apologists or by Soviet critics, in the end runs afoul of stubborn realities. There is no substitute for painstaking theoretical, historical and logical analyses—doctrine by doctrine, case by case.

Limitations of space make it possible only to suggest an appropriate method. And since the case *against* the impact and continuity of Marxist theory is better known in the West, I shall be concerned almost entirely with the opposing one. Additionally, I wish to deal more fully with arguments advanced by those quoted earlier in these pages who have maintained that Marxist theory has little or no relevance for an understanding of the operative Soviet order. Before I proceed, however, I categorically cite a few illustrations (without attempting substantiation) of the disparity and discontinuity of Marxist theory and Soviet practice.

I believe that Lenin's justification for the seizure of power in a country without a highly developed capitalism and a mature and massive proletariat represented a repudiation of Marx's theory. So, also, Lenin's conceptions of the role of the Party, both in prerevolutionary theory and in postrevolutionary practice, constituted significant departures from Marxism. In practice, too, the dictatorship of the Communist party (which in Lenin's day became rule by an oligarchy and, under Stalin, one-man rule) bore and, despite some apparent dispersion of power since Stalin, bears no relation to the Marxist conception of the dictatorship of the proletariat. Closely linked to this conception was Marx's doctrine of the withering away of the State—an ideal professed by Marx in his very early writings. The failure of the Soviet state to wither away, in the face of the claim that the U.S.S.R. has already achieved socialism, a classless society and, according to the New Party Program, "a state of the entire people" (itself a formulation in conflict with basic theory)—however rationalized—is in fundamental contradiction with Marxist theory.

Divergence of premise and practice, myth and reality with respect to these (and other specific) Marxist doctrines would not be difficult to document. But it is quite another thing (and, in my view, egregious error) to dismiss the whole ideology as totally and unconditionally lacking in relevance for an understanding of Soviet practice.

I come now to my primary task: to support the proposition that key Marxist doctrines (however modified or distorted in practice) have nonetheless, in a truly vital sense, maintained basic and significant meaning, and exercised important and continuing influence on the operative Soviet order. In support of my thesis, I shall give consideration to three Marxist conceptions of fundamental importance.

Socialized Property

In the Communist Manifesto, Marx and Engels wrote that "the distinguishing feature of communism" is "the abolition of bourgeois property," a system based "on class antagonisms, on the exploitation of the many by the few." They added, "In this sense, the theory of the Communists may be summed up in a single sentence: Abolition of private property."

A powerful and persuasive argument may be made (as Erich

Fromm, for example, does) that Marx, in seeking the end of capitalism, was essentially concerned not with maximizing production, but with the "full and free development of every individual," and that his "idea" was "deformed and corrupted" by the Communists.[60] Or, as put by Robert Tucker, what Marx had sought was "the spiritual regeneration of man" and "to end human alienation by changing the world."[61] In this view, the perversions and distortions of Marxism in Soviet practice have been so far-reaching and so fundamental as to justify the conclusion that the U.S.S.R. cannot truly be called a Marxist state. The fact, however, cannot be gainsaid that—from a *Marxist* point of view—the basis for the development of unalienated man was the abolition of private ownership of means of production and the substitution of common ownership, a thoroughly planned economy, and production for use rather than for profit. Insofar as the U.S.S.R. corresponds to this conception, it may be said, in a real and meaningful sense, to derive from, and to have been influenced by, Marxism.

The Soviet constitution proclaims that "the economic foundation of the U.S.S.R. is the socialist system of economy and the socialist ownership of the instruments and means of production." It provides that "the economic life of the U.S.S.R. is determined and directed by the state national-economic plan," and declares work to be "a duty and a matter of honor for every able-bodied citizen."[62] While some provisions of the Soviet constitution are devoid of significance and others more honored in the breach than in the observance, these institutions are so fundamentally rooted in the beliefs of the people and their leaders that, for the foreseeable future, they are as unlikely to be abolished as is the basic system of private property in the United States.

It is true that dictatorial controls in the U.S.S.R. mean that the Marxist scheme, particularly in its conception of socialist democracy, has not been realized. This lack of freedom, in turn, affects and limits the common ownership of property, but—and this is critical to understanding—it does not negate it. Milovan Djilas, for example, goes too far when he maintains that, in effect, the Communist political bureaucracy owns the nationalized property because it "uses, enjoys, and disposes" of it.[63] While their controls give the bureaucrats important and special benefits, so long as marked fluidity prevails and national property may not be inherited, the privileges of the party leaders fall far short of ownership.

Not only does the fundamental organization of the economy reflect the Marxist scheme, but the strength of ideology is shown by frequently stubborn adherence to doctrine at the expense of rationality and efficiency. For example, much waste and neglect would be eliminated or reduced, and incentives increased, if small producers and traders were permitted to operate on a personal profit basis. The storekeeper and the restaurateur, among many others, would have compelling motives to reduce labor and other costs while improving service. But to permit private profit would mean a return to private enterprise, and this is ideologically unacceptable.

Consider another case. Planners in the U.S.S.R., basing themselves on Marx's proposition that only labor creates value, were ideologically debarred from imposing an interest charge for the use of capital. If used, it would serve as a means of efficient allocation and rationing of scarce capital and tend to set rational limits to the amounts of capital which planners would find it attractive to use in projected plants. But, as Professor Robert W. Campbell writes, "the Russians have been unable to use this simple approach because it is contradictory to the Marxist theory of value." And, despite the fact that, as Nicolas Spulber points out, "the labor theory is a poor tool for tackling problems of rational allocation of resources, it was called upon to serve as a normative principle of valuation." [64]

It is true that recently the Russians have succeeded, in part, in getting around the difficulty by using certain other devices, but these are not entirely satisfactory substitutes. So also, recent proposals for a system of plant (not individual) "profit" incentive, interest on capital, a new pricing system to reflect more accurately labor and material costs and stimulate production of new items, fines for delivery delays, and other techniques, if adopted, would be designed to improve the planning system, not to replace it.[65] In any event, ultimate intrusion of elements of rationality into the planned economy is akin to the fact that welfare state measures are permitted to alter our free enterprise system without destroying it. Adaptations and modifications in both systems do not mean that beliefs or ideologies are lacking in force. On the contrary, continuing adherence to essentials, and the time lag required to make sensible modifications, suggest that theory, *qua* theory, plays an important role in guiding practice in both cases. But this is more particularly true within a relatively closed, doctrinaire society like that of the U.S.S.R.

Agriculture presents an even clearer and more dramatic example of the compulsions of theory. Now, it must first be said that there are many explanations for the failure of the U.S.S.R. to achieve the repeatedly promised high level of agricultural production. These include the infertility of much Soviet land; inadequate rainfall; lack of mechanization, storage, and transport facilities; and heavy dependence on the labor of women and children—but surely a primary factor is the basic inadequacy of the system of collectivization itself. It simply does not give the peasant sufficient incentive to produce abundantly.

This failure is pointed up by the vitality of the dwarf private farm sector. Although only 1.4 per cent of the total agricultural land area and 3.3 per cent of the total sown area in 1962, this sector, on the basis of official Soviet statistics, contributes a heavily disproportionate share of the total output of many important foods such as vegetables, potatoes, meat, milk, and eggs. That year, according to the (1963) American Agricultural Exchange Delegation to the U.S.S.R., it "accounted for about a third of gross agricultural output—including almost half of the total output of livestock products." [66] By contrast, the figures for labor productivity and the care of livestock in the public agricultural sector are so incredibly low as to be almost unbelievable.[67]

Khrushchev repeatedly admitted the comparative inefficiency of Soviet agriculture. In 1956, at the 20th Party Congress he said, "Available data show that in our country considerably more labor is spent to produce a ton of milk or meat than in the United States." [68] In 1959, at the 21st Congress, he conceded that agriculture had been "in a critical state, fraught with dangerous consequences. . . ." [69] In March 1962, at a special plenary meeting of the Central Committee of the Party (following the 22nd Party Congress), he admitted that "the Party and all Soviet people" were "seriously concerned with the state of agriculture," [70] and in June he commented that "many" Soviet farms "have no clear notion of the value or production cost of products. The state farm director who carries on his work in this manner knows that his farm will be given a subsidy."[71] A homely illustration, pointing up the contrast in attitudes of the Soviet and American farmer, was given by Khrushchev who, late in 1963, said that "at some railroad stations in the Soviet Union, mountains of mineral fertilizer accumulate; snow falls and covers them, and children slide down them on sleds. This is inconceivable to an American farmer. He pays money for fertilizers and knows that if they aren't used he will, as they say, go broke."[72]

Why, then, in face of these difficulties, does the U.S.S.R. reject private enterprise in small-scale industry, commerce, and agriculture? While it has been argued that internal power drives or practical considerations "converged" with ideology to make socialized property desirable, the explanation is hardly convincing. The Communists were committed to achieve this goal as a central, unalterable aspect of a creed for which many had languished in Tsarist prisons. It seems more reasonable to suppose that the collectivization program in particular, with its loosing of a hornet's nest of opposition and concomitants of ruthless discipline, belt-tightening, and even famine, involved serious, calculated risks to *personal* power to serve the ends of preservation and extension of the *socialist* system.

Furthermore, it was not possible, once recovery from the ravages of war and civil war had been achieved, for any Bolshevik leader who aspired to achieve or hold power, to oppose in principle or long delay nationalization of property—just as it is impossible today for any such leader to seek to dismantle or fundamentally alter the collectivist industrial and agricultural systems in the U.S.S.R. And this is true despite the fact that, in specific regard to agriculture, as Inkeles and Bauer have shown in their probing study of the U.S.S.R. (based mainly on interviews with Soviet refugees), "nothing approaches the directness, simplicity, and pervasiveness of hostility toward the collective farm system. Only 2 per cent of the sample had no opinion on this subject. All groups without distinction and virtually unanimously wanted it eliminated. On a direct question, nine-tenths of the entire sample said flatly that the *kolkhoz* should be abolished and all the land distributed."[73] It is true that for reasons of economic necessity, the private farm sector is tolerated. At times, particularly in periods of political transition, the leaders will actually pander to popular desires. Thus, Khrushchev, in September 1953, just on the eve of his election as First Secretary of the Party, in addition to affirming that each collective farm household must be allowed a small holding "as private property" with "personally owned productive livestock," called for the elimination of the "prejudice" that it is "disgraceful for a worker or an employee to own livestock as private property."[74] Similarly, Brezhnev, within weeks of his accession announced the removal of some restrictions (imposed under Khrushchev) on private farming and livestock raising, although he did so with the caveat that "the economic conditions are not yet ready for such . . . restrictions."[75]

Nonetheless, with every improvement in the public farm situation, pressure against the private plots is renewed. And for the future, the New Party Program anticipates that "at a certain stage," as *kolkhozes* increase production, "supplementary individual farming will gradually become economically superfluous." Beyond that, "in the long run" there will be "the merging of *kolkhoz* property and the property of the entire people into a single communist property."[76]

Materialism

Fundamental to Marxism is its materialist philosophy which rejects supernaturalism in any form, insisting that "The material, sensuously perceptible world to which we ourselves belong is the only reality" and that "the ideal is nothing more than the material world reflected by the human mind and translated into terms of thought." In this view, "It is not religion that creates man but man who creates religion," which serves as "the opium of the people." Lenin characterized this dictum as "the cornerstone of the whole Marxist view on religion" and insisted that "We shall always teach a scientific world outlook." On the other hand, purely as a matter of tactics, he was not always prepared "to put the religious question in the forefront."[77]

Similarly, Lenin's successors have pursued the antireligious campaign with varying degress of intensity at various times, but the convictions and goals have never been altered and the campaign has never been fully relaxed. During the war, to be sure, the regime, while engaged in a life and death struggle, felt it necessary to make some concessions to the religious sentiments of the people, particularly in the villages. These concessions served also to appease allies and promote pan-Slavic support.

By 1947, only two years after the end of the war, however, the official Komsomol journal again called for an "aggressive ideological struggle" against those who did not recognize "the incompatibility of religious convictions and membership in the Komsomol," and by 1950, *Science and Life* flatly announced that "Marxism-Leninism and religion are as irreconcilable as materialism and idealism." [78]

That this irreconcilability is a fundamental premise of Soviet society today is manifest in many ways. It is reflected, despite some concern with methods, in the New Party Program adopted in October 1961.[79] It is propagated and urged on a variety of fronts: in Party and youth organizations; in special associations and conferences; in films, television and radio programs; in books, articles, and editorials; and, perhaps, most important and pervasive, in the educational system. Party directives require the schools, as instruments of Communist policy, to be antireligious, not simply nonreligious, and to ensure that young people become "conscientious and convinced atheists, ready to fight effectively against various religious superstitions and points of view." Manuals explain in precise detail how teachers must introduce antireligious education into their teaching.[80] This campaign was intensified when the Communist Party Central Committee, early in 1964, announced a new, extensive, and coordinated program to attempt to eradicate religion from every aspect of Soviet life.[81]

It is possible to argue that the antireligious campaign in the U.S.S.R. is not *basically* a matter of ideological commitment, but an aspect of a power struggle. The church, after all, had bitterly opposed the revolution. If given a free hand to propagate its views, it might become an opposing center of power. But the argument is not very persuasive. The leaders of the U.S.S.R. were schooled in and, there is no reason to doubt, believe in Marxist materialism. Apart from making temporary and tactical retreats—dictated by immediate exigencies—they seem determined to spread materialist doctrine even at some risk to Communist and personal power.

It is reasonable to suppose that if the Party came to terms with the church, already rendered thoroughly subservient under pervasive surveillance, it might well serve to make the leaders more acceptable to the masses. Other rulers have known how to use and bend the state religion for their purposes. Why not the Communists? That the church might prove agreeable is not at all to be excluded.[82] Of course, no Communist could make a real accommodation with the church without risking ouster. But this is simply another way of saying that personal power and position, in this instance, depend upon continuing commitment to fundamental Marxist materialism.

The evidence is clear, too, that ideology and philosophical criteria, such as materialism, have often been invoked in the U.S.S.R., with harmful consequences to Soviet scientific progress. One of the best known examples was the whole controversy over Lysenkoism. Under pressure from the lay Central Committee of the Communist Party, the Presidium of the Academy of Science, in 1948 found it necessary to hold that

> Michurin's [Lysenko's] materialist direction in biology is the only acceptable form of science, because it is based on dialectical materialism and on the revolutionary principle of changing Nature for the benefit of the people. Weismannite-Morganist idealist teaching is pseudo-scientific, because it is founded on the notion of the divine origin of the world and assumes external and unalterable scientific laws.[83]

Similarly, Einstein's theory of relativity, which seemed to Soviet philosophers to have elements of the metaphysical or mystical, was, as early as 1938, described by the Astronomical section of the U.S.S.R. Academy of Sciences as "counter-revolutionary."

"It is still fresh in the minds of many," wrote Peter Kapitsa, a brilliant Soviet physicist, "how a few of our philosophers, dogmatically applying the method of dialectics, proved that the theory of relativity was without foundation." So, also, he added, the philosophers first reacted with hostility to the development of "cybernetics," which they characterized as "a reactionary pseudo-science that arose in the U.S.A. after World War II" and as "a form of contemporary mechanicism." [84]

Now it is true that within the U.S.S.R., Lysenko's biological theories are no longer the *only* acceptable form of science, and that many experimental scientists ignored the postulates of the philosophers with respect to Einstein's theory and cybernetics. As

Kapitsa commented, "the physicists carried out nuclear reactions and verified Einstein's law not on separate atoms but on the scale of the atom bomb." "It would have been a good thing indeed," he wryly added, "if the physicists had followed the conclusions of some of the philosophers and discontinued work on the problem of applying the theory of relativity to nuclear physics." If the scientists had accepted the philosophers' definition of cybernetics, "it can be said that the conquest of cosmic space . . . could not have taken place." [85]

It should be observed, however, that Marxist theory dictated (or appeared to dictate) scientific theory and how considerable—in face of error and risks to progress—was its force, at least for a time. And basic philosophical theory continues to maintain its importance as a point of general reference and frequently retarding influence. The New Party Program, for example, provides that "In an age of rapid scientific development, the working out of the philosophical problems of contemporary natural science, on the basis of dialectical materialism as the only scientific method of cognition, acquires greater urgency." [86] This is to be the standard and the guide. It was cited, for instance, in a resolution of the All-Union conference on *philosophical* problems affecting physiology and psychology with the comment that "Contemporary physiology and psychology are developing on the methodological basis of dialectical materialism, in an irreconcilable struggle between materialism and idealism, between dialectics and metaphysics." [87] And even in biological research, the intrusion of Marxist criteria still continues to exercise an inhibiting influence. In August 1963, M. A. Olshansky, President of the Lenin All-Union Academy of Agricultural Sciences, categorically asserted that "Every Soviet scientist understands, of course, that peaceful coexistence of materialism and idealism in science cannot take place. This is why the Michurin school in genetics decisively casts away the reactionary conceptions of 'classical genetics.' " [88]

If, as suggested by some quoted earlier in these pages, the Soviet leaders are practical and/or power-driven men, with no real theoretical commitment, then the scientific area would seem to be the least congenial (and most damaging to their own purposes) for the intrusion of philosophical ideas which they value little or not at all.

Egalitarianism

A fundamental, theoretical "end" of Marxism is the realization of a thoroughly egalitarian society. It was Marx's view that in the socialist phase, the economic system would provide payment to its workers "proportioned to the labor they supply," and equality would consist "in the fact that measurement is made with an equal standard, labor." But true equality would be achieved only in the higher, communist phase, "after the productive forces have also increased with the all-round development of the individual, and all the springs of cooperative wealth flow more abundantly." Then would the standard prevail, "From each according to his ability, to each according to his needs." [89]

In the aftermath of the Bolshevik revolution, equality to its uttermost limits was the order of the day. As David J. Dallin wrote:

> Everything that stood in the way of equality was to be abolished, at once, completely: that was the spiritual crux of the November revolution and of the ideology of the early period of the Soviet regime. Equality in consumption and strict rationing were to eliminate inequality in the distribution of food supplies. The floor space of houses and apartments was carefully measured and the available space equally distributed among the population. The peasants divided landlords' estates, the workers seized the factories and drove the old owners into the street. Expeditions from the cities requisitioned grain supplies from the villages for the hungry cities. Soldiers tore shoulder straps from officers' uniforms. All ranks were abolished to make sure that not a vestige of the old inequality would be left.[90]

In this period, wages tended toward equality. By 1921, workers of widely varying qualifications, skill, or performance received nearly equal wages.[91] But this equality, extorted from an economy of want and scarcity (a base that made a travesty of Marx's vision), had to be abandoned to restore the ravaged economy. Under NEP, the traders and small entrepreneurs were invited back and peasants given the right to sell their products in the free market. The inevitable effect was marked differentiation in income. With the ebbing of revolutionary élan and under conditions of poverty, higher earnings provided the strongest incentive to more productive and skilled work for the working class as well. By June 1931, Stalin was decrying "the consequences of wage equalization" which deprived unskilled workers of incentive to become skilled workers and lead to heavy turnover in labor. "In order to put an end to this evil," he said, "we must abolish wage equalization and discard the old wage scales." [92]

In typical fashion, Stalin sought to make a virtue of what may well have been a necessity. What is more, he carried the inequalities far beyond the needs, or even utility, of the case. Accordingly, in 1934, Stalin characterized the views of those who "think that Socialism calls for equalization, for levelling the requirements and the individual lives of the members of society" as "petty-bourgeois views of our leftist blockheads." With regard to their "one time" attempt to organize industry to provide equal compensation for skilled and unskilled workers, he added: "You know what harm these infantile equalitarian exercises of our 'left' blockheads caused our industry." [93]

More inequality became the fashion and the cry. As a consequence, the piecework wage became the prevailing system, and gross disparities developed between the earnings of the skilled and unskilled. (At the same time, Stalin instituted ruthless and Draconic measures of labor discipline.) And, in 1940, a decree was issued requiring payment of tuition fees for upper secondary and higher education.

In light of these developments, it was quite generally predicted in the West that egalitarianism had been permanently and irrevocably abandoned as a goal of Soviet policy. Quite typical was the statement of Arthur Koestler that a survey of the trends in the U.S.S.R. "contradicts the alleged temporariness of these expedients and reveals a continuous and coherent movement in a direction opposed to fundamental principles of socialism." [94]

Consequently, it is noteworthy that with postwar recovery and further progress in building a high industrial base, a number of measures were adopted to restore greater equality. These included currency devaluation (which had a particularly adverse effect on high income groups as well as black marketeers), the ending of the tuition system (making education generally available to the talented, at all levels, without tuition fee), an increase in minimum wages and pensions, extension of the pension system to farm workers, special tax concessions for low-income groups, and reduction in the use of the piece work system, all of which have been of special and substantial benefit to those at the bottom of the economic scale. Labor benefited, too, from a shorter work week and from reform and liberalization of the labor code. In addition, the Soviet people for many years have had access to cultural opportunities and to hospital and medical facilities on a widespread and generally egalitarian basis.

While motivation does not alter the facts involved, it does bear upon the role of ideology and prospects for the future. Some Western observers have explained the Soviet program of popular education and other welfare measures, as W. W. Rostow does, "mainly as a reflex to its power goals." [95] Or, as put by Solomon M. Schwarz, "The need to adjust Soviet realities to the imperatives of modern industrialism is thus the *main* cause of the recent development of social welfare in the U.S.S.R." [96] (Schwarz's emphasis.) In similar vein, Bertram Wolfe queried, "Does not advancing industrialism—under any 'system'—require more literate, better trained workers?" [97]

There is, I believe, little doubt that increased welfare is an important and, in the long run, indispensable concomitant of developing industrialization. But, as Alec Nove pointed out in a carefully documented analysis, "the fact remains that in relation to national income the Soviet Union spends more on health, education and so on, than highly industrialized Western countries do, and it is therefore wrong to assume that her present rate of spending is in some sense economically predetermined, regardless of political decision or system of government. . . ." [98] Under the circumstances, is it not reasonable to assume that while the motivations for social welfare may be varied and complex, the egalitarianism suggested in Marx's vision of a socialist society—a vision in which the Soviet leaders, like the Soviet people, have been educated and reared—may form a real and important element in the composite? [99]

As for the future, the New Party Program envisages that national income will rise 150 per cent in 10 years and by 400 per cent in 20 years, that agricultural production will attain two and a half times its present volume in 20 years, and that the disparity between high and low incomes will be steadily reduced; that within 10 years there will be a general 35- or 36-hour work week; and that a variety of free benefits, services, and facilities will be provided within 20 years to such extent that "public consumption funds will total about half of the aggregate real income of the population." The program further promises that by 1980 "Soviet society will come close to a stage where it can introduce the principle of distribution according to needs. . . ." [100]

In light of the continued emphasis on heavy industry, the great deficiencies of collectivized agriculture, imbalances of the Soviet economy, chronic shortages, and the record of broken promises, it seems highly improbable that the U.S.S.R. will achieve its overall production goals within the times set. Add the recalcitrance of human nature and it is extremely doubtful that by 1980 the Soviet Union will "come close" to realizing the ultimate Marxist conception—which, in any event, may be visionary and utopian.

On the other hand, there is no reason, barring war, to doubt that the U.S.S.R. will be able, in the next several decades, to make *substantial progress* toward the realization of many of the important economic and welfare goals outlined in the New Party Program. That program is consistent in conception and formulation with *certain* fundamental Marxist egalitarian principles and it seems to me fatuous to believe that Marxist ideology, *per se,* has played and will play no real or substantial part in its implementation.

V. CONCLUSIONS

The conclusions of this essay will not appeal to those who are attracted to tidy and monistic explanations. Soviet leaders may in the future, as they have in the past, subordinate Marxism and the welfare of the Russian people to a variety of considerations and pressures. Certain Marxist doctrines have been attenuated, perverted, deferred, and, in some instances, discarded. But the whole truth is far more complicated than is suggested by those who ascribe little or no importance to the continuity and influence of Marxist theory.

It would, in fact, be most surprising if Marxist ideology had little or no hold on Soviet leaders. They have been nurtured in the Marxist creed since birth, and have been advanced, in many instances, because of uncritical loyalty to it. As for the people, while no doubt much cynicism prevails among them, it remains true that they exhibit a "peculiarly Soviet style of thinking, and of formulating problems," and "seem to absorb a good deal of the 'metaphysics' of Marxism." As Inkeles and Bauer conclude from their study of Soviet attitudes:

It is impossible to be exposed to a system of propaganda as all pervasive and monopolistic as that of the Soviet regime and escape without some influence. The areas where greatest influence was exerted were precisely those our knowledge of human learning points to, namely the basic values of the individual and the implicit dimensions of his thought.[101]

Nicholas DeWitt has pointed out that it is a major premise of Soviet education that "the basic truths of human life, of nature and of the universe, and of social, political, and economic reality, have been discovered and proclaimed and are beyond debate, so that the task of the teacher and of the scholar is to demonstrate and apply these truths rather than to question them or to seek alternative truths." While, as he also suggests, ideological conformity is often tempered by the need for professional competence, conformity remains an important element of the Soviet educational process and Soviet mentality.[102]

Paradoxically, some who argue that a fundamental *ideological* cleavage exists between the West and the U.S.S.R. at the same time refuse to endow the Soviet ideology with any content. But, as R. N. Carew Hunt has said, "the movement would not be the force it has become were there not in every country men and women who sincerely believe in the ideas behind it, which form collectively what we call its ideology. To represent this ideology as a species of opium with which the Soviet leaders contrive to lull the people while taking care never to indulge in it themselves is to attribute to them an ability to dissociate themselves from the logic of their system—an ability which it is unlikely they possess."[103]

Even in the areas where distortion or perversion of Marxism has manifestly taken place, it is revealing to observe how the "old truths" persist so that a measure of relaxation promptly brings people to the fore who seek to restore Marx's true meaning and purpose. Typical is that group of intellectuals in the U.S.S.R. today, whose attitude is perhaps best (or at least most overtly) expressed by Yevtushenko, who, in his recent autobiography, wrote that "those who speak in the name of Communism but in reality pervert its meaning are among its most dangerous enemies, perhaps even more dangerous than its enemies in the West," [104] and in the poem of Boris Slutsky: "Time to bring the dreams to pass. Yes, with neither doubt nor hesitation—To get to work and bring the dreams to pass." [105]

I conclude that the U.S.S.R. is most rationally to be explained as a complex and unique interpenetration and amalgam of Marxist ideology and a host of other forces including the compulsions of expediency and power, the old Russian tradition, and the recalcitrance of the human condition. As such, I believe it is *sui generis* and defies monistic interpretation and characterization. To maintain that because departures from Marxism have been far-reaching in some areas, Marxism cannot possibly have *any* continuing impact or significance, is to insist upon the absolute indivisibility of Marxist doctrine—a test we would be unable to apply to other doctrines. By so rigorous a standard, it would be impossible to explain the coexistence of democracy and slavery in the United States for nearly 100 years, or the coexistence of Christianity (and other religions) and un-Christian autocracy for nearly two thousand years.

If this conclusion is sound, the task of evaluating Soviet society is extraordinarily complicated and challenging. It is necessary, as Whitehead suggested, to "seek simplicity, and distrust it." One must avoid the temptation to compress, to find symmetry and consistency unjustified and unsupported by the complexities of the real Soviet world. One must take account of and grapple with all the significant forces and pressures acting and interacting to mould Soviet reality, including both the revolutionary and antirevolutionary dynamic. Above all, one must recognize that oversimplification of the "socialist" world will no more contribute to true understanding than oversimplification of the "capitalist" world. As E. H. Carr has truly said, "the *homo politicus* who pursues nothing but power is as unreal a myth as the *homo economicus* who pursues nothing but gain." [106]

NOTES

1. See, especially, Michael Rywkin, "Generation in Conflict: The Literary Arena," *Problems of Communism,* July-August 1964, pp. 1-10; David Burg, "The 'Cold War' on the Literary Front," *Problems of Communism,* July-August 1962, pp. 1-14, Sept.-Oct. 1962, pp.

33-46, Jan.-Feb. 1963, pp. 44-58; Priscilla Johnson, "The Regime and the Intellectuals" (Spec. Supplement), *Problems of Communism,* July-August 1963, pp. I-XXVII; Max Hayward, "The Literary Purge in Retrospect, *Survey,* October 1963, pp. 54-62; Patricia Blake and Max Hayward, eds., *Dissonant Voices in Soviet Literature* (New York, 1962); Max Hayward and Leopold Labedz, eds., *Literature and Revolution in Soviet Russia, 1917-1962* (New York, 1963); and Hugh McLean and Walter N. Vickery, *The Year of Protest, 1956* (New York, 1961).

2. Quoted by Michael Rywkin, *op. cit.,* p. 3.
3. "Stalin's Heirs," *Pravda,* October 21, 1962, p. 4.
4. *Pravda,* March 10, 1963.
5. *Ibid.* See also his speech of June 21, 1963, in *Pravda,* June 29.
6. See V. Yermilov, *Izvestia,* Jan. 30, 1963, and L. F. Ilyichev, *Pravda,* March 9, 1963.
7. *Pravda,* March 10, 1963.
8. *People, Years, Life.* Quoted in *Current Digest of the Soviet Press,* September 5, 1962, p. 6.
9. New York *Times,* September 5, 1964, p. 2.
10. New York *Times,* October 19, 1964.
11. New York *Times,* October 22, 1964.
12. See his "Victory of the Clerks," *New Republic,* Nov. 14, 1964, p. 18. Severyn Bialer, in "Twenty-four Men Who Rule Russia," New York *Times Magazine,* Nov. 1, 1964, comments that "the Central Committee is likely to have an increasing influence in deciding who the top leaders will be."
13. New York *Times,* October 17, 1964.
14. New York *Times,* October 20, 1964.
15. Harrison E. Salisbury, "Fatal Flaw in the Soviet System," New York *Times Magazine,* August 25, 1957, pp. 13 ff.
16. For a pertinent discussion of succession crises beginning with Stalin's death, see Howard R. Swearer, *The Politics of Succession in the U.S.S.R.* (Boston, 1964).
17. New York *Times,* October 17, 1964.
18. New York *Times,* October 17, 1964.
19. New York *Times,* October 20, 1964.
20. Khrushchev's Report to the Supreme Soviet, *Pravda,* July 14, 1964, and Report of the Central Statistical Administration, *Pravda,* July 23, 1964.
21. See Alec Nove, "The Soviet Consumer—A Discussion," *Problems of Communism,* July-Aug. 1964, p. 70.
22. Joint Economic Committee of Congress, *Annual Economic Indicators for the U.S.S.R.* (Washington, D. C., 1964), pp. 95, 91.
23. New York *Times,* Jan. 8, 1964. For 1958-1962, the United States' growth rate (with a much larger base) averaged 4.3 per cent. Joint Economic Committee, *op. cit.,* p. 95. Over a longer period, how-

ever, with the exception of war years, our growth rate has been between 2.5 and 3 per cent.

24. See, for example, Nove, *op. cit.,* p. 70.

25. See Joint Eco. Comm., *op. cit.,* p. 91, and *Pravda,* Nov. 7, 1963.

26. *Pravda,* July 14, 1964 and Edward Crankshaw, "The Farmer Frustrates Khrushchev," New York *Times Magazine,* Sept. 20, 1964.

27. Joint Eco. Comm., *op. cit.,* p. 91 and New York *Times,* Sept. 16, 1964.

28. See *Pravda,* July 14, 1964, Alec Nove, *op. cit.,* p. 70, and Harry Schwartz in New York *Times,* July 23, 1964.

29. See New York *Times,* June 28, 1964. This question is discussed further in a different context at a later point.

30. See Lynn Turgeon, "The Soviet Consumer," *op. cit.,* pp. 65-66, and Joint Eco. Comm., *op. cit.,* p. 91.

31. Joint Eco. Comm., *op. cit.,* p. 92.

32. Quoted in New York *Times,* Jan. 8, 1964.

33. See Leon Smolinski and Peter Wiles, "The Soviet Planning Pendulum?", *Problems of Communism,* Nov.-Dec. 1963, p. 24.

34. There has been considerable discussion of these questions in Soviet journals and press over the past few years. Representative is one by Trapeznikov which appeared in *Pravda,* Aug. 17, 1964.

35. Khrushchev's Report to the Supreme Soviet, *Pravda,* July 14, 1964.

36. Isaac Deutscher, *Russia After Stalin* (London, 1953), p. 113.

37. See, for example, Julian Towster, *Political Power in the U.S.S.R.* (New York, 1948), p. 12.

38. Nicholas P. Vakar, *The Taproot of Soviet Society* (New York, 1961, 1962), pp. 112, 114, 132.

39. W. W. Rostow, *The Dynamics of Soviet Society* (New York, 1952, 1953), pp. 7, 8, 29, 86, 247, and *passim.*

40. W. W. Rostow, *The Stages of Economic Growth* (Cambridge, 1960), pp. 160, 161.

41. Vakar, *op. cit.,* p. 132.

42. *The Dynamics of Soviet Society, op. cit.,* pp. 46, 48, 78.

43. *XXII S'ezd Kommunisticheskoy Partii Sovetskogo Soyuza Stenograficheskyi Otchyot* (Moscow, 1961), pp. 258, 266.

44. Sidney Hook, "Challenging Study: Challenge of Communism," New York *Times Magazine,* Oct. 13, 1963, p. 34.

45. Robert V. Daniels, "Soviet Power and Marxist Determinism," *Problems of Communism,* May-June 1960, pp. 12, 16.

46. Robert V. Daniels, *A Documentary History of Communism* (New York, 1960), p. xxviii.

47. Daniel Bell, *The End of Ideology* (Glencoe, 1960), pp. 373-374.

48. *Ibid.*, pp. 331-333.

49. Nikita S. Khrushchev, *For Victory in Peaceful Competition with Capitalism* (New York, 1960), p. 443.

50. Edward Hallett Carr, *Socialism in One Country, 1924-1926* (New York: The Macmillan Co., 1958), pp. 3, 4.

51. *Ibid.*, pp. 4-6.

52. *Nation,* Jan. 3, 1959, p. 14.

53. Isaac Deutscher, *The Great Contest* (New York, 1960), pp. 33, 34.

54. Isaac Deutscher, *Russia in Transition* (New York, 1957), p. 9.

55. *The Great Contest, op. cit.*, p. 21.

56. *Russia After Stalin, op. cit.*, p. 159.

57. Leonard Schapiro, "Has Russia Changed?," *Foreign Affairs,* April 1960, p. 397.

58. Bertram D. Wolfe, "The Durability of Soviet Despotism," *Commentary,* August 1957, pp. 95, 96.

59. George F. Kennan, "The Confusion of Ends and Means," from comments made on September 21, 1959 and reproduced in Samuel Hendel, ed., *The Soviet Crucible* (Princeton, 2nd ed., 1963), p. 638.

60. Erich Fromm, *May Man Prevail?* (New York, 1961), pp. 41-43, 72-73.

61. Robert Tucker, *Philosophy and Myth in Karl Marx* (Cambridge, 1961), pp. 24, 100.

62. Articles 4, 11, 12.

63. Milovan Djilas, *The New Class* (New York, 1957), p. 44.

64. Robert W. Campbell, *Soviet Economic Power* (Cambridge, 1960), pp. 102, 103; Nicolas Spulber, *The Soviet Economy* (New York, 1962), p. 232. Alec Nove in *The Soviet Economy* (New York, 1961), p. 276, has characterized the effect of this practice on the Soviet economy as "stultifying." Joseph S. Berliner called it "a clear instance of ideological thinking" ("Experimentation in the Soviet Economy," in Changing Communist World, Proceedings of a Conference held by The United Nations Association in Canada, May 1963).

65. Campbell, *op. cit.*, pp. 101-104; Spulber, *op. cit.*, pp. 233, 240-241, and *passim;* Nove, *op. cit.*, pp. 270-284. See also Trapeznikov, *op. cit.*

66. "Soviet Agriculture Today," Foreign Agricultural Economic Report, No. 13, U. S. Department of Agriculture (Washington, D. C., Dec. 1963), p. 11; Joseph W. Willett, "The Recent Record in Agricultural Production," Joint Economic Committee of Congress, *Dimensions of Soviet Economic Power* (Washington, D. C., 1962), pp. 112-113; see also W. A. Douglas Jackson, *The Nature and Structure of Soviet Agriculture* (a pamphlet published by the Institute of International Education, New York, 1963), p. 3.

67. Campbell, *op. cit.*, pp. 70, 74.

68. "Report of the Central Committee of the CPSU to the 20th Party Congress" (Moscow: Foreign Languages Publishing House, 1956), p. 84.

69. "Report to the Special 21st Congress of the CPSU," *Soviet Booklet No. 47* (London, 1959), p. 8.

70. *Pravda,* March 6, 1962, p. 1.

71. *Pravda,* June 30, 1962, p. 4.

72. *Pravda,* October 2, 1963. Reported in *Current Digest of the Soviet Press,* Oct. 30, 1963, p. 10.

73. Alex Inkeles and Raymond A. Bauer, *The Soviet Citizen* (Cambridge, 1959), p. 244.

74. *Pravda,* September 15, 1953.

75. The New York *Times,* November 7, 1964.

76. *XXII S'ezd . . . , op. cit.*, p. 285. In a technical theoretical sense it is only at the last stage that agriculture will have become fully socialized property.

77. Quoted in Jesse Clarkson, *A History of Russia* (New York, 1961), p. 571.

78. *Ibid.*, pp. 712, 713.

79. *XXII S'ezd . . . , op. cit.*, p. 318.

80. Alessio U. Floridi in George Z. F. Bereday and Jaan Pennar, eds., *The Politics of Soviet Education* (New York, 1960), pp. 91-92.

81. See *Partiinaya zhizn,* No. 2, Jan. 1964, pp. 22-26.

82. See, for example, S. P. Pavlov, First Secretary of the Central Committee of the Young Communist League, in *Pravda,* April 17, 1962, p. 4.

83. Quoted in Julian Huxley, *Soviet Genetics and World Science* (London, 1949), pp. 39, 171.

84. *Ekonomicheskaya gazeta,* March 26, 1962, p. 10.

85. *Ibid.*

86. *XXII S'ezd . . . , op. cit.*, p. 324.

87. *Voprosy psykhologii,* July-August 1962. Reported in *Current Digest of the Soviet Press,* Dec. 12, 1962, p. 15.

88. *Selskaya Zhizn,* August 18, 1963, p. 2. See also "Report on Soviet Science," *Survey,* July 1964.

89. Karl Marx, *Critique of the Gotha Program,* in Lewis S. Feuer, ed., *Marx and Engels: Basic Writings on Politics and Philosophy,* pp. 118, 119.

90. David J. Dallin, *The Real Soviet Russia* (New Haven, 1944), p. 89.

91. Legislative Reference Service of the Library of Congress, *Communism in Action* (Washington, D. C., 1946), p. 33.

92. Joseph V. Stalin, *Problems of Leninism* (Moscow, 1953), p. 463.

93. *Ibid.*, pp. 635-637.

94. Arthur Koestler, *The Yogi and the Commissar* (New York, 1946), p. 180.

95. *The Dynamics of Soviet Society, op. cit.*, p. 133.

96. Solomon M. Schwarz, "Why the Changes?" *Problems of Communism,* Jan.-Feb. 1960, p. 12.

97. Bertram D. Wolfe, "Facts and Polemics," *ibid.*, p. 12.

98. Alec Nove, "A Reply to My Critics," *Problems of Communism,* May-June 1960, p. 50.

99. When asked whether the goal of Soviet policy was the welfare of the individual, with its totalitarian character only a means to the rapid realization of this end, or whether totalitarianism has become an end in itself with the ultimate aim merely "to bring about total tyranny in the name of abundance and liberation," George F. Kennan replied: "On countless occasions, when I have been asked which of two seemingly contradictory and incompatible realities is true in the Soviet Union, I have been obliged to say: both. This, too, is one of these instances." "The Confusion of Ends and Means," *op. cit.*, pp. 635, 638.

100. *XXII S'ezd . . .* , *op. cit.*, pp. 276, 284, 296, 297, 299, 301-302.

101. *The Soviet Citizen, op. cit.*, pp. 178-179.

102. Nicholas DeWitt, *Soviet Professional Manpower* (Washington, D. C., 1955), pp. 3-4.

103. R. N. Carew Hunt, "The Importance of Doctrine," *Problems of Communism,* March-April 1958, pp. 14-15. See also Herbert Marcuse, *Soviet Marxism* (Vintage, New York, 1961), pp. 24-25, Alfred G. Meyer, *Communism* (New York, 1960), pp. 43-45, and Merle Fainsod, *How Russia Is Ruled* (Cambridge, 1963), pp. 591-598.

104. Yevgeny A. Yevtushenko, *A Precocious Autobiography* (New York, 1963), p. 81.

105. *Literaturnaya gazeta,* Nov. 24, 1962, p. 2.

106. E. H. Carr, *The Twenty Years Crisis* (London, 1941), p. 125.